OH, WILD WEST!

OH, WILD WEST!

| THE CALIFORNIA PLAYS |

Culture Clash

THEATRE COMMUNICATIONS GROUP | NEW YORK | 2011

Oh, Wild West!: The California Plays is published by Theatre Communications Group,
Inc., 520 Eighth Ave., 24th Floor New York, NY 10018-4156

This publication is made possible in part with funds from the New York State
Council on the Arts, a State Agency.

TCG books are exclusively distributed to the book trade by Consortium Book Sales
and Distribution.

LIBRARY OF CONGRESS CATALOGING-IN-PUBLICATION DATA
Oh, wild west! : the California plays / by Culture Clash.
p. cm.
ISBN 978-1-55936-327-3
1. California—Drama. 2. American drama—21st century. I. Culture Clash
(Comedy troupe)
PS634.2.O38   2011
812'.608—dc22   2011013339

Text design and composition by Lisa Govan
Cover design by Soap Design Co.
Front cover photos by Craig Schwartz (left and right)/Kevin Berne (center);
back cover photo by Eric Schwabel

First Edition, June 2011

To Mick Vranich,
Motor City Poet

CONTENTS

PREFACE

By Richard Montoya

Oh Wild West. Oh Wild California. Oh Westward Expansion. Why are we so obsessed with you? Your history, your myth, your bloody bloody trail of grim white men and Hollywood Latin heartthrobs even. Is it because in that last gasp—that final westward ho of treaties, trails or tears, and broken promises that we find ourselves? We find Brando as Zapata and Elvis as a sexy Apache warrior, too. We find and connect The Beats to Russell Means, Trudell, Mick Vranich, and the MC5. From the Motor City to a Cave up in the Hills, where we can write and reframe our history. We now find the great-grandsons and great-granddaughters—the descendents of Manifest Destiny—in hipster garb from Williamsburg to Silver Lake. We Culture Clash with them in the quaint Echo Park cantinas and Brooklyn bistros and we tell them that Jack London was a bully and a braggart, but he would have kicked the Cisco Kid's butt on principle alone. And we are of both!

And more! Romantics like a Fenimore Cooper novel and Chicano neorealists with Indian roots. Oh Wild West indeed. The grim pioneer is at the door again, and he looks a lot like Arizona Sheriff Joe Arpaio—we need a barroom fight; we need to laugh—so send in Zorro and his Mestizo Postmodern Clowns to the Ninth Circuit Federal Courthouse to fight for William Shakespeare, Culture Clash and ethnic studies—all banned by the Arizona Attorney General.

On guard!

CHAVEZ RAVINE

To Mr. Frank Wilkinson,
Tireless advocate for human rights
and L.A. affordable housing

GHOSTS OF L.A.

An interview with Culture Clash by John Glore

This interview with Richard Montoya and Ric Salinas of Culture Clash took place in L.A.'s Bunker Hill district, with Dodger Stadium visible on a nearby hillside.

JOHN GLORE: The story you dramatize in *Chavez Ravine* took place half a century ago, but it seemed that it wouldn't stand still as you began investigating it.

RICHARD MONTOYA: The story shifted like an L.A. earthquake. On the face of it we thought, well, the Dodgers kicked out the poor Mexican people, and it's going to be one more for the annals of Chicano theater. But as we kept digging, what we found was a much more complicated story. It goes back to the turn of the century when Mexicans were fleeing Mexico because of the revolution. These immigrants found a kind of hamlet nestled in these hollows, these hills that we can see from where we're sitting. But one man's hamlet was another man's blighted slum area. So in the forties and fifties, that barrio becomes the focus of well-intentioned people in the L.A. City Housing Authority who want to provide decent, affordable public housing. Of course, this was the time of McCarthyism, and the Housing Authority was full of intelligentsia, of dreamers who advocated for poor people, so they were branded socialists by people who wanted to stop the public housing plan. Our first tragedy really begins there, 10 years before the Dodgers ever thought of coming to L.A.

The story seemed to undergo an emotional shift when you interviewed Frank Wilkinson (site manager for the Housing Authority in the late forties and early fifties).

MONTOYA: Absolutely. In coming upon Frank Wilkinson, who actually served time in prison because he wouldn't answer questions about Communist affiliations, we find a kind of hero, really, a real advocate for the poor. He lost the most, because he stood up against McCarthy and Hoover. He risked assassination, he risked everything. We really were able to hang our hats on Frank; he becomes a kind of a Jimmy Stewart hero.

RIC SALINAS: And, of course, there wouldn't be a story if there wasn't the resilience of the families that stayed on the hill. If they had decided to take the city's money and go, there would be no story.

How did the Watchman and Mr. Mover and Mr. Shaker find their way into the play?

SALINAS: One of the difficult challenges was to portray that display of power that goes on in back rooms, behind closed doors: in City Hall, in the police department, in private clubs. The film noir approach was fun. It allowed us a kind of visual shorthand: When you see dark figures shaking hands, or exchanging a briefcase . . . it's *L.A. Confidential.* But the majority of what we put on stage was from transcripts, from newspaper clippings. The mayor really was promised a new Cadillac to run against the housing plan. O'Malley really did take a helicopter ride over Chavez Ravine. The *L.A. Times* did have a guy who wrote columns as "the Watchman," and he did manipulate the mayor and the city council's activities.

MONTOYA: L.A.'s got a really dark side, historically. Pick your police chief; your newspaper publisher, Hearst or Chandler; your Red Squad, your assassination detail. Throw in labor, throw in Hollywood, throw in activists like Fred Ross—you've got all the makings there for something that shaped film noir. And *Chavez Ravine* lands smack-dab in the middle of that dark, dark period for L.A. And the flipside of it was this jolly good time in the fifties when, you know, who in the heck could be against a baseball stadium? I think what gave *Chavez Ravine* a lot of its magic is that we were doing the play at the epicenter of that civic crucible, in the vortex of civic power.

Why frame the play with the Fernando game?

MONTOYA: It was the first time that Latinos began to make a pilgrimage back to Dodger Stadium. It really took a kind of miracle, that incredible season of '81, when they won the World Series, all the amazing games that Fernando had in his rookie season. The mysticism of Fernando being an Indian Mexican, the sense of there being ghosts and spirits rising up out of that piece of land: It really became a kind of ghost-play.

How does *Chavez Ravine* fit into the continuum of your work?

SALINAS: This play is a little bit vaudeville, *carpa*, which is how we started out, but it also uses the documentary work, the interviews, oral histories that we've been doing more recently. And we've always had a kind of Brechtian style in our work. But what's new is we decided to portray characters and story through dialogue rather than monologue after monologue. We created scenes that tell a specific story in a way that we really haven't done before.

Is it just an L.A. story?

MONTOYA: Well, it's also a story about the shaping of America. Every city in the country has some kind of stadium or freeway or airport issue, and that's where you'll find your Movers and Shakers, and that's where you'll find poor people being moved out to make room for the city's growth. The audience was also able to make correlations between McCarthy's war on commu-nism and our war on terrorism today. Who's an American, who's not an American? Who's a patriot?

John Glore was the resident dramaturg for the Mark Taper Forum and worked with Culture Clash for two years on the development of Chavez Ravine. *He is currently Associate Artistic Director of South Coast Repertory. This interview first appeared in* American Theatre *magazine November 2003.*

PRODUCTION HISTORY

Chavez Ravine was commissioned by Center Theatre Group's Mark Taper Forum (Gordon Davidson, Artistic Director; Charles Dillingham, Managing Director) and received its world premiere there on May 17, 2003. It was directed by Lisa Peterson; the set design was by Rachel Hauck, the costume design was by Christopher Acebo, the lighting design was by Anne Militello, the sound design was by Dan Moses Schreier, musical direction and arranging were by John Avila and the original music and lyrics were by Scott Rodarte, Randy Rodarte, John Avila and Richard Montoya; the dramaturg was John Glore, the production stage manager was James T. McDermott and the stage manager was Susie Walsh. The performers were:

Actors	Musicians	Understudies
Richard Montoya	John Avila	Roberto Alcaraz
Ric Salinas	Randy Rodarte	Minerva Garcia
Herbert Siguenza	Scott Rodarte	Edgar Landa
Eileen Galindo		

JULIÁN CHÁVEZ'S RAVINE, 1840–1981

The following is a timeline of important moments in the history of the area known as Chavez Ravine and the people associated with it. Culture Clash's play follows this chronology closely, only occasionally making minor alterations to the sequence of events for the sake of clarity and/or dramatic effect. One bit of history that has been left out of the play is the fact that the Dodgers relocated to Los Angeles long before ground had even been broken for their new stadium, playing four seasons in the Los Angeles Coliseum before they played their first game in Chavez Ravine.

1840s Julián A. Chávez, a City Councilman, acquires land near the center of the Pueblo of Los Angeles, in an area that becomes known as Chavez Ravine. Appraised value, $800.

1910–11 Mexican Revolution leads to resignation of President Porfirio Díaz in 1911, followed by years of unrest. Many of the first residents of Chavez Ravine are refugees from the revolution and its aftermath.

1949 National Housing Act passed by Congress; $110 million is made available to L.A.'s City Housing Authority (CHA, a federal agency), to build subsidized low-income housing.

August 1949 L.A. City Council unanimously approves public housing project for eleven sites around Los Angeles, including Chavez Ravine.

July 24, 1950 CHA sends letter to residents of Chavez Ravine announcing public housing plan; soon thereafter begins land purchase in Chavez Ravine; initiates eminent domain proceedings against reluctant landowners.

December 26, 1951 City Council votes 8–7 to cancel contract with CHA and to block its plan for public housing. The following April, California Supreme Court orders city to honor contract.

June 1952 Citywide referendum upholds Council's decision to cancel public housing, but CHA continues to move forward.

August–September 1952 CHA site manager Frank Wilkinson is asked about his possible communist affiliations and is subsequently forced to testify to the California Senate Committee on Un-American Activities. When he refuses to answer questions, he is fired from CHA.

December 26, 1952 On behalf of a small group of powerful businessmen, Norman Chandler, publisher of the *L.A. Times*, sends letter to Congressman Norris Poulson, drafting him to run for mayor as an anti-public housing candidate against pro-housing incumbent Fletcher Bowron.

May 26, 1953 Poulson defeats Bowron in L.A. mayoral election. Immediately cancels Chavez Ravine housing project.

1953 Roz Wyman elected as youngest City Council member and first woman on the Council. Her campaign includes support for bringing major league baseball to L.A.

1953–58 Only a dozen or so families remain in the Ravine, having resisted eminent domain condemnation: the city leaves them alone for five years while looking for a use for the city-owned land.

1955 Wyman sends letter to Walter O'Malley, owner of the Brooklyn Dodgers, suggesting she and fellow Council member Ed Roybal travel to Brooklyn to discuss possible Dodgers move to L.A. O'Malley rebuffs the offer.

October 1955 Dodgers win World Series.

October 12, 1956 Dodgers stop in L.A. on way to exhibition games in Japan. First meeting of O'Malley and L.A. County Supervisor Kenneth Hahn. O'Malley, unhappy that he can't get a new stadium built in Brooklyn, tells Hahn he intends to move the team, but swears him to secrecy.

January–February 1957 O'Malley buys minor-league L.A. Angels and their stadium, Wrigley Field, in South Los Angeles.

March 1957 Poulson and a delegation of L.A. leaders travel to Dodgers spring training camp in Vero Beach, Florida, to convince O'Malley to move the team.

May 1957 O'Malley and Hahn take helicopter ride over the city; when O'Malley sees Chavez Ravine, he comments on its suitability for a ballpark.

October 7, 1957 City Council votes 10–4 to grant O'Malley three hundred acres in the Ravine in exchange for Wrigley Field; city will pay $2 million dollars to clear and grade land; county will spend $2.75 million for access roads. O'Malley will set aside and develop forty acres for recreation, will pay to build his own stadium.

October 8, 1957 O'Malley publicly announces his intention to move to L.A. Sends Poulson telegram: "Get your wheelbarrow and shovel. I'll see you at Chavez Ravine."

April 1958 Dodgers begin first season in L.A., playing in the Coliseum.

June 3, 1958 Proposition B to approve city's deal with O'Malley passes by a narrow margin (25,000 votes).

January 1959 California Supreme Court dismisses lawsuits brought by private citizens attempting to challenge validity of L.A.'s contract with the Dodgers.

April 1959 L.A. radio station KWKW begins first regular Spanish-language broadcasts of major league games, with René Cárdenas doing play-by-play. Jaime Jarrín joins him in the booth the next year.

May 8, 1959 Sheriff's deputies evict last family from house in Ravine. Bulldozers begin final demolition. Family continues to camp on land for another week.

September 1959 Dodgers break ground for new stadium. Team ends its second season playing in Coliseum by winning World Series.

1961 Poulson loses bid for third term to Sam Yorty. Blames loss on Dodger Stadium controversy.

April 10, 1962 Opening of new Dodger Stadium in Chavez Ravine.

April 1981 Fernando Valenzuela begins his rookie season by pitching opening-day shutout against Astros. Wins first eight starts, including five shutouts. Becomes first to win Rookie-of-the-Year and Cy Young Award (for best pitcher) in same season.

A NOTE FROM THE AUTHORS ON STAGING

Chavez Ravine is a play full of ghosts, flashbacks and flash-forwards. Lisa Peterson staged it very much like a film-noirish radio play or chamber piece, meaning that, even though there were movable backdrops, a few chairs and tables, set designer Rachel Hauck, for the most part, kept the stage bare (bare like Richard Nuetra architecture, that is). There were no realistic sets. This freed the performers to easily move from scene to scene, from decade to decade, from character to character. The play moved as swiftly as a Santa Ana wind. Chavez Ravine is a play about an American city in constant flux: the action onstage flowed without the cumbersome trappings of a traditional play.

Vintage Chavez Ravine photographs by Don Normark. Chavez Ravine community portrait courtesy of Henry Cruz (RIP) and the Bishop Boys. Excerpts from "Cuervos" by Victor Valle used by permission; excerpts from the poem "Memories Around a Bulldozed Barrio" by Manazar Gamboa used by permission of Michelle Kholos for the Gamboa Literary Estate; "Barrio Viejo" words and music by Lalo Guerrero used by permission.

| ACT ONE |

Dodger Stadium—first inning, 1981.
The theater is the infield of Dodger Stadium, the pitcher's
mound faces the audience, we see part of the scoreboard and the
infield bases. We hear the final notes of the "National Anthem."
The crowd cheers.
   Lights up. Sportscast announcer Vin Scully stands in front of
a microphone wearing headphones.

VIN: Hello everybody, and a pleasant good afternoon to you,
   wherever you may be. Welcome to the 1981 opening day at
   Dodger Stadium. Vin Scully here on a perfect Southern
   California day. The sun is shining over brilliant azure skies
   and let me tell you the ballpark never looked prettier,
   resplendent in Dodger blue!
      Today's broadcast brought to you by Farmer John meat
   products, the only Southern California packers of Iowa
   corn-fed pork. Farmer John, the way ham oughta be, west-
   ern style. Next time, try a shank or butt portion with the
   bone left in.

Rookie Fernando Valenzuela (Herbert Siguenza).

Today's broadcast brought to you by the good folks at the Department of Water and Power.

(Fernando Valenzuela runs to the pitcher's mound.)

And here comes rookie Fernando Valenzuela, tapped by skipper Tommy Lasorda because of an injury to starting pitcher Jerry Reuss. My oh my, Fernando looking trimmer and leaner than he did in training camp. Today will be quite a test for young Valenzuela. Imagine folks, here's a young kid, speaks no English, and a little more than a year ago was playing far away, in the childhood sandlots of a sleepy Mexican village, in a place called Etchohuaquila, Sonora. This screwballing south paw is the youngest player since Catfish Hunter to start an opening day game. And after a quick scratch of the crotch, here we go.

Fernando taking the hill with a twenty-year-old heart beating—I'm sure a little bit harder than normal. There's fifty thousand plus in the ballpark and a million butterflies. Valenzuela takes a breath, getting ready to make his first pitch of the year to these Houston Astros. He looks in, takes the sign, the arms flailing, the eyes rolling to the back of the head . . . weird. Curveball for the first strike of the game. A nice start for this matinee crowd. *(Crowd cheers)* Fernando getting the folks on his side early. Valenzuela checking in, Scoscia wig-wagging a couple of signs, the wind-up, eyes looking skyward, tapped foul off to the left of the plate, strike two! *(Crowd cheers)*
The unorthodox Valenzuela backing off the mound now, mops his brow, runs his left index finger along his greasy forehead. Valenzuela now looking over to the second base area, he seems distracted folks.

(Small houses gently fall onto the outfield from above. Two Chavez Ravine residents enter like ghosts from another era: Maria, in a 1940s dress, carries a small house and places it on second base. Her brother, Henry, appears in WWII military dress. They look toward Fernando.)

I can't tell from here if Fernando is trying to say something to second baseman Davey Lopes or if something has caught his eye in center field.

(Maria places something underneath the house, on second base.)

I can tell you this, this home crowd is growing restless as Fernando holds up the game. He's never pitched in front of this many wild Dodger fans. What on earth is Valenzuela looking at?

(Henry, the soldier boy, speaks to Fernando:)

HENRY: Fernando, I was born behind second base and raised right here on La Bishops Road. I wanna tell you about a place very close to my heart, a place most people know as Chavez Ravine, but to the familias who lived here, these were neighborhoods.

MARIA: La Loma, Palo Verde and Bishop. We never called it Chavez Ravine.

HENRY: La Bishops Road ran through the base of a canyon located in the midst of five ravines:

MARIA: Chavez, Cemetery, Solano, Reservoir and Sulpher.

HENRY: This area was bordered by Echo Parque, North Broadway and Elysian Park. Some people called it a slum, Fernando.

MARIA: It was no slum, man. It was home.

HENRY: It was hard times to be sure.

MARIA: It was familia.

HENRY: My name is Henry Ruiz, this is my kid sister:

MARIA: Maria Salgado Ruiz.

FERNANDO *(Bewildered)*: Hola.

(Back to the game at Dodger Stadium.)

VIN: Valenzuela talking to Steve Garvey perhaps. That would be strange, Garvey no habla español. Here comes Skipper . . . Skipper Tommy Lasorda trotting out to the rubber to calm his rookie down. Tommy's looking trimmer and leaner than he did last season.

(An overweight stagehand in Dodger uniform enters from the audience as Tommy Lasorda.)

Lasorda's speaking a mouthful of Spanish to Valenzuela. He seems to be saying, hey kid, no more stalling, que la chingada!

(Tommy Lasorda hands Fernando a rosin bag and quickly exits.)

HENRY: Fernando, when I was born, my grandmother buried my umbilical chord under that house right there.

MARIA: All the abuelas did that.

HENRY: I don't really know why, I never questioned it.

MARIA: La Sobadora, the herb lady told us to do it.

HENRY: She lived near center field.

MARIA: La Sobadora's name was Juana de los Perros, she was a full-blooded Yaqui Indian. She was the lady in the neighborhood that could help you when you ate too many green apples or peaches from la Moore Park.

HENRY: Golly, some babies were born right on the kitchen table, te acuerdas, little sister?

MARIA: Sure I do. When babies were born, when people died in their homes, La Sobadora, La Juana de los Perros was there every time. These are sacred lands you're pitching on, Fernando. Long ago burial grounds for the Tongva, Chinese and Jewish gente.

(We hear bits and pieces of funeral services: the recorded sound of Native American/Chinese/Yiddish voices.)

These were all beautiful hills, Nando. May I call you Nando?

FERNANDO: Bueno.

MARIA: One hill, sloped down from the ridge overlooking our street. If you happened to walk down that hill's footpath, you would run directly into our back fence. And if you opened the fence's gate, you would be entering my universe. My universe consisted of my father's garden . . .

HENRY: . . . nopales, fig, loquat and apricot trees everywhere.

MARIA: Don't forget the fish ponds Papá made by hand . . .

HENRY: . . . and the billy goats, rabbits, roosters and sheep that ran around like they owned the pinche place!

MARIA: And at certain times of the year, the scent of wild, night jasmine filled the ravines.

HENRY: I think he's got the picture, Sis.

MARIA: Sacred land Fernando, don't ever let anyone tell you otherwise.

HENRY: Hey, hermana, take it easy, we're holding up the game, let's let the man pitch.

MARIA: You're not my father, Henry.

HENRY: Suave.

MARIA: Bonarue.

HENRY: Que la chingada.

(Back to Vin at Dodger Stadium.)

VIN: 0 and 2 as Fernando returns to the game. The youngster may have gotten dust in his eye, light winds are known to whip around the infield. He looked positively possessed from here. He takes the sign, the wind-up, the high-kick fly ball into right field, Pedro Guerrero turning now . . . and makes the grab.

(The crowd cheers. Fernando Valenzuela runs off.)

And so Valenzuela keeps the Astros on the launching pad. And at the end of half an inning, the Astros nothing and the Dodgers coming up. And, boy oh boy, do we have an unusual beginning to the twentieth season here at Chavez Ravine, que la chingada!

(The crowd roars. We hear church bells toll and the lights change as we are now in the courtyard of Santo Niño church, 1946. A large group has formed, including Maria, the Rodarte Brothers, a Kid and Lencho.)

ALL *(Singing)*:
Estas son las mañanitas
Que cantaba el rey David
A las muchachas bonitas
Le cantamos así,
Despierta, mi bien despierta
Que ya el sol amaneció . . .

(They trail off, forgetting the words to the traditional folk song.)

LENCHO: Who knows the words?

(Father Tommy enters.)

ALL:
>   For he's a jolly good fellow . . .

FATHER TOMMY: Ay, gracias hermanas y hermanos! Look, everybody's here, Señor Rosini, the Johnson brothers, Uri the sheepherder and, of course, the Arechiga clan with all fourteen of their children. You all bring such joy to my corazón.

MARIA (*Carrying a birthday cake*): Here you go, Father Tommy.

(Father Tommy blows out the candles on the cake. They all cheer.)

FATHER TOMMY: Every year on my birthday you wake me up at four in the morning, que Dios los bendiga.

KID: Hey, Father Tommy, you speak pretty good Spanish for a gringo!

FATHER TOMMY: That's right, sonny, yo sabo mucho!

LENCHO: Hey, Padre, how do, how do.

FATHER TOMMY: Lencho?

LENCHO: I'm only here for the free bagels and pan dulce. Let's party, daddy-o!

FATHER TOMMY: Pasen, pasen adentro, let's all go inside and enjoy some hot chocolate on the house . . . of the Lord.

MARIA: Happy birthday, Father Thomas.

FATHER TOMMY: Maria Salgado Ruiz, the ringleader! How are you this morning?

MARIA: Good as you and twice as fresh.

FATHER TOMMY (*Clearing his throat*): I have to say, Maria, you have organized another perfect party.

MARIA: I think I've found my calling, Father.

FATHER TOMMY: And is that calling serving the glory of our Lord as a nun?

MARIA: Nah, that's for squares, man. C'mon, it's 1946! I either want to be a back-up singer for the Chick Webb band or help underprivileged pachucos at the Lincoln Heights jail.

FATHER TOMMY: Oh Lord . . . (*He crosses himself*)

MARIA: Oh, Father Tom, I almost forgot, can we still have the Garment Union fundraiser here next Friday?

FATHER TOMMY: I wanted to talk about that Maria . . .

MARIA: Thank you, Padre, you're swell.

FATHER TOMMY: Say, Maria, you never bring your union organizer friends to mass.

MARIA: They're mostly Jewish, Padre.

FATHER TOMMY: Never mind then.

KID: Hey, Padre, what's the movie in the patio this week?

FATHER TOMMY: *The Grapes of Wrath.*

KID: Is it scary?

FATHER TOMMY: Yes it is.

(An elderly Señora with a cane enters.)

SEÑORA: Buenos dias, Father Tommy . . .

FATHER TOMMY: Ah, Señora Sanchez, buenos dias. How are you feeling this morning?

SEÑORA: Not too good on account of my arthritis. Mira no más. Se acabaron mis pastilles. And I'm a little gassy too. Escúchame, Father Tommy, vienen los Mariachis de Boyle Heights?

FATHER TOMMY: No, señora, but the Rodarte Brothers are here from City Terrace and they will play till your heart's content.

SEÑORA: Ay, me encanta cuando los hombres tocan la guitarra, toda la noche, toca toca toca toca! By the way, Father Tom, that was a beautiful service you did at the velorio for Bobby Casos's grandmother, rest in peace, pobrecita.

FATHER TOMMY: Thank you, señora, but I was very worried, it rained so hard up here they couldn't move the body from the house for five days.

SEÑORA: Oh no, Father Tommy, she's still there lying on the table dead as you please, Padre, right next to la potato salad.

FATHER TOMMY: Dear God. *(He crosses himself again)*

SEÑORA: Oh si, she's not ready to leave the Ravine yet.

FATHER TOMMY: Adiós, señora.

SEÑORA *(To the Rodarte Brothers)*: Marihuaneros!

(The Señora exits. Henry sneaks up behind Father Tommy.)

HENRY: Happy birthday, Father T.

FATHER TOMMY: Henry, the World War II veteran! Welcome home, son. We're all real proud of you.

(They embrace warmly.)

HENRY: It was an honor to serve my country, sir.

FATHER TOMMY: You don't have to sir me, Henry.

(Henry shuffles.)

Look at you. You make a better soldier than you did an altar boy.

HENRY: Are you still sore at me, Padre?

FATHER TOMMY: You're the only altar boy I ever fired from Santo Niño for pouring too much wine in the chalice.

HENRY: Well, you kept drinking so I kept pouring.

FATHER TOMMY: I did slur the scriptures that morning! Oh, but the collection baskets were full.

(They chuckle.)

You must be glad to be home?

HENRY: I suppose . . . *(Looks around)* Nothing ever changes around this place. *(Pointing off)* Still have that same dirt road coming up from Solano.

FATHER TOMMY: Oh yes, the car at the bottom has to wait for the car at the top to come down.

HENRY: And Pingüino the Ice Man?

FATHER TOMMY: . . . . Still delivers frozen blocks of water . . . up those one hundred and forty-four steps.

HENRY: Ah, cherry raspados, those were the best . . .

(Silence.)

FATHER TOMMY: Will you be living on your father's lot?

HENRY: I don't know, Padre.

FATHER TOMMY: Our Lord has a plan for you, Henry.

HENRY: Didn't see much of the Lord in Sai Pan.

FATHER TOMMY: He was there with you and your brother Arturo. Que descanse en paz.

(Father Tommy crosses himself. Henry's Mother enters.)

MOTHER: There's my mijo. I've been looking everywhere for him. Look how handsome he looks in his uniform. Give your mamá a kiss . . . on the lips, cabrón, on the lips. I suppose he's too . . . He's too high tone to kiss his mother anymore.

HENRY: Gee, Ma.

MOTHER: He came back skin and bones que no, Father Tom?

FATHER TOMMY: He looks like a soldier. He reminds me of his papá.

MOTHER: You should see the house, Father Tom, I have it all fixed up for Henry and his Soledad.

FATHER TOMMY: Swell.

MOTHER: Con las cortinas blancas y las hierbas, you have to come by and bless the casa, Father Tom.

HENRY: I already told ya, Ma, Hank Junior's getting big and we wanna have another baby right away.

FATHER TOMMY: That's wonderful.

HENRY: The house is too small.

MOTHER: But it's your house, Henry. Your daddy wanted you to live there, isn't that right, Father Tommy? And I won't hear another word about it.

HENRY: We'll see, Ma. I gotta go help Soledad. Con permiso.

FATHER TOMMY: Pásale Henry.

MOTHER: Mijo, there's a two-foot stack of homemade tortillas and menudo on the stove.

HENRY: I hate menudo, Ma.

MOTHER: Since when?

HENRY: I'll just get a French Dip at Phillipe's.

(Henry starts to exit.)

MOTHER: ¡Como que French Dip y la chingada! Sorry, Father Tommy.

MARIA: Hey everybody, let's jitterbug!

(Maria grabs Henry as the Rodarte Brothers strike up a few bars of "La Loma Boogie.")

RODARTE BROTHERS *(Singing)*:
    La Loma La Loma boogie . . .
    La Loma La Loma boogie . . .
    La Bishop La Bishop boogie
    La Bishop La Bishop boogie
    Palo Verde . . .
    That's where my baby's from!

(Lights change as two men enter.
We are high in the rolling hills of Elysian Park, 1949.)

NEUTRA: Slow down Wilkinson, you are walking too fast!

WILKINSON: You architects don't get out much, do ya? Aren't these rolling hills of Chavez Ravine a perfect site for a brand-new housing project? The sunshine, the fresh air . . . Take it in, man.

NEUTRA *(Hacking)*: But I cannot breathe.

WILKINSON: Well, what do you think of the land, Richard Neutra?

NEUTRA *(Catching his breath)*: I'm quite taken by this rural area, surrounded by rugged hills and rustic unpaved roads.

WILKINSON: These "rustic roads" are dangerous and impassable after hard rains.

NEUTRA: I find it astonishing that modern downtown Los Angeles is only two miles away from this charming "Aztec Village."

WILKINSON: It's a shanty town, Dick.

NEUTRA: Down on Bishops Road, I ate tacos with old men. I even met a Negro family on relief.

WILKINSON: A Negro family on relief? Why that's terrific. Don't you see, man, these are exactly the kind of people who will benefit most from your modular, low-slung, abstractly asymmetrical buildings.

NEUTRA: Exactly, but I am afraid it may not be possible to develop this area without destroying its rich assets.

WILKINSON: It is possible. But only with the modern designs of Richard Neutra, possibly the greatest architect of the twentieth century.

NEUTRA: You make me blush.

WILKINSON: You build it, Richard, build it right here in these hills, our dream project. You genius, you master of shape, you Bauhaus bohème, and it is you and Robert Alexander that they will remember, not Frank Lloyd what's-his-name.

NEUTRA: My legacy? Keep talking, Frankie.

WILKINSON: You know, Richard, I am somehow reminded of 1939, when I rode a bicycle across Palestine.

NEUTRA: You rode a bicycle across Palestine?

WILKINSON (*Pointing to himself*): When this kid from the Hills of Beverly saw the poor of the very poor, I made a vow then and there to always help the destitute.

(Breaking into song with the band:)

Lovely homes in the hills of Chavez,
My heart sings this true refrain,

Frank Wilkinson (Richard Montoya).

> Blighted are the homes of Chavez,
> We'll use th'eminent domain . . .

NEUTRA: Eminent domain?
WILKINSON: Sure . . . Like we did in Aliso Village . . .
NEUTRA: Never heard of it.

WILKINSON:
> And the garden homes of
> Ramona and Watts . . .

NEUTRA: Watts that?

WILKINSON:
> Sign today for a brand-new unit
> And leave behind your dirt-filled plot!

NEUTRA: I don't know, Frank.
WILKINSON: As site manager for the Housing Authority of the City of Angels, I will name this project . . . Elysian Park Heights!
NEUTRA: Not bad, Frank. Not bad.
WILKINSON: Think of it, Dick, thanks to the Federal Housing Act of 1949, we now have the resources to realize my dream, a dream for all Los Angeles, a city without slums. Real homes for the people, I say! Will you come along with me to make history, Richard Neutra? Don't make me drag this band all over town. Are you with me, Dick?
NEUTRA: Ya vol, I can see it Frank . . .

> . . . the promise of the grand revolution!
> Building homes for every average Joe.

NEUTRA AND WILKINSON:
> Toilets with a flushing handle,
> Water running hot and cold.

NEUTRA:
> Lovely homes in the hills of Chavez,

WILKINSON:
> For the underprivileged and the common man

NEUTRA AND WILKINSON:
> Finger parks for the kids to play in,
> Modern kitchens for Mom and Dad.

WILKINSON: Let's rush downtown . . . to present our master plan.

NEUTRA: Our master plan?

WILKINSON: Our master plan!

NEUTRA AND WILKINSON:
> Our master plan, our master plan,
> Our master plan plan plan plan plan plan plan plan plan!

(A sudden interruption: the sound of a woodpecker.)

WILKINSON: Look, Dr. Neutra, above the hedge, a woodpecker building a home.

NEUTRA: Biological realism, natural ingenuity!

NEUTRA AND WILKINSON:
> Our master plan!

(Neutra and Wilkinson exit. The band plays and sings.)

RODARTE BROTHERS *(Singing)*:
> Take me downtown
> To the center of the city.
> The future's being planned
> It's a town without pity.
> Downtown, there's movers and there's shakers.
> Downtown, there's givers and there's takers.
> Downtown, Downtown, Downtown, Downtown.

(Two men wearing gray trenchcoats and fedoras emerge from the shadows. They have been observing all. These shadowy and

powerful figures meet at center stage. They survey the land.
There is an exchange. The men shake hands and exit.
The photo of the village on a panel at the back of the stage
comes to life with the warm glow of the lights.
Enter Manazar, the dead poet. He will serve as narrator
remaining onstage, freely entering and exiting scenes.)

MANAZAR: Q'volé, my name is Manazar. I am a poet who grew up aquí in La Bishop. When I died, not too long ago, they spread my ashes all through these hills. Now, before we proceed with the play I have to take you back to the beginning, the genesis of this place. Hey, it's my job as your dead poet-slash-ghost presence-slash-narrator device que la chingada.

Now, the original familias came here in the 1920s, refugees of the Mexican Revolution. They came with very little and they found themselves in these empty hills and, sabes que, they needed houses, so the people worked together to build their casitas.

Now, I'm going to bring out some professional actors to help me dramatize these historical events, but first I have to read you the rules, gente. *(Pulls a piece of paper from his wallet)* What I got right here is rule number one. OK: the other actors will pretend not to hear or see me. Rule number two: only you, the audience, can hear or see me, so feel free to buy me a drink after the show, ay! Rule number three: any similarity between me and the Stage Manager in *Our Town* is purely coincidental.

(The actors walk on, wearing ponchos and signs delineating their characters: Chavez Ravine residents—"old man," "child," "campesino." They act in an overly exaggerated agitprop style.)

Órale, please welcome the Eminent Domain Players!
CAMPESINO: We have a very serious problem, gente. The ground on most of these lots has to be leveled before we can do any work.
OLD MAN: Pues, let's get a bulldozer!

CHILD: Pero Don Jorge, we can't afford it.

OLD MAN: Bueno. ¡Ni modo! ¡Vamos!

MANAZAR: Hey, I never said they went to the Actors Studio.

RESIDENTS: Hey . . .

MANAZAR: Soon more picks were swinging up and down, while shovels and wheelbarrows joined in, and before you know it . . .

RESIDENTS: We changed the face of the land.

Manazar (Herbert Siguenza, front) with the Eminent Domain Players (from left to right: Richard Montoya, Eileen Galindo and Ric Salinas).

MANAZAR: And a long caravan of ragtag cars and trucks, causing a large trail of dust, made its way up la Bishops Road hauling all sorts of building materials. Before long, a few casitas started to take shape. Frames of houses like skeletons appeared. Finalmente, after many months of intense labor, the gente climbed the eastern ridge to admire their creation.

RESIDENT 1: Casitas had been built everywhere.

RESIDENT 2: Improvised on the basins of canyons.

RESIDENT 1: The slopes of hills, the crests of ridges.

RESIDENT 3: And one small house stood sentry atop a hill.

RESIDENTS: Mira.

MANAZAR: They all stood there, proud.

RESIDENTS: Ahhhhhh . . . We had raised a Mexican village with nails, screws and faith.

(Meanwhile, in the downtown office of the City Housing Authority:)

HOLTZENDORF: Wilkinson, in my office, now!

WILKINSON: On my way, boss. Mr. Holtzendorf, I've been up at the Ravine all day with the architect Richard Neutra. Wait till ya get a load of these plans, Dicky boy!

NEUTRA: Guten morgen, Herr Holtzendorf.

HOLTZENDORF: We speak English here at the City Housing Authority, amigo.

NEUTRA: Very well.

(Drum roll.)

We propose building twenty-four thirteen-story buildings, and 162 two-story structures.

WILKINSON: In other words boss, seventeen thousand souls living in a racially integrated community, get it?

HOLTZENDORF: Thirteen stories, huh?

NEUTRA: Oh yes, I will integrate my modernistic designs, with the inside and outside fused—near-nature bio-realism. That gives me another idea: cul-de-sacs!

Neutra (Herbert Siguenza) and Wilkinson (Richard Montoya) present plans to the Residents.

HOLTZENDORF: Where the hell is this fella from?

NEUTRA: Vienna.

HOLTZENDORF: And you, Wilkinson?

WILKINSON: UCLA.

HOLTZENDORF: I'm a Trojan man myself.

WILKINSON: Very sorry to hear that, boss.

HOLTZENDORF: Listen, fellas, Mayor Bowron is behind us one hundred percent, but how are we going to sell this Chavez Ravine housing project in the court of public opinion?

WILKINSON: I can go up to the Ravine with Nacho Lopez—he speaks Spanish, boss—knock on every door and talk to the people face to face.

HOLTZENDORF: It's the bigwigs I'm worried about. Look, Wilkinson, I want you to round up every society dame, politician and two-bit newspaperman. Take them on your slum tours see, show them the blight firsthand.

WILKINSON: Slum tours are swell, boss, but I have another idea. Feature this, I know some film students over at USC, your alma mater. These kids are terrific. They could make a motion picture see, that would expose to the entire city the plight of the slums, up close and personal. We'll use dramatic music and all.

NEUTRA: Tan tan tan. That's a wonderful idea, Mr. Holtzendorf. We'll shoot in grainy black-and-white with smoke and shadows.

WILKINSON: We'll use real people boss, no phony actors. You could make a cameo.

NEUTRA: Reality cinema!

HOLTZENDORF: All right, but I want top billing and no subtitles. Now hit the highway and convince everyone that we need public housing here in Los Angeles!

NEUTRA AND WILKINSON: Yes sir. *(They exit)*

HOLTZENDORF: I'm gonna be in pictures . . . *(Whispering)* "Rosebud . . ."

(Meanwhile, back at the Ravine:)

BAND AND RESIDENT:
  Alpine,
  Dog Town,
  Happy Valley,
  La Macey,
  Clover,
  Las Avenues,
  Frog Town,

ALL:
  Hazard . . .

MANAZAR: I wanna talk about this picture right here.

(Manazar slowly moves a panel, revealing a large photo of actual Ravine residents, circa 1941.)

I see uncles, primas, I see my sister, mira, there's Joe Guerra and his brother Johnny. See that morenito kid right there in the middle? That's me with my carnal, they used to call me Nonio.

OFFSTAGE VOICES: Hey Nonio!

MANAZAR: If you look closely at the photo, some of the señoras are wearing the army hats, and on the hats are little stars. Those little stars are for their sons and daughters who were away—over there—serving their country. Some of the fellas never made it back.

My neighbors were Italians, Slavs, Russians and some Germans, but for the most part era pura Mexicanada, puro frijol. And on holidays, pura aroma de tamal y hecho al menudo, y los compadres tocando la guitarra till late at night. *(The Rodarte Brothers strum an old corrido)* That was our community. That's something you can never erase from your cabeza.

There was conflict, fist fights. Once in a while, un filero, a knife . . . *(A man shaves with a switchblade)* you know, for shaving, hardly no guns. Sometimes we'd rumble right in the parking lot at St. Peters. There were fights even between the viejas. One time Carol's mother and Genoveva were scratching and pulling their trensas.

(A woman fights with a female dummy.)

WOMAN: ¡You fucking bitch te mato!

MANAZAR: Those viejas were vicious man!

On Friday and Saturday nights, we would go to the dances. *(We hear some boogie-woogie)* Sometimes the Pachucos came, those guys were like knights in shining armor. They had a language all their own.

PACHUCO: Órale high-tone, ay te watcho in the ranfla with the two crazy rucas chichonas de Mary Queen of Angels ese vato loco camita, simón que yes.

MANAZAR: That was easy for him to say.

PACHUCO: La Tuya. Pinche Nonio.

MANAZAR: Nonio. See, we all had nicknames back then. Let's see, there was . . .

HANK JUNIOR: Whitey, Willie 77, She-Dog, Tarzan, Speedie . . .

MARIA: Silent Joe, Shy, You Bet as Will . . .

MANAZAR: Peewee, Pegleg, Peanut . . .

LENCHO: El Ripper, Golpes, Old Butter Milk Sky . . .

ALL: La Living Monster, Nonio, Little Blackie, Headlights, Six-pack, Mocoso and Once.

MANAZAR: We called him Once ("Eleven"), because he always had a runny nose. His twin brother was named Doce ("Twelve"), he had a harelip. And Two Nickel Donuts: she would roll her stockings all the way down to her ankles, so it looked like she had donuts on top of her shoes. Some-times they called me El Peludo ("The Hairy Guy"). When we would go skinny-diving, the guys would see the hairs all over my body, they said I looked like . . .

ALL: King Kong!

MANAZAR: And I was only ten years old, too. Bobby, Pete and me roamed the whole area up here: Bishops Road, Effie Road, Puto Hill. Climbed every darn tree, swam in the L.A. river . . . big rocks, clean water, earth, not concrete, big trout, you could cast a line, we would go skinny diving in there, walk downtown, Lincoln Avenue, La Temple, La Broadway . . . La Chinatown, take all the coins out of the good-luck fountains, hop the trolley over to the Coliseum and jump the fence. We would hang out all day at Elysian Park drinking moonshine and smoking reefer. Radio was big. On Sunday night, we would gather around and listen to Baby Snooks, Amos 'n' Andy, Red Skelton. We had our own comedians, too. We had a little stage right there. It's still there, they would get up there and talk all kinds of trash. Nicky Apodaca, he was the main one, he would have us laughing so hard our panzas would hurt!

(The band strikes up a few bars as Nicky appears.)

NICKY APODACA: OK, OK, thank you, gracias, ladies and ger-manies, carnales y carnalas, buenas nalgas! OK, OK, what kind of chickens do they raise in Palo Verde?

RESIDENTS: What kind, Nicky?

NICKY APODACA: Mexican chickens: they lay eggs with the chorizo already inside.

RESIDENTS: That's funny.

NICKY APODACA: OK, OK, OK, what kind of cans do they shoot over at the police academy?

RESIDENTS: What kind, Nicky?

NICKY APODACA: Mexi-cans!

RESIDENTS: That's a good one, Nicky.

NICKY APODACA: How many coppers does it take to find a stolen jukebox up here in Chavez Ravine?

RESIDENTS: How many, Nicky?

NICKY APODACA: One, because there's only one plug in the whole pinche neighborhood . . . Only one plug . . .

(Silence. Nicky bows his head and exits.)

MANAZAR: Nicky died onstage that day, and later he died in the war in Korea.

RESIDENT: Poor vato.

MANAZAR: Everything was here. We had a malt shop, pool parlors and a beauty shop. Once in a while we would go to Sears & Roebuck on Soto.

RESIDENT: That's right.

MANAZAR: When we went downtown, when we left the barrio, it was like going to el *Twilight Zone.*

(At the offices of the City Housing Authority, Wilkinson and Holtzendorf watch the finished Chavez Ravine film in the dark. A shadowy figure, wearing a trenchcoat and fedora, enters and delivers a letter to Holtzendorf.)

NARRATION *(On film)*: Well, what did ya find out? Does Los Angeles need ten thousand new houses?

BOB, THE HOUSING MAN *(On film)*: Brother, and ten thousand more!

(Dramatic music. Shadowy figure exits. Lights up.)

WILKINSON: So, what d'ya think of the motion picture, boss?

HOLTZENDORF: Frank, I'm gonna have to ask you to sign a loyalty oath.

WILKINSON: A loyalty oath? To whom?

HOLTZENDORF: To the goddamned U.S. of A., that's who!

WILKINSON: Supposing I don't sign a loyalty oath, boss?

HOLTZENDORF: Supposing you do!

WILKINSON: Well I've done nothing wrong, Mr. Holtzendorf.

HOLTZENDORF: That don't matter, Frank, we've all signed them. Look, we've got a hundred million dollars from Uncle Sam on the line and the feds already have a burr up their ass with the Hollywood Ten.

WILKINSON: What's that got to do with the Housing Authority?

HOLTZENDORF: There's a war on communism. Now sign the oath or we lose the dough!

WILKINSON: Well, all right.

HOLTZENDORF: That a boy. Now, where's that letter to the Chavez Ravine residents?

WILKINSON: It's right here in my satchel, boss.

HOLTZENDORF: This should have gone out months ago.

WILKINSON: I'm trying my level best. We've been awful busy, Mr. Holtzendorf.

(Holtzendorf begins to read the Chavez Ravine letter. As he begins to read, a light comes up on Maria reading the same letter in Spanish.)

HOLTZENDORF: July 24, 1950. To the families of Chavez Ravine areas, this letter is to inform you that a public housing development will be built on this location for families of low income. The attached map shows the property that is going to be used. The house you are living in is included. You will be visited by representatives of the Housing Authority who will inspect your house in order to estimate its value. It will be several months before your property is purchased. Later, you will have the first chance to move into the new . . .

MARIA *(Overlapping)*: A las familias de Chavez Ravine, Esta carta es para informarles que un proyecto de vivienda pública será construída para familias de bajos recursos. El mapa incluido muestra la propiedad que se utilisará. La casa en que vive está incluída. Usted será visitado por un representate de la Autoridad de vivienda para inspeccionar su casa y estimar su valor. Su casa y propiedad serán compradas por la ciudad. Usted tendrá la primera oportunidad de mudarse al nuevo proyecto . . .

MARIA AND HOLTZENDORF: Elysian Park Heights Development.

HOLTZENDORF: Good.

MARIA: Dios mío, Mamá, Henry, have you read this letter?!

(We hear "I'm Dreaming of a White Christmas.")

MANAZAR: One night, it snowed in Chavez Ravine. It really only snowed on a few streets, but it was magical. The kids got up to go to school, but no way did anybody go. We could hardly believe it, white snow falling on La Loma, the muddy streets and cotton willows. Christmas must be coming to Bishop, I just hope St. Nick doesn't lose his way and get jumped in the Ravines.

HENRY: Merry Christmas, everybody.

MARIA: Merry Christmas, Henry.

MOTHER: Merry Christmas, mijo. Oye, where's Soledad and the kids? We should all be together en la Nochebuena, no?

MARIA: Did you see the snow, Henry, isn't it beautiful?

HENRY: It's just swell.

MARIA: Don't be a scrooge.

HENRY: Mamá, Soledad and I have been talking.

MOTHER: Qué bueno mijo, married couples should talk every once in a while, your father was so quiet. Are you hungry?

HENRY: We have to talk about the city's offer.

MOTHER: Oh, not now, mijo, it's Christmastime. Siéntate.

HENRY: I think we should take it.

MARIA: Have you lost your marbles, Henry?

HENRY: It sounds like a good thing.

MOTHER: It's not a good thing, Henry.

HENRY: It's good money, Mamá.

MOTHER: It's not about the money mijito.

HENRY: Look, I talked to the Housing Authority man yesterday, they'll pay what the house is worth.

MARIA: You talked to the gringo behind Mamá's back?

HENRY: Yeah, I did. I've been wanting to move outta here for a long time.

MOTHER: Well I don't want to move out of here. This is where you were born, this is where your abuelos died.

HENRY: This place is full of pinche ghosts.

MANAZAR: Hey, hey, hey!

MOTHER: Watch your mouth, it's Christmastime.

HENRY: Sorry, Ma.

MOTHER: This is where my compadres are, Henry.

HENRY: Your compadres are moving.

MOTHER: That's not so.

HENRY: Don't you want to move to San Gabriel?

MOTHER: I hate San Gabriel.

HENRY: What about San Fernando?

MOTHER: I hate San Fernando more than I hate San Gabriel.

MARIA: Saints make lousy cities, soldier boy.

HENRY: Mamá, Soledad and I are going to sell the house.

MOTHER: What did you say?

HENRY: We're selling, Ma.

MOTHER: No, mijo, no, your daddy gave you that house.

HENRY: Father didn't give us shit! He left that house, he left you.

MOTHER *(Slaps Henry)*: Desgraciado.

MARIA: Go ahead and leave then, Henry, I'm staying here with Mamá.

HENRY: What do you know, little sis? You're too busy hanging around those pachucos and the Reds at the Union Hall.

MARIA: Those Reds are gonna help us fight the city.

HENRY: Sooner or later you are going to have to sell. And the longer you wait, the less they offer.

MARIA: I don't care about money, I'm Red remember?

HENRY: You better watch what you say, little sis.

MOTHER: ¡Ya basta!

MARIA: We're gonna stay.

HENRY: Stay here then, with your billy goats and your hand-me-downs.

MOTHER: Cállense los dos, already. Hank, do what you have to do, you have your own familia now. Your sister and I are staying put. But do me a favor, si vendes tu casa, if you dare sell that little house that your father built with his hands and sweat and blood, don't look back, mijo, because you will never ever set foot in this house again, mentiendes?

(Henry walks out the door. Maria stops him on the porch.)

MARIA: Henry, wait! Where are you going?

HENRY: Soledad is waiting for me. We're gonna stay with her family in Boyle Heights for a while.

MARIA: Ma's just trying to keep us all together.

HENRY: I have my own family to worry about now.

MARIA: Don't you remember when Dad left here?

HENRY: Sure I do.

MARIA: He waved at us and then just walked away.

HENRY: He walked all the way to the Mexican border looking for work, they said.

MARIA: The guy just disappeared.

HENRY: I am not my old man, Maria.

MARIA: You're taking the kids away from Mamá.

HENRY: It's a free country, little sis. I'm taking my GI Bill and the city dough and never looking back. I'm gonna give my kids more than footprints in the dirt and chicken shacks. It's a goddamned slum up here.

MARIA: You don't mean that, Henry.

HENRY: Sure I do, Maria, there's a world over this hill. I fought for it, our brother Arturo died for it and I want my kids to see it. We're gonna move west, Maria.

MARIA: West?

HENRY: Echo Park maybe.

MARIA: You can't afford Echo Park.

HENRY: There's nothing here.

MARIA: We have everything here.

(A car horn honks.)

HENRY: I gotta go.

MARIA: So long, Henry.

(Henry leaves.)

(To nobody) Feliz Navidad.

(Manazar silently joins Maria on the porch. The porch light flickers on her. Maria disappears into the house. Lights up on Manazar.)

MANAZAR: Henry never set foot in his mother's house again. Hey, six thousand dollars seemed like a fortune back then. When I left la Bishop, I was riding in the back of my father's pickup truck. I didn't even have time to say good-bye to my friends, nada.

(We hear the rumbling of an old pickup truck.)

I was just sitting in the back, looking at the houses, trying to memorize the streets, the trees, the gullies, the little arroyos. I tried to burn it into my cabeza, so that I would never forget.

(The band reprises the "Downtown Song": "There's movers and there's shakers . . ."
     Two men talk: Mover and Shaker. They wear white trench-coats and fedoras.)

SHAKER: This public housing program is stinko, I tell ya. It's like three-day-old fish and I ain't buying.

MOVER: Mayor Bowron and his liberal do-gooders have been able to muster up plenty of lettuce from the feds to build their dream houses.

SHAKER: A hundred million clams and they don't have to answer to anyone.

The Watchman (Herbert Siguenza) spooks the Mover (Richard Montoya, left) and Shaker (Ric Salinas).

MOVER: I smell a rat, I tell ya.

SHAKER: We got to put a stop to it, see.

MOVER: I got forty acres up at the Ravine and I ain't selling at their price, see.

SHAKER: I got three lots up Bunker Hill with the DWP. That's still the big game in town.

MOVER: Not this subsidized housing for the poor! Cry me a river!

SHAKER: It's un-American.

MOVER: That land should be used for private real-estate interests.

SHAKER: Preserve the free enterprise system for all Americans. And I mean all *Americans!* Except the japs, the chinks, the hebes, the spics, the fags and the niggers. I leave anybody out?

MOVER: The micks, the guineas and the krauts.

SHAKER: Them, too. We need to stop the Housing Authority before they break ground, see.

MOVER: Hell's bells, how we gonna do that?

(We hear a voice from the shadows as a cigarette lighter flicks on:)

VOICE: Light is the one thing communist vermin cannot stand, and publicity is the most effective way a free society can control them.

SHAKER: What's the big idea you sneaking up on us with that dramatic voice and all?

(It's the Watchman, in black fedora and trench coat, smoking a cigarette.)

MOVER: Yeah, who are you?

WATCHMAN: Who are you?

SHAKER: Who are you?

WATCHMAN: Who are you?

MOVER: Who are you?

WATCHMAN: You first.

SHAKER: You first.

WATCHMAN: You first.

MOVER: Ah right, ah right. I'm Mr. Mover and he's Mr. Shaker.

SHAKER: We're the Pep Boys, see. What's your racket, fella?

MOVER: Spill!

WATCHMAN: Let's just say I share your interests, gentlemen. You can call me . . . the Watchman.

MOVER AND SHAKER: The Watchman?

WATCHMAN *(Wicked)*: Ha ha ha ha ha ha ha ha ha.

SHAKER: Hey, Watchman. I'll take a Rolex for Hannukah, ha ha . . .

WATCHMAN: Save the comedy for Howdy Doody. You wanna stop the Housing Authority?

SHAKER: Sure we do, plenty awful.

WATCHMAN: We need to kill this public housing project by calling it socialistic, see? We need to convince everyone that the top brass at the City Housing Authority are communist infiltrators, see?

MOVER AND SHAKER: We see.

WATCHMAN: Maybe we'll get Joe McCarthy to make a house call.

SHAKER: Say, Joe McCarthy is swell.

WATCHMAN: Marx is working down at the CHA.

MOVER: Which one, Groucho or Zeppo?

SHAKER: Why, that's the most ridiculous thing I ever heard.

(Mover and Shaker laugh at their joke.)

WATCHMAN: Shut your pie-holes and listen up! I'm putting together a committee of twenty-five of the most powerful men in Los Angeles. You fellas should come down and take a steam with us at the Jonathon Club.

SHAKER: Say, the Jonathon Club is flossy!

WATCHMAN: Sure it is. You haven't lived till ya seen Fritz Burns and Asa Call snapping wet towels at each other.

MOVER AND SHAKER: Oooh.

WATCHMAN *(Impatiently)*: So, what d'ya say? You're either with us or you're against us.

MOVER: Wait a minute, Watchman, what about the mayor?

SHAKER: Fletcher Bowron's sweet on the housing plan, ain't he?

WATCHMAN: Mayor Bowron will testify to HUAC . . .

MOVER AND SHAKER: House Un-American Activities Committee.

WATCHMAN: You think the voters will want to reelect a commie sympathizer? Besides, I got the perfect stooge and my money says he'll be the next mayor.

SHAKER: Meanwhile, we let the City Housing Authority continue to do our dirty work.

WATCHMAN: Bingo.

MOVER: Getting rid of the Mexicans?

WATCHMAN: Bingo again. So what d'ya say?

MOVER: I'll get all my highfalutin' real-estate friends from Bel Air to Pasadena onboard.

SHAKER: I'll call in my marker on the Chamber of Commerce.

MOVER: Say, Watchman, what are you bringing to the party?

SHAKER: Yeah.

WATCHMAN: Let's just say: "The pen is mightier than the sword."

SHAKER: What do ya mean by that, fancy fella?

WATCHMAN: Don't you fellas read the *Times*?

(The Watchman exits.)

MOVER: That fella scared me plenty. I peed in my pantalonees.

SHAKER: Look at ya. They can drip-dry standing while we grab a burger at Tommy's—let's roll!

(We hear the scratchy, sad, antiquated sounds of Russian marching music. Lights come up on a small shack in the Ravine. We are in the dreary universe of Uri, the Russian Sheepherder. He sits in his shack, singing to the Russian marching music, which he plays on his phonograph. There is a knock at the shack door. It is Maria. She holds a plate of hot food.)

MARIA: Uri? Uri the Sheepherder, are you in your shack?

(Aggressive sheep nip at her heels.)

URI: Maria, come in, hurry, close door, don't let the sheep in! Vohr. Vohr.

MARIA *(Entering the shack)*: Hello, Uri, I wanted to make sure you had a hot meal this week.

URI: Always thinking of others, Maria. Can I offer you some Russian vodka?

MARIA: Sounds like a capital idea.

URI: I make myself.

MARIA: Nice pinup poster.

URI: My girlfriend, Jane Russell. Nastrovia!

(They clink glasses and drink.)

MARIA: Have some tamales while they're still hot.

(Uri tears into the plate of tamales with great skill.)

URI: I not have tamales like this since Mexico City.

MARIA: Mexico City?

URI: In the home of Frida Kahlo and her husband what's-his-name, the big fat painter guy. My boss Leon Trotsky is there. Uri was personal valet to Trotsky.

MARIA: How exciting.

URI: Poor Trotsky bite right into tamale without removing corn husk, he almost choke to death. Uri have to pull tamale from Trotsky throat. And Frida, lovely Frida, with her unibrow, laughing like the devil. Those Mexicans, always trying to kill Comrade Leon. *(He laughs. Maria is silent)* What is wrong, Maria, you not like Uri's story?

MARIA: It's a swell story. —Uri, families all over the Ravine are taking the city offer.

URI: I'm sorry to hear about your brother.

MARIA: The city shouldn't be able to force people away from their homes, off their land. Goddamnit, Uri.

URI: Take it from a communist, it is un-American.

MARIA: I agree.

(Maria gulps the remaining vodka.)

URI: "It is better to die on your feet than to live on your knees."

MARIA: Is that Russian?

URI: No, Emiliano Zapata say this.

(Maria's spirits are lifted for the moment.)

MARIA: What do we do?

URI: At the Workman's Circle, Maria, we are talking about building coalitions.

MARIA: I heard Carey McWilliams speak about that last week at the Figueroa Hotel.

URI: Good. Strength in numbers!

MARIA: What if we form a homeowners coalition?

URI: Now Maria is thinking.

MARIA: I want you to be the chairman, Uri.

URI: Nyet, nyet, no!

MARIA: No?

URI: This is job for Maria!

MARIA: But I'm not ready.

(Uri reaches for a dusty book from his nightstand.)

URI: I give you this book. Read it and you will be ready.

MARIA *(Reading)*: Karl Marx.

URI: Autographed by the author himself!

MARIA *(Reading inscription)*: "To Uri, love and kisses, Karl." Why I couldn't . . .

URI: You need this more than I, comrade. Come back tomorrow, Maria, we read *Communist Manifesto* and the *Treaty of Guadalupe Hidalgo*, written in the same year!

MARIA: You are a kind old gentleman.

URI: I am just lonely old sheepherder, with fleas.

(Maria moves to the door.)

MARIA: Oh, Uri? I wanted to thank you for helping me with the elementary school theater project this year.

URI: Maria, do you think Stanislavsky might be too much for second graders?

(Lights fade to black. Lights come up on a town hall meeting at Santo Niño church:)

MOB OF RESIDENTS: No nos moverán, we won't move . . .

(They all break into song: "This Land Is Your Land.")

MARIA: Hello, gente, and welcome everybody to the first Palo Verde Home Owners Protective Society Fundraiser!

(Cheers as the band vamps.)

MOB OF RESIDENTS: No nos moverán. We won't move!

MARIA: It gives me great pleasure to introduce a surprise guest. Please welcome a new friend to the neighborhood, el Señor Pete Seeger.

PETE SEEGER: Hello everybody. Sure is swell to be here with you. Gracias para invitarlo.

RESIDENT 1: ¡Tócate un pinche corrido gringo!

PETE SEEGER: Whatever it is you said, muchas gracias, señor. I wanna thank Maria for organizing this swell event. Why, she's getting to be quite an organizer. I know she's been workin' with ol' Fred Ross over at the Brooklyn Avenue CSO. Before you know it, Maria might be hobnobbing with the big boys downtown: the Ahmansons, Chandlers and the Tapers . . . *(Crowd boos)* Don't worry folks, none of those fat cats are here tonight (well, some of the Taper folks are here but that's an entirely different story).

Here's a couple verses Woody wrote you never get to hear anymore. Let's pick up the tempo, fellas!

(Pete sings a few, more obscure, verses of "This Land Is Your Land" with the band. The crowd cheers. Pete exits.)

MARIA: Thanks, Pete! Hey everybody, don't forget to support our production of the *Cherry Orchard* tomorrow night, starring the second graders of Palo Verde grammar school, co-directed by Uri the Sheepherder and myself.

URI: Next year, *War and Peace*, with the first graders!

MOB OF RESIDENTS: No nos moverán, we won't move . . .

SEÑORA: ¿Maria, Maria, mijita cuándo vienen los Mariachis de Boyle Heights? Me encanta cuando los hombres tocan la guitarra, toda la noche, toca, toca, toca . . .

MARIA: No Mariachis tonight, Señora Sanchez, but we do have the Rodarte Brothers from City Terrace.

SEÑORA: Estos pachucos, greñudos. ¡Andale marihuaneros! A one, a two, a you know what to do!

(The Rodarte Brothers play. Señora plays the trumpet.)

MARIA *(To Señora)*: Thank you, you're a regular Dizzy Gillespie.

SEÑORA: But I couldn't get my solo, mija.

MARIA: I'm sorry.

SEÑORA *(To the Rodarte Brothers)*: You messed me up, you motherfuckers.

(Maria notices Nacho Lopez and Richard Neutra standing in the back of the hall.)

MARIA: Excuse me, you two gentlemen standing in the back, would you please step forward and tell us who you are?

(There is a rustle in the crowd.)

NACHO LOPEZ: Claro que sí. *(Clearing his throat)* Muchas gracias, señorita. Buenas noches, amigos. Damas y caballeros, venimos para explicar la importancia y la necesidad del proyecto de vivienda . . .

MAN: We speak English, buey!

NACHO LOPEZ: Very well. I am with the City Housing Authority.

MOB OF RESIDENTS: Boo . . .

NACHO LOPEZ: I am translator Nacho Lopez.

MOB OF RESIDENTS: Vendido! Sellout!

NACHO LOPEZ: This gentleman is architect Richard Neutra.

NEUTRA: Halo.

MOB OF RESIDENTS: Boo . . .

NEUTRA: Bye-bye . . .

MOB OF RESIDENTS: No nos moverán . . . We won't move . . .

(Nacho Lopez tugs on Neutra to stay put.)

NACHO LOPEZ: Where's Wilkinson?

(Nacho Lopez and Neutra go back and forth looking for Wilkinson. Neutra hits Nacho with his blueprints.)

Pete Seeger (Richard Montoya, foreground) and the Residents.

MOB OF RESIDENTS: No nos moverán . . . no nos moverán . . .

MARIA: Por favor, gente. Let's settle down, cálmense. These señores had the courage to come here from downtown. Why don't we show them more respect than the city usually shows us, eh?

WILKINSON *(Entering)*: And we certainly do appreciate that, young lady. My name is Frank Wilkinson and I am with the City Housing Authority.

MOB OF RESIDENTS: Boo!

WILKINSON: I only ask for a few minutes of your time, brothers and sisters. I'll take it from here, fellas.

NEUTRA: Thank God you arrived, Frank. The Aztecs were getting restless.

(The Mob of Residents reacts.)

NACHO LOPEZ: Mr. Wilkinson, these people won't listen.

WILKINSON: Nacho.

NACHO LOPEZ: Yes, boss.

WILKINSON: Go wait in the car. Keep the motor running.

(Nacho Lopez exits.)

Folks, consider this . . .

MOB OF RESIDENTS: Why are you taking away our homes? Fuck you! Go away, gringo!

MARIA: People are angry, Mr. Wilkinson, we never had a chance for a public hearing.

WILKINSON: I assure you that will not happen again.

MARIA: Is that a promise?

WILKINSON: You bet it is.

MARIA: We're gonna hold you to that, sir.

WILKINSON: Go right ahead, young lady. Folks, think of the positive effects this brand-new housing project will have on all of you and your children.

ONE-ARM VET: I fought in the war, and this is how you pay me?

RESIDENT 1: You tell 'em, Lefty.

WILKINSON: May I tell you a little something about the war, brother? A couple of years ago, I accompanied some military men to deliver a bronze star to a dead soldier's family up here in the Ravine. They called our office because they couldn't even find the street on a city map. They figured I could find the place. I did. Well, we finally found the dead boy's ma and pa living in the squalor of a filthy tent, next to an open sewage ditch, and I'm here now and I can see that nothing's changed. *(Crowd reacts)* We've already found bubonic plague at Terminal Annex just down the road and you've got a terrible vermin problem up here. Now come on, you folks deserve better and this is it. *(Crowd reacts)* Los Angeles could be the first large American city without slums.

ELDER WOMAN: This is no slum! This has been my home, and I do not want to sell or move or be chased out like a pack of wild dogs. I'm too old to find a new casa.

WILKINSON: I appreciate your concerns, señora, believe you me. We will do everything possible to help you find affordable, temporary housing until the project is built.

MARIA: How can these folks buy a home in another part of the city with the money you offer us?

OLD MAN: I have thirteen grandchildren and a large hat collection, where do we go?

WILKINSON: We will assist you in finding a home big enough for you and your clan of thirteen. And, remember, we will give you a certificate saying you all have first priority to return to the new housing project as soon as it's complete.

MARIA: Is that another promise, Mr. Wilkinson?

WILKINSON: You bet it is. We'll build day nurseries for the children, an outdoor auditorium for entertainment. Three-, four-, and five-bedroom homes with flushing toilets and washing machines on every floor.

MOB OF RESIDENTS: Ooooh . . .

WILKINSON: And you will not pay utilities.

MAN: How much is the rent?

RESIDENT 1: Yeah, how much is this gonna cost us?

WILKINSON: According to what you can pay, fellas. The average rent is thirty, forty dollars or so.

OLD MAN: Do you want to live in houses stacked on top of each other so high our children might fall out the windows?!

RESIDENT 2: We'll be packed in like sardines!

NEUTRA: Let me address the sardine issue, if I may. Ladies and gentlemen, I have designed a new modern village with plenty of light, air and space. Interior streets will end in cul-de-sacs that are very safe for children to play. The two-story units will face wonderful gardens and finger parks.

RESIDENT 3: What the hell are finger parks?

RESIDENT 1: What the hell are culo-sacs?

NEUTRA: Amigos, the thirteen-story buildings will have communal space and kitchens on every other floor, to create a sense of tribal unity. (Boos) You people do not understand architecture!

WILKINSON: Richard . . . go wait in the car with Nacho.

(Neutra exits.)

RESIDENT 2: Mr. Wilkinson, what if we decide not to move?!

WILKINSON: Folks, this is a court-ordered condemnation, the city will enforce her Eminent Domain law to the fullest.

MARIA: This Eminent Domain, isn't that just a weapon the city uses when it wants to steal our land?

(The crowd reacts.)

WILKINSON: It's in the Constitution, folks, the U.S. Government gives cities the power to take private land if it's for the greater public good.

MARIA: But it's not for *our* greater good, Mr. Wilkinson! Why don't you take your Eminent Domain law back to the Westside?

(The crowd cheers.)

WILKINSON: The city of L.A. doesn't need the Westside just yet, thank you very much. What I mean to say is there are no slums on the Westside.

OLD MAN: Have you been to Venice Beach?

WILKINSON: Look, you folks need this.

RESIDENT 3: This is a trick!

OLD MAN: You're getting rich off our land!

WILKINSON: I don't make a gosh darn penny from any of this. You've gone a little too far, señor. Look, I know this is a very difficult time for you all. I know a thing or two about change. But, this will be for the betterment of all your lives. I believe in public housing, I do. I've lived in public housing with my wife and children. I've stood in silent vigils till the restricted covenant laws of Central and La Brea Avenues were lifted, allowing Negro families to move in for the first time, by the way. Believe me, Frank Wilkinson is for the people, I tell ya.

(The crowd reacts.)

RESIDENT 4: Why should we believe you?

MOB OF RESIDENTS: No nos moverán . . . no nos moverán . . .

DON MAGDALENO: ¡UN MOMENTO! ¡UN MOMENTO! ¡UN MOMENTO! *(Fires a gun into the air. Silence)* Lo que dicen estos señores, francamente yo lo veo bien. ¡Yo soy comunista! ¡Soy del club socialista de Morelos! Yo peleé con Emiliano Zapata con el moviemiento. Tierra y Libertad.

URI: Viva Zapata!

DON MAGDALENO: Gracias Uri. Todos tenemos que sacrificar algo para el bien de todos. ¡Eso es el progreso, señores! ¡No sean pendejos, háganlo por sus hijos, por su futuro, chingado! I have the deed to my land right here, and I am ready to sign, sir! ¿Quién me sigue? Who else?

OLD MAN: Don Magdaleno is right. We must do this for our children. And our children's children. I'll sign, Mr. Wilkinson.

(The Mob of Residents ad-lib agreement.)

DON MAGDALENO: Who's got a fountain pen? I need a fountain pen, chingado.

(The crowd applauds as Wilkinson hands Magdaleno a pen and shakes a few hands.)

MARIA: Well, Mr. Wilkinson, looks like you got what you wanted.

WILKINSON: They won't be sorry, Maria. Right?

MARIA: Vamos a ver, Mr. Wilkinson. We'll see.

RODARTE BROTHERS *(Launching into their "This Land Is Your Land" parody, singing)*:
This land is your land,
But it once was my land,
Before we sold you Manhattan Island,
You pushed our nations
To the reservations
Remember,
This land belongs to you and me.

(At the darkened end of a train platform at Union Station:)

UNION STATION VOICE: Starlite Express departing to Bakersfield, Fresno, Sacramento, Eureka, Redding. Final destination Eugene, Oregon. All aboard.

WATCHMAN: Norris Poulson, where ya headed?

POULSON: I'm going fishing up in Oregon, congressional recess.

WATCHMAN: We've kept close tabs on your voting record, Congressman Business: anti-labor, anti-communists, chasing all those pinkos outta Hollywood . . .

POULSON: Thank you. Say, who are you?

WATCHMAN: You can call me the Watchman.

POULSON: You scare me. I have a train to catch.

WATCHMAN: This train doesn't move till I say it moves. Listen to me and listen carefully, I want you to run for mayor of Los Angeles.

POULSON: The next mayor of Los Angeles? I don't think so. I've been working like a horse lately. I have to take nervous pills now.

WATCHMAN: Easy, boy-o. There are powerful interests in this city with plenty of cash and influence to help you beat the pants off that liberal, Mayor Bowron.

POULSON: "Powerful interests"?

WATCHMAN: I've put together a group called the Committee of Twenty-Five.

POULSON: Angelinos?

WATCHMAN: No, Anglos.

POULSON: Like who for instance . . .

WATCHMAN: Oh, the boys over at Pacific Mutual Life, Barker Brothers, some oilmen, a little outfit called O'Melveny & Meyers, and yours truly from the *Times*.

POULSON: Is that you, Mister Chandler? I love your column.

WATCHMAN: Shut your trap. Don't disappoint us, Poulson.

POULSON: How can you guarantee my victory?

WATCHMAN: It's already done. And in return you'll help *us* out with some real-estate deals, a water diversion plan or two, and, oh yeah, a particular housing project . . .

POULSON: I need time to think about this.

WATCHMAN: We have no time. The campaign starts tomorrow. Your first speech is in your pocket.

POULSON: In my pocket? . . . I'm nervous . . . nervous like a turkey in November.

(The Watchman is gone. Poulson fumbles retrieving the speech from his pocket. He looks bewildered as he is pulled along by "The Poulson Jingle":)

RODARTE BROTHERS *(Singing)*:
    Choo choo,
    All aboard
    The Poulson Express!
    Take the red line or
    Angels Flight.
    We got a knockout
    Who won't stop the fight.
    Vote Poulson for mayor
    Of Los Angeles!
    Choo choo!

(Back at the Ravine, we hear a knock on a door.)

MR. ROSINI: Signora, *buona pasqua*, may I come in?
MOTHER: Claro, claro que sí, Señor Rosini.
MR. ROSINI: Signora, I will not stay long. I miss Henry and his little bambinos.
MOTHER: They moved away to Pacoima.
MR. ROSINI: Sounds terrible.
MOTHER: Oh, it's ugly out there.
MR. ROSINI: Not too many families left, eh?
MOTHER: No, not too many of us left.
MR. ROSINI: Very sad. I want to say happy Easter and give to you a bottle of vintage wine. I made it myself today! This morning was a very good year, eh!
MOTHER: Ay, gracias, Señor Rosini.
MR. ROSINI: Signora, we are all so proud of your sons. With them we beat the crap out of Mussolini, eh? Fascist Pig! *(Spits)* Oh sorry. I must go, eh?

MOTHER *(Bending down to clean up his spit)*: Adiós. Tell Señora Rosini to come over anytime, mi casa es su casa.

MR. ROSINI: That's a nice. Don't forget, Bosco's Car Agency on Broadway is giving away the Happy Easter baskets to all the bambini. I tell my children to get a basket, come home, put on different sweater and go back and get another basket. Old Sicilian trick. Ha ha ha.

MOTHER: Señor Rosini, you're a regular Italian Buddy Hackett.

MR. ROSINI: Signora, I almost forgot to tell you . . . we take the city offer. We find a nice little house. *(Teary)* Tomorrow we move to Glendale. Ciao!

(Mr. Rosini exits crying. We hear "The Poulson Jingle":)

RODARTE BROTHERS *(Singing)*:
    Choo choo,
    All aboard
    The Poulson Express!
    Take the red line or
    Angels Flight.
    We got a knockout
    Who won't stop the fight.
    Poulson for mayor
    He won't let you down
    He'll kiss the babies, the mommies
    And kick out the commies.
    Poulson for mayor of
    Los Angeles!
    Choo choo!

(The sound of a flashbulb.)

NEWSREEL VOICE-OVER: Mayoral candidate Norris Poulson hits the campaign trail like a storm trooper! *(Flash)* Here's our next mayor being kissed on the cheek by five-year-old "Miss Sugar Beet Queen." *(Sound of an air kiss) (Flash)* Here's Nervous Norrie riding a burro on Olvera Street.

("Viva Poulson!" Flash) Here's Mr. Poulson with the buxom blond "Miss Frozen Food 1953." *(Whistle!)*

POULSON: I am the anti-housing candidate and proud of it, and I will strike out . . .

WATCHMAN *(Lowers his L.A. Times)*: Creeping socialism.

POULSON: Creepy socialism! Thank you.

(Applause. "The Poulson Jingle" is sung under. A phone rings.)

CHIEF PARKER: Police Chief Parker here. Hello, Watchman. Yes, dirt on Frank Wilkinson from the Housing Authority? My intelligence man has been eyeballing the pinko for months. I'll call the Bureau myself, we'll go right to the top.

(Another phone rings.)

DIRECTOR HOOVER: J. Edgar Hoover here. Hello, Chief Parker. Why, I've got a dossier on Wilkinson bigger than Uncle Miltie's pecker. The poor bastard will never know what hit him.

(Another phone rings.)

WATCHMAN: Watchman here. Why thank you, J. Edgar. We certainly know who wears the pants in Washington. We'll get this information to the right hands. Frank Wilkinson's dead; he just don't know it yet.

("The Poulson Jingle" ends with:)

RODARTE BROTHERS *(Singing)*:
Choo choo.

(Later. Downtown. Maria pays a visit to Mr. Wilkinson. A knock at the door.)

WILKINSON: Maria.

MARIA: What's going on, Mr. Wilkinson?

WILKINSON: Come in, have a seat.

MARIA: No thank you.

WILKINSON: What can I do for you this morning?

MARIA: What you can do for me is tell me exactly what is going on. Families are up-rooted, their houses are dark and empty with NO TRESPASSING signs all over the place. Did you read the *Times* this morning? "HOUSING PROJECT DOOMED."

(She hands him the L.A. Times.)

Did you know all along when you handed us those certificates, did you know we would never come back?

WILKINSON: Don't be cross with me, Maria. Of course I didn't know.

MARIA: What am I to tell the families that are ready to move into your tall buildings and cul-de-sacs? What do I say to the families left on the hill? What do I tell them, Mr. Wilkinson?

WILKINSON: You can tell 'em this—tell 'em that Fritz Burns, Asa Call, Joe McCarthy, J. Edgar Hoover, William Randolph Hearst, Chandler and the *Times* make a powerful foe, young lady.

MARIA: What are you saying?

WILKINSON: I've been subpoenaed to testify before the California Un-American Activities Committee.

MARIA: My gosh, Frank, when did this happen?

WILKINSON: Last week. I was at the hospital, recovering from surgery. When I came to I found the subpoena pinned right to my hospital gown.

MARIA: Was that some sort of sick joke to put the scare in ya?

WILKINSON: It's no joke, Maria.

MARIA: And what about your boss?

WILKINSON: The pragmatic Mr. Holtzendorf? He told me to find myself a lawyer. A lawyer who was not a communist.

MARIA: What are you going to do?

WILKINSON: Fight.

MARIA: I can help you, Frank.

WILKINSON: Thank you, Maria, but you need to be awful careful yourself.

MARIA: What about your family?

WILKINSON: I had to move them away.

MARIA: I'm scared, Frank . . .

WILKINSON: I'm scared, too, kid. I'm scared, too.

(Lights fade to black.
Lights up on a podium with Mayor Poulson. We hear "The Poulson Jingle" music. The sound of a flashbulb.)

NEWSREEL VOICE-OVER: May 26, 1953. Norris Poulson defeats pro-housing candidate Fletcher Bowron.

(We hear audience applause.)

POULSON: My fellow Angelenos, as your new mayor, my first plan is to stop the public housing project in Chavez Ravine. I know there are some families illegally living up there, but that is city land now, and they will not be able to stand in the way of progress.

If you are not prepared to be a part of this modern city, if you want Los Angeles to revert back to pueblo status, then my best advice to you is to be prepared to settle elsewhere because you cannot stop the momentum which is thundering this city to greatness!

("The Poulson Jingle":)

RODARTE BROTHERS *(Singing)*:
We got a knockout
Who won't stop the fight.
Poulson's the man
The man who is right.
Poulson, the new mayor
Of Los Angeles!

(Lights fade out.
Lights up on Wilkinson at a hearing of the California
Senate Un-American Activities Committee, aka Baby HUAC.)

COMMITTEE CHAIRMAN: Please state your name and occupation.

WILKINSON: My name is Frank Wilkinson, I am the Information Director and Site Manager for the Housing Authority of the city of Los Angeles.

COMMITTEE CHAIRMAN: Tell us the names of all organizations, political or otherwise, of which you have been a member from the date of your commencement at the University of California at Los Angeles to the present.

WILKINSON: No, sir, I would want to recollect much further before I answer that question.

COMMITTEE CHAIRMAN: You haven't the discretion. You may answer the question.

WILKINSON: Do I have any rights at all to refuse to answer a question regarding organizations?

COMMITTEE CHAIRMAN: No, you do not.

WILKINSON: May I have a moment to discuss this matter with my attorney?

COMMITTEE CHAIRMAN: I beg your pardon?

WILKINSON: Do I have any rights here, Mr. Chairman?

COMMITTEE CHAIRMAN: You do not! State the names of all the organizations you have belonged to!

WILKINSON: I would hold that to answer such a question might incriminate me.

COMMITTEE CHAIRMAN: Mr. Wilkinson, are you now or have you ever been a member of the communist party?

(Pause.)

WILKINSON: I respectfully refuse to answer that question, Mr. Chairman.

(There is rumbling from the senate chambers.)

The greatest threat to our country today is fear; this hysteria that grips the land jeopardizes everything our country was founded on. *(Crowd noise)* My past associations are irrelevant to these proceedings. What this committee is doing is only ensuring that the working poor, the average man and woman will never have a right to dignified affordable housing. And that will have dire consequences for generations to come.

COMMITTEE CHAIRMAN: Order! Order!

WILKINSON: Fire me, send me to jail, but don't push the poor out of the cities by golly, and don't kill public housing in this country.

COMMITTEE CHAIRMAN: That will be enough, Mr. Wilkinson.

WILKINSON: History will find us guilty of destroying democracy today . . . I am an American, Mr. Chairman . . . I am an American!

(We hear the pounding of the gavel. All hell breaks loose.)

COMMITTEE CHAIRMAN: Order! Order! This hearing will come to order . . .

(Maria listens to the radio.)

NEWSREEL VOICE-OVER: Strike three for former CHA Information Officer Frank Wilkinson, who refused to answer questions at the hearings of California's "Baby HUAC" Committee today. Red Wilkinson was immediately fired by CHA bossman Howard Holtzendorf. It's the end of public housing in Los Angeles.

(We hear radio static . . . the sound of a radio being dialed. We hear news from the fifties . . .)

MANAZAR *(Entering)*: The homes, the barrios, the people scattered into dark oblivion, the city pushing down on the heart of memory . . .

(*The radio static turns into the sound of wind. We now also hear Lalo Guerrero's "Barrio Viejo."*

A Chavez Ravine Resident carries a suitcase across the stage. The Man reaches down for a handful of dirt, sniffs it, makes an offering of it, sprinkling it, then walks away. He is followed by other Residents one by one. A slow procession of suitcases. They all exit.

Two shadowy figures in trenchcoats and fedoras enter. They shake hands and exit.

Wind.

Lights fade to black.)

| ACT TWO |

MANAZAR:
    Lonely winds whip across the hills
    Passage of time—yet time stands still.
    Five years have passed
    Golden dusk
    Cold blue night
    A flock of ravens like shadows passes
    Across the Palo Verde schoolyard where chavalios once
        squealed with delight.
    Dust, ghosts and spirits stir as these Santa Ana winds
        whip through the hills.
    Dawn.

The Ravine is no more heaven. Walter O'Malley and Kenneth Hahn fly high in a whirlybird. It's 1957.

(Manazar creates a wooshing sound with an ancient Indian instrument. He continues this throughout the scene. County Supervisor Kenneth Hahn, Walter O'Malley and a pilot fly a helicopter over Los Angeles.)

O'Malley (Richard Montoya) and Hahn (Ric Salinas, front left) fly above the Ravine, with Pilot (Eileen Galindo), powered by Manazar (Herbert Siguenza).

O'MALLEY (Pointing): What's that down there to the left?

PILOT AND HAHN: Chavez Ravine!

HAHN: It's an abandoned housing project site, Mr. O'Malley. It's been vacant for nearly five years now, it's the perfect location.

O'MALLEY: My people tell me that land is restricted for public use only.

HAHN: What's more public than a ballpark, Mr. O'Malley? We'll convince the Council that this is a good thing for the city!

O'MALLEY: I see some houses down there.

VOICES: ¡No nos moverán!

O'MALLEY: What was that?

PILOT: Squatters.

HAHN: It's the Santa Ana winds whippin' around, sir.

(The helicopter hits some turbulence.)

Well, Mr. O'Malley, they're really gonna love your Dodgers here in Los Angeles . . . you'll be glad you moved from Brooklyn!

O'MALLEY: Not so fast Supervisor Hahn, they'll skin me alive on Flatbush Avenue if the fans catch wind of this.

HAHN *(Pointing down)*: The Ravine's a beaut, ain't she?

O'MALLEY: The land looks rough, the leveling and grading would cost a fortune.

HAHN: We'll get you what you need and that's a promise.

O'MALLEY: Where's the subway line, Kenneth?

HAHN: Subways are the past, freeways are the future. Notice the constant flow of happy motorists? Mr. O'Malley, Angelinos love to drive, and all roads lead to Chavez Ravine.

O'MALLEY: What's all this smoke?

MANAZAR *(Coughing)*: Smog.

HAHN: It's what we call a "marine layer," sir. It makes for spectacular sunsets!

O'MALLEY: Tell me, how come Walter Disney didn't want to build his Magic Kingdom in the Ravine?

PILOT: He's fuckin' goofy.

O'MALLEY: Maybe I should build my stadium in Anaheim.

HAHN, MANAZAR AND PILOT: Anaheim?!

HAHN: You don't wanna do that, sir, nothing good will ever come outta Anaheim.

O'MALLEY: Wrigley called Los Angeles a bush town, bush league, second rate. Say, is that the Pantry down there? I could use a juicy steak.

HAHN: Don't you see, Mr. O'Malley, there's not a major league team this side of the Mississippi.

O'MALLEY: Don't tell that to St. Louis.

HAHN: You bring the Dodgers out west, you make history, your legacy is assured. Imagine, the '55 World Champs in beautiful Southern California. So what do ya say, Mr. O'Malley, do we have a deal?

O'MALLEY: I can't hear you, Hahn.

HAHN: Can you hear me? Can you hear me now? Can you hear me? Do we have a deal?

O'MALLEY: No deal.

HAHN: I think I'm getting airsick.

MANAZAR: And my arm's getting tired.

O'MALLEY: Pilot, put me down.

PILOT: What'd you say?

O'MALLEY: Put me down!

PILOT: OK, you're a potato-eatin' paddy.

> (*Hahn barfs. The propellers thump thump thump, then the helicopter flies away.*
> *Manazar takes the stage, pushing a wastebasket on wheels.*
> *The crack of a bat, the echo of a roaring crowd.*
> *Manazar picks up a newspaper from the ground. He reflects on the headline:*)

MANAZAR: The paper says, "Walter O'Malley Not Happy in Brooklyn," but he wasn't sold on L.A. yet. Baseball fever was in the air over City Hall. The game was heating up. The big-time city chingones wanted baseball downtown worse than a tecato needs a fix.

Things might have been slow in the Ravine, but the mayor's office was about to get as busy as a triple baptism at San Conrado church on a Sunday afternoon. Now watch me make myself invisible. (*Spins and picks up a broom, becoming a janitor at City Hall*) Órale . . .

> (*The mayor's office. Poulson is asleep. An intercom buzzes.*)

POULSON: Hello.

INTERCOM VOICE: Mr. Mayor, wake up, your two o'clock appointment is here.

POULSON (*Surprised*): I have a two o'clock?

INTERCOM VOICE: With a reporter from the *Herald*.

POULSON: All right, send him in.

(A blond Cub Reporter from the Los Angeles Herald *enters, all energetic.)*

Say, you're not a him—you're a her!

CUB REPORTER: You are very perceptive. Millie Miller, cub reporter for the *Herald.* Nice digs.

POULSON: Thank you.

CUB REPORTER: Mr. Mayor, the boys at the city desk are rumbling that the Dodgers won't be playing in Brooklyn next year. Gimme the danish and not the tutti-frutti. What is your opinion on the matter?

POULSON: My opinion? I'll let you know as soon as somebody gives me one.

CUB REPORTER: I have plenty of questions for you, Mr. Mayor . . .

POULSON: Well, I can answer all your questions, Miss Cub Reporter. *(Grabs her notebook and puts it to his head like a fortune-teller)* Yes, yes, no, no, maybe and yes! Have a nice day, I am a very busy man. *(Intercom buzzes)* See.

INTERCOM VOICE: Mr. Mayor, your two o'clock hot cocoa is ready.

POULSON: Oooh! A-hem, tell him I'll be right there.

CUB REPORTER: Is it true Kenny Hahn took O'Malley on a helicopter ride up the Ravine?

POULSON: Look, I just had lunch with Supervisor Hahn at the Brown Derby . . .

(She takes notes furiously.)

. . . he tells me the deal's gone south.

CUB REPORTER: Never give up, Norrie. May I call you Norrie?

POULSON: Well, OK.

CUB REPORTER: If I listened to every fella who said I couldn't become a *newspaperman,* why I wouldn't be sitting here next to you now.

POULSON: Gee, you're pretty smart for a girl.

CUB REPORTER: And you're pretty . . . much the mayor.

POULSON: O'Malley doesn't want to play ball with us, kid.

CUB REPORTER: Why, O'Malley is a keen businessman. Why would he sell Ebbett's Field? Why is he nudging Horace Stoneham to move the Giants to Frisco? Why did he buy Wrigley Field in South Central Los Angeles?

POULSON: I suppose you're gonna tell me.

CUB REPORTER: These are clues, Norrie, clues that he's serious about moving. Seems to me that you have to get in the batter's box before San Diego and Minneapolis do. Just think, Mr. Mayor: jobs, growth, civic pride . . .

POULSON *(Realizing)*: . . . property taxes.

CUB REPORTER: You already have the support of the Downtown Chamber of Commerce, the sports writers—and Councilwoman Roz Wyman has most of the Council on board.

POULSON: She does?

CUB REPORTER: Why don't you give the valley a reason to drive south? The Westside a reason to come east?

POULSON: People are saying that City Hall is just sitting on that land.

CUB REPORTER: You can fire a darn cannon through Chavez Ravine and you wouldn't hit a soul, it's the most underused land in the county.

POULSON: Who's firing cannons through Chavez Ravine?

MANAZAR *(Watching from the side)*: Nicky Apodaca did on the Fourth of July.

BAND *(Joining Manazar)*: Órale.

CUB REPORTER: Why don't you catch the next aeroplane to Vero Beach, Florida, and make O'Malley an offer.

POULSON: Florida scares me: alligators, flamingos, senior citizens, oh my.

CUB REPORTER: You're in the bottom of the ninth with two outs and the bases loaded. You, Mayor Poulson, are at bat with a big stick.

POULSON: I am?

CUB REPORTER: Big league ball for a big league town.

POULSON: You're a dreamer, kid.

CUB REPORTER: I'm an Angelino.

POULSON: And you love your city, right?

CUB REPORTER: I'd love to scoop the *Times*, Mr. Mayor.

POULSON: You newspapermen are all alike.

CUB REPORTER: Why thank you, sir. Would you get me an auto-graphed baseball from Sandy Koufax, I think he's dreamy.

POULSON *(Concerned)*: Koufax is a Jew, you know.

CUB REPORTER: Really? I thought he was a pitcher.

(Music and the sound of a twin engine airplane. We see a small shadow of a plane cross the entire stage floor.)

MANAZAR: Vero Beach, Florida, training camp, Dodger Town. The promise of a new baseball season. Mira, there's Duke Snyder, y el Pee Wee Reece. Ah, the smell of freshly cut grass chingao, sends me back to my childhood at the Palo Verde schoolyard.

Órale, I'm gonna just kick back right here for a little whiles ay, que suave.

(A figure in a trench coat enters and helps to change Mayor Poulson into a Hawaiian shirt. He gives the mayor a small valise and finally puts a dab of suntan lotion on his schnoz. Manazar appears as the water boy with buckets of balls and a baseball bat.)

POULSON: I'm here!

MANAZAR: Get behind the batter's cage, pendejo.

(We hear the smack of a bat, Poulson narrowly avoids decapitation from a ninety-mile-an-hour ball.)

POULSON: Ooh! *(Another smack, another narrow miss)* Aah! *(Another smack)* Eeh!

(The sound of a single ball hitting Poulson on the noggin as O'Malley enters. So much for first impressions.)

O'MALLEY: Well, well, let me guess, you must be the mayor of Los Angeles?

POULSON *(Out of it)*: Mr. O'Malley . . .

O'MALLEY: Over here, buddy.

POULSON: Porris Noulson here with a delegation of civic leaders to make you a serious offer, but first, Mr. O'Malley,
you're really gonna love this . . . *(Pulling something from his
valise)* . . . the Dodger Dog?! *(O'Malley looks displeased)*
Forget the Dodger Dog. *(Puts the Dodger Dog back in his bag)*
Mr. O'Malley, I'm ready to build you a stadium on the moon
if I have to.

O'MALLEY: I can't play ball on the moon, Poulson. And I don't
wanna play in Secaucus, see.

POULSON: Yessir.

O'MALLEY: So start talkin', Mr. Mayor.

*(Poulson and O'Malley move a few steps downstage to negoti-
ate. Manazar provides the blow by blow account. The men
mime Manazar's descriptions as klezmer music is played by the
band.)*

MANAZAR: Nobody really knows what happened that day, so I'll
sort of summarize, freely mixing fact with fiction. The
negotiations were like a sparring match . . . *(Poulson and
O'Malley, the negotiators, shadow box)* Like a game of
roshambo . . . *(They play roshambo, "rock, paper, scissors")*
chest-thumping . . . *(They thump their chests)* and tap-danc-
ing just like Riverdance . . . *(They tap-dance)* Some say
Mayor Poulson gave O'Malley the shirt off his back . . .
(Poulson offers his shirt to O'Malley)

O'MALLEY: No.

MANAZAR: And his chonies.

(Poulson offers his underwear.)

O'MALLEY: You got style, kid.

POULSON: Thank you, sir.

O'MALLEY: I like your moves. I'll tell you what, if you can get a
hit off Don Drysdale, you gotta deal.

POULSON: Don Drysdale?

(Manazar hands Poulson a bat.)

O'MALLEY: Hey, Don, how 'bout pitching to the nervous Nellie?

(A very nervous Poulson backs away.)

MANAZAR: Órale, just do it.

(O'Malley ad-libs batting advice to Poulson, who takes his awkward stance. In a blur, a ninety-mile-an-hour fastball comes in. Poulson swings the bat like a spaz, causing him to twirl many times. He somehow connects with the ball.)

¡Chingado!
O'MALLEY: Holy Cardinal Mahoney, you just hit Don Drysdale clean out of the park!
POULSON: There must be cork in it.
O'MALLEY: Say it ain't Sosa. Listen, I'd like me a Spanish ballplayer. Have you any Spanish ballplayers out on the coast?
POULSON: I'll get you the dishwasher at Clifton's Cafeteria if I have to, sir.
O'MALLEY: Swell. The Dodger Dog, huh? Ha ha ha . . .

(O'Malley and Poulson exit.)

MANAZAR: At the end of the day, it looked like L.A. was gonna get those Brooklyn Bums after all. The city was gonna spend a pile a dough to clear and level the land. And O'Malley would build himself a dream stadium. Safe. ·

(Manazar cleans up, picking up baseball stuff.
On another part of the stage, a man stands in front of an old radio microphone.)

RADIO MAN: It's time for the Yiddish Radio Hour broadcasting live from Brooklyn in New York City. It's a very dark day in Gotham, goys and girls. We're sitting shiva here in the radio studio as we've learned an hour ago that yes, it's true, it's official, the Brooklyn Dodgers are no more. They're leaving Ebbets Field, the Bums have broke our collective borough hearts!

MRS. MARACCINO *(Low, smoker's Bronx accent)*: May they die in a fiery plane crash on their way to the coast.

RADIO MAN: Now, now Mrs. Maraccino!

MRS. MARACCINO: Well, all right. May their aeroplane have a five-hour stopover in Cleveland. And may their children suffer brain cancer!

RADIO MAN: Always nice hearing from Mrs. Maraccino in the Bronx.

TOUGH NEW YORKER: I feel like somebody stabbed me in the eyeball with a butter knife. But I'd take it if the Bums would stay in Brooklyn.

RADIO MAN: Well said, Staten Island! And ten-year-old Gordie Davidson sent this letter in today . . .

TEN-YEAR-OLD GORDIE *(With gray hair, Brooklyn Dodger cap and glove)*: I dunno, it's really sad, I dunno, maybe one day I'll produce a hit play about it, I dunno . . .

RADIO MAN: Thank you, Flash Gordie from East Flatbush. Today's show is brought to you by Spellman's Matzo Ball Mix, you'll wish every night was Passover. And remember, Mothers, if you have a bar mitzvah boy, you can find all his clothing needs at Joe & Paul's in Manhattan!

(Radio Man sings the "Joe & Paul's" jingle, as Ten-Year-Old Gordie and Tough New Yorker dance.)

Joe & Paul's a bargain-igen
Joe & Paul's you can a bargain-igen
A suit, a coyt, a gabardine
Namt a rayn a clane duh zine.
Joe & Paul's, OY!

(Segues into "This Land Is Your Land." A few Residents are gathering at a fundraiser at the church meeting hall—1957. Maria presses on. She sings one more verse, this time all on her own.)

MARIA: Come on, gente, we can't quit now! La lucha continúa!

ELDER WOMAN: ¿Sabes qué, Maria, we've been fighting for eight years now mija, first the housing project and now with this new stadium measure, chingado qué más quieren?

BENNY THE WORRIER: We don't want to make any more trouble, they could deport us like they did in '32!

ELDER WOMAN: The Bracero Program!

BENNY THE WORRIER: Operation Wetback . . .

ELDER WOMAN: There's only twelve families left and francamente I'm thinking of leaving, too. I'm tired, mija.

MARIA: We can't give up now, gente! We have support from a few City Council members. Councilman Ed Roybal says it's morally and politically wrong to take our land and use it for private gain, you see?

ELDER WOMAN: Pinche políticos!

RESIDENT: Órale.

BENNY THE WORRIER: Maybe we should just keep our mouths shut and move out.

MARIA: No, gente, sí se puede, look, we were able to get enough signatures to put Proposition B—the stadium referendum—on the ballot and the vote is tomorrow. So you see, we can do this, we just need to keep up the good fight. No nos moverán . . . No Prop B . . . C'mon everybody!

MOB: No nos moverán . . . No Prop B . . . No nos moverán . . .

SEÑORA: Maria, Maria . . .

MARIA: ¿Ah, Señora Sanchez?

SEÑORA: ¿Dónde están los Mariachis del Boyle Heights? Me encanta cuando los hombres tocan la guitarra, toda la noche toca, toca, toca . . .

MARIA: Lo siento, señora, we couldn't afford them tonight. But one of the Rodarte Brothers is here.

SEÑORA: ¿Lástima, no hay champurrado?

MARIA: No, señora, I'm sorry.

SEÑORA: ¿No ay vino rojo de Señor Rosini?

MARIA: Tampoco.

SEÑORA: ¿No, ay, homemade vodka de Uri the Sheepherder? (Maria shakes her head no) No weesky? What is happening to our comunidad? (Looks over to the Rodarte Brothers) ¡Y tú, cabrón! ¿Traes marihuana? (*A Rodarte Brother nods his head yes*) Por lo menos vamos. Toca toca toca . . .

BENNY THE WORRIER: Maria, I'm sorry, but I have to go home now.

MARIA: What do you mean you have to go?

BENNY THE WORRIER: I don't want to miss *I Love Lucy*.

MARIA: But the meeting's not over yet.

REBOSO: Bye bye, Maria. I'm going, too.

MARIA: Well, thank you all for coming. Remember vecinos, we're working the polling booths, mañana, seven A.M. sharp, I'm not talking Mexican time, OK? Don't be late!

RESIDENTS: Good night. Buenas noches. Hasta mañana.

ELDER WOMAN: What time?

MARIA: Seven A.M.

ELDER WOMAN: Eleven?

MARIA: Seven.

ELDER WOMAN: Eleven?

MARIA: No, seven, señora.

ELDER WOMAN: OK, I'll see you at eleven.

MARIA: If anyone needs a ride to the polls let me know . . . Oh goodness. Ma! . . . Ma!

MOTHER (*Entering*): ¿Qué paso with your coalition building? Mija, where is everybodies?

MARIA: Meeting ended early; not a very good turnout.

MOTHER: Well, that's just swell. I've got a five-foot stack of homemade corn tortillas back there.

MARIA: Sorry, Ma. Where are the santitos for the shrine?

MOTHER: Father Thomas came for them earlier for the kermés.

MARIA: What?

MOTHER: He said they would be safer at Mission San Conrado.

(*Maria sweeps up after the meeting.*)

MARIA: But I needed them to build the altar to protect the remaining familias.

MOTHER: I know, mija, even the saints have abandoned us, eh.

MARIA: Ah, that's OK, saints don't vote anyway . . .

(Maria and her mother exit.
A cold wind blows—we hear the Dodger song—we are at a
television studio for the Dodgerthon Fundraiser, 1958.)

VOICE-OVER: Quiet on the set. Cameras rolling in five, four,
three . . .

CLEVE *(Wearing an eye patch)*: Cleve Herman here and we're
coming to you live from the Erroll Caroll theater in beautiful Hollywood for the five-hour Dodgerthon. And we have
boatloads of entertainment coming your way including the
Dodgerthon dancers. Look at 'em back there. *(Cleve points
upstage to a very silly dancer)* Ah, to be young, happy and gay.
Folks, we've got dozens of personalities from the television
and motion picture business here to show their support for
Proposition B, which will decide whether or not Walter
Frances O'Malley gets to build his beautiful new stadium
in Chavez Ravine for our Los Angeles Dodgers. *(Canned
audience applause)* By all accounts it's going to be a very
close race, every vote counts and we're counting on Mom
and Dad there at home to be sure to hit the polls before
suppertime tomorrow night, folks. So, let's get things
started with our leadoff slugger, the assistant general manager for the Los Angeles Dodgers, say hello to Dick Walsh
everybody.

DICK WALSH: Hi ya, Cleve.

CLEVE: What ya got there, Dick?

DICK WALSH: I have a relief model of the most modern baseball
stadium in history, with four tiers that will accommodate
fifty-six thousand fans.

CLEVE: She sure is a beaut, Dick!

DICK WALSH: I'll say, with room for sixteen thousand automo-
biles.

CLEVE: That's a lot of Packards and Plymouths in the parking
lot, Dick. Thanks for coming by.

DICK WALSH: So long, Cleve.

CLEVE: So long, Dick. Say hello to your lovely wife, Susie.

(Dick falls, crushing the stadium model.)

Make that three tiers. What a beautiful three-tiered stadium she will be. Folks, we have a real treat in store for you this evening, let's hear from an old friend of ours, Hollywood film star and president of the Screen Actors Guild, ladies and gentlemen, say howdy to Ronnie Reagan. Gipper!

REAGAN: My fellow Angelinos, the moment is here. If you stand for mom, baseball and apple pie, well, then you must vote for the passage of Proposition B. That's B for baseball. We'll see you on opening day. I know Nancy and I will be there, and Bonzo, too. Isn't that right, Bonzo?

BONZO: Oooo, ooh, aah, aaaaagggg!

REAGAN: God bless America and God bless the Los Angeles Dodgers.

CLEVE: There goes Bonzo, or was that Nancy? I can never tell . . . *(Audience boos)* Bunch of Nancy Reagan fans, my goodness. Things have gone bananas here in the studio and Bonzo's just joined the fellas in the band. *(Rim shot)* Everybody OK with the Taft Hartley players? The drummer just got a case of monkey pox. *(Audience boos)* Lot of monkey pox fans out there . . . Now folks, nobody's worked harder to bring the Dodgers to Los Angeles than our next guest, the first woman ever elected to the City Council, the firebrand of the Fifth District. Let's welcome to the batter's box, Councilwoman Rosalind Wyman. Rozzie!

ROZ: Thank you, Cleve. Ladies and gentlemen, what we're talking about here today is public use, the greatest good for the greatest number of people. Los Angeles is a sad, sad city and do you know why?

CLEVE: Why, Rozzie?

ROZ: I'll tell ya, Cleve, because she has no seasons. What is spring without spring training? What is fall without the fall classic? What is a real city without baseball? Baseball will unite our city, give us a purpose, a center, a heart. A vote for proposition B is a vote for Los Angeles. Thank you.

CLEVE *(Wiping his eye)*: Very powerful and emotional speech. Thank you, Roz. Brought a tear to my one eye. The cavalcade of stars and supporters for Proposition B doesn't stop here, why we've got Jerry Lewis, Milton Berle, Connie

Francis, Joe E. Brown, and none other than my good friends, Bud Abbott and Lou Costello! Jimmie Mac, bring out Bud and Lou!

BUD ABBOTT: Well, Costello, you know Walter O'Malley just asked me to be coach for the Los Angeles Dodgers.

LOU COSTELLO: Look Abbott, if you're the coach you must know all the players.

BUD: I certainly do.

LOU: Well, I've never met the guys, so you're going to have to tell me their names and then I'll know what players are on the team.

BUD: Let's see who we have on the bags: Who's on first, What's on second, I Don't Know is on third . . .

(Bud and Lou perform their famous "Who's on First" routine until . . .)

LOU: . . . I'm not talking about third base.

BUD: Take it easy, Lou!

LOU: Yo sólo quiero saber quién está en primera.

BUD: Quién.

LOU: ¿Quién está en primera base?

BUD: Sí.

LOU: ¿En la primera base?

BUD: Quién.

LOU: ¿Y por qué me preguntas a mí?

BUD: Te estoy diciendo, Quién está en primera.

LOU: Yo sólo quiero saber cómo se llama.

BUD: ¡No, Cómo está en segunda!

LOU: ¿Y por qué estamos hablando en español?

BUD: I don't know, why are we speaking in Spanish?

LOU: Yo no sé.

BUD AND LOU: Third base!

(On another part of the stage, in Chavez Ravine, three men stand around a small fire. Lencho plays the harmonica as softer Santa Ana winds blow. Dogs bark and howl in the distance. Red sky, a large moon hangs low peeking over the mighty San

Gabriel mountains to the east of the baby Santa Monica foothills. Maria ambles over. The men warm their hands over the flame.)

MARIA: Say fellas, it's Maria, Henry's little sister.

THREE MEN: Say Maria, q'volé, it's Henry's little carnalita . . .

(One of the fellas offers Maria a nip from a bottle.)

MARIA: Oh no, gracias.

(The man keeps holding the bottle to her.)

Oh, what the hell.

SAL: Es todo.

(Maria takes a hit and reacts.)

MARIA: Whoa, that'll warm up your insides, que no?

LENCHO: Hey, clean the bottle, ese, clean the bottle . . .

MARIA: Did you fellas vote yet, we still got an hour before the polls close.

(A few coughs, but mostly silence.)

LENCHO: Uh, yeah, we voted at the Jonathan Club, we're all members.

JOE: What's the use in voting, Maria, this place is history.

MARIA: I think we need to have a more positive attitude, fellas. People outside the Ravine are fighting for us.

LENCHO: Like who?

MARIA: Eli Kovner and the *Eastside Sun*. There's even a rabbi from the old schul in Boyle Heights who is willing to go to jail for us.

JOE: Puro pedo.

LENCHO: La Effie Street is dust, already.

SAL: Bishop and Solano are next.

LENCHO: They're tearing up the land like crazy.

Maria (Eileen Galindo) talks to the last Residents (Herbert Siguenza, front; Richard Montoya, center; and Ric Salinas, right).

SAL: Yesterday they buried the old Palo Verde Elementary School. They took the roof off, and filled it with dirt.

LENCHO: ¡Qué bárbaro!

JOE: I saw some white men from a movie studio this morning, and they took a whole row of houses for a dollar a piece.

LENCHO: ¡Fubar loco!

JOE: No, it's true, es cierto vato. They're gonna use the houses for a movie called *Tequila Mockingbird*.

LENCHO: *Tequila Mockingbird?* That sounds good, man.

SAL: We're gonna be movie stars. I'll be the Lone Ranger.

JOE: Chale, I'll be Tonto.

LENCHO: No, you'll be *tonto*.

(They laugh.)

MARIA: I'll drive you to the polls myself, right now, vámonos.

SAL: Can you drive us to the liquor store?

MARIA: I'm not fooling around, guys, your three votes could make the difference and we could win this thing, c'mon, Lencho.

LENCHO: I'm a reality man, Maria, and I'm telling you this town ain't never gonna let us win nada.

SAL: Mayor Poulson sold it all.

MARIA: You guys don't want a baseball stadium up here, do ya?

LENCHO: Remember Pete Aruthia, Maria?

MARIA: Sure I do, Lench.

JOE AND SAL: Oh yeah . . .

LENCHO: When I was a peewee at Nightingale Grammar School, Pete Aruthia taught me and some of the Bishop Boys how to play baseball real good . . .

JOE: . . . we had some good athletes up here . . .

(The guys start throwing around a ball over the fire.)

SAL: . . . from Lincoln, Cathedral, Mary Queen of Angels . . .

LENCHO: . . . semi-pro even, the Elysian ACs . . .

JOE: . . . the Palo Verde Pirates.

LENCHO: The Japanese ballplayers at Garfield and Roosevelt were tremendous ballplayers, too, very fast. Those Japanese vatos, very fast and short . . . But up here, in our neck of the woods, every morenito wanted to be Jackie Robinson, remember vatos? Your brother Arturo was a beautiful shortstop, Maria. Good enough to play with those Negro players allá in Watts.

JOE: Rest in peace.

LENCHO: We took championships—championships, Maria! With torn shoes and our fathers' gloves.

SAL: We would make the white kids cry all over their new uniforms.

(The guys share in a rare warm moment.)

MARIA: Those are wonderful memories guys, they truly are, that's why we have to fight, so our children will have memories, too. We gotta fight, man! ¡No me moverán, guys!

LENCHO: You're missing the point, Maria.

MARIA: What's that, Lencho?

LENCHO: Fight or no fight, we all love baseball.

(*A beat. The guys exit, leaving Maria alone as the lights slowly fade on her.*
The Band plays "Election Night Blues.")

RODARTE BROTHERS (*Singing*):
Somebody's gonna win,
Somebody's gonna lose,
Democracy is brewin'
In the Red, White and Blue
Still countin' ballots,
Got the Election Night Blues
'Cause there's winners and there's losers
Got the Election Night Blues
Yeah . . .

(*At the Pacific Dining Car—two men sit in a private room.*)

WATCHMAN: Looks like a major league baseball stadium is finally coming to downtown Los Angeles.

SHAKER: With this Proposition B matter behind us, thank God . . .

WATCHMAN: O'Malley and his Dodgers can break ground next week.

SHAKER: Hey, Watchman, can I get box seats?

WATCHMAN: You can sit under the catcher's nut sack if you like. Raise a glass to the committee of twenty-five.

WATCHMAN AND SHAKER: Cheers.

(*Poulson crosses the stage with balloons and a silly Dodgers hat.*)

POULSON: We won! We won! . . . We have a new stadium, we have a new stadium!

SHAKER: Holy Mexican fuckin' jumping beans. Looks like your boy Poulson's trippin' the light fantastic.

WATCHMAN: Let him enjoy it.

SHAKER: He was a good empty suit.

WATCHMAN: He's out.

SHAKER: Sam Yorty's on deck, can we work Yorty like we did your boy Poulson?

WATCHMAN: Don't know about Yorty yet, he's a bit of a loose cannon.

SHAKER: Loose cannon.

WATCHMAN: We'll see.

SHAKER: We'll see.

WATCHMAN: We'll see.

(Mover enters with a newspaper.)

MOVER: Jeez fellas. The paper says we barely squeaked by. I didn't think this Prop B election was gonna be such a tight race. It was closer than a priest on an altar boy!

(Enter Cub Reporter.)

CUB REPORTER: Hello Movers and Shakers!

MOVER: Well well well, if it isn't that pesky cub reporter dame from the *Herald*.

WATCHMAN: They'll let anyone in the Pacific Dining Car.

SHAKER: I smell a rotten green tomata.

CUB REPORTER: Aw, come on, fellas, it's a great day for baseball in the City of Angels.

SHAKER: Sure it is, cookie.

CUB REPORTER *(Whipping out a notebook)*: So what's next, Bunker Hill?

MOVER: That's up to City Council, sister.

SHAKER: And we have great respect for our city's elected officials and the democratic process.

CUB REPORTER: I hear Buffy Chandler's got plenty of ideas, maybe a symphony hall?

SHAKER: Who knows? Maybe we'll build a watchamacallit, where them fairies dance around in tight little clothes?

MOVER: The ballet.

SHAKER: Yeah, the ballet.

CUB REPORTER: I hear you suits stand to rake in plenty of dough from all of this.

SHAKER: You hear too much, ya hear.

WATCHMAN: Why don't you get on your little pink bicycle and deliver papers for old man Hearst?

CUB REPORTER: Just doing my job, fellas.

MOVER: Do it somewhere else.

CUB REPORTER: From where I'm standing you fellas still got one big problemo.

MOVER: Those Mex families on the hill?

WATCHMAN: Goddamn squatters been living rent free for years.

SHAKER: The jig is up, we'll put the pinch on 'em. They're as good as gone.

CUB REPORTER: I hear some of those old folks are gonna fight till the end, could get real messy up there boys, could turn into a regular feeding frenzy for a newspaperman like myself . . .

SHAKER: What are ya saying there?

CUB REPORTER: You can bet Channel Thirteen will send a television crew up the Ravine. Egg everybody on for the cameras, eh? Plus, there's a boatload of lawsuits heading your way challenging the contract with the Dodgers. Lawyers are already talking Supreme Court. That's out of your jurisdiction, ain't it?

WATCHMAN: We have friends in Washington.

CUB REPORTER: You can't play that Red card much longer. You gotta ask yourself: Why was the election so close? Maybe the voters in this city are getting tired of backroom politics. Did you feel that fellas . . .

WATCHMAN: What . . .

CUB REPORTER: . . . was that a tremor or a shift in power?

(Cub Reporter exits.)

ALL: Broads.

(An earthquake. The three men tremble. Lights out.
Dodger Stadium, 1981. A baseball game is in progress. We
hear the classic organ melody used to get the crowd worked up
. . . tan tan tan tan . . . then the roar of the crowd, the seventh
inning stretch and the Dodger Dog Girl.)

VIN: We're here at the seventh inning stretch and if you're just
joining us, this crowd is going absolutely loco for Fernando
Valenzuela, who has kept these Astros scoreless through
seven innings. You never want to say shut-out too early,
but the youngster is making a very strong showing. Now,
before I describe to you what Fernando mania looks like, let
me tell you that I am happy to be joined by Spanish com-
mentator Jaime Jarrín.

JAIME *(Speaking with a heavy accent)*: Muchas gracias, Veeeeeen
Scully. Es un placer estar aquí contigo y la comunidad de
Los Angeles. ¡Con Feeeeeerrrr-nando! El Toro Valenzuela.
Veen.

VIN: Well, Jaime, the Mexican Hat Dance will certainly be the
anthem around these parts whenever Fernando's working.

JAIME: Claro que sí, Veeeen, es un baile típico de México, pero
no tiene nada que ver con béisbol. Veen.

VIN: That's right, Jaime. We may be watching the Rookie of the
Year today.

JAIME: Oh sí, Veeen, rookies como Don Newcombe, Jim Gilliam,
Frank Howard and Jim LeFebre . . . qué casualidad, ahí está
mi amigo Supervisor Kenneth Hahn, hola Kenny . . .

VIN: Claro que sí, Jaime. The honorable Kenneth Hahn is here
with his entire family, and little Jimmy Hahn was a batboy
here on another opening day nearly twenty years ago. We're
in the middle of the seventh inning.

JAIME: And you know what that means . . .

VENDORS: It's the seventh inning stretch. C'mon, everybody on
your feet.

JAIME: "Take Me Out to the Ball Game." You know the words.

Dodger Stadium Vendors (Eileen Galindo and Herbert Siguenza) and Jaime Jarrín (Ric Salinas) sing.

(The Vendors throw peanuts and popcorn into the audience and get them up to stretch and sing:)

VENDORS AND JAIME:
Take me out to the ball game,
Take me out with the crowd,

Get your peanuts!

Buy me some peanuts and crackerjacks
I don't care if I never get back
'Cause it's root root root for the Dodgers,

Cold beer!

If they don't win it's a shame
For it's one, two, three strikes you're out
At the old ball game!

(We hear a female voice:)

DODGER DOG GIRL: Dodger Dogs, get your Dodger Dogs. World Famous Dodger Dogs. Heavenly Dodger Dogs.

(The Dodger Dog Girl descends from high above the stage, and sings:)

I'm the Dodger Dog Girl,
I'm the Dodger Dog Girl,
Today Fernando is on the mound,
I'm the Dodger Dog Girl,
When I see him
My feet don't touch the ground,
I'm the Dodger Dog Girl . . .

BAND:
She's the Dodger Dog Girl.

DODGER DOG GIRL:
I'm the Dodger Dog Girl . . .

BAND:
She's the Dodger Dog Girl.

DODGER DOG GIRL:
Mustard no ketchup,
Jalapeños, extra onions,

My feet are numb,
I have two bunions,

'Cause I'm the Dodger Dog Girl . . .

BAND:
> She's the Dodger Dog Girl.

DODGER DOG GIRL:
> I'm the Dodger Dog Girl . . .

BAND:
> She's the Dodger Dog Girl.

(She speaks the rest in verse as the music plays on:)

DODGER DOG GIRL:
> I lit many candles for Fernando,
> get your Dodger Dogs here,
> with a pop or a beer,
> another strike,
> another cheer,
> I'm the Dodger Dog Girl,
> who will levitate in the
> center field bleachers,
> but nobody will see me,
> except maybe a few cholos in the gangbangers section,
> nobody will know,
> except my Fernando,
> he looks right at me,
> and I tell him,
>
> Sweet Nando, may I call you Nando?
> It is our prayers and forgiveness
> that make you great.
>
> Only Fernando sees this Dodger Dog Girl,
> levitate in center field.
> and Fernando knows,
> all the spirits of
> La Loma,
> Bishop and

Palo Verde
the Pachuco zones
and spirits of Native peoples of
Las Cienegas
the opium dens of Chinatown ghosts
Tecato blues
and Jewish spirits
of so many cemeteries
buried deep
under the shortstop
are
with
you
now.

Fernando nods to me,
and he knows that I am more than
a Dodger Dog Girl,
he knows I am the one who
secretly blows out the
candles my abuela lights every year so the Dodgers will
    never advance to the World
Series,
damn, I wish it wasn't so effective!
I am
Sister Aimee Semple McPherson
and the song of Bernadette
he knows that today
I am La Nuestra Señorita
la Reina de Los Angeles.

I love you fat dark little Indian boy!
I'm a Chicana who loves Vin Scully too!

(She rises ten feet: the levitation of the Dodger Dog Girl.)

Aaaaaaaah . . . Shit, this is high . . . *(Composing herself)*

(The Dodger Dog Girl finally comes down to the stage. She ad-libs thanks to her savior, Tommy Lasorda, who unhooks her from the harness.)

Dodger Dogs . . . Get your Dodger Dogs.

(She exits.

> *Maria sits in a pinspot. From the upstage shadows two Detectives ask her questions.)*

DETECTIVE 1: Maria Salgado Ruiz?

MARIA: Who's asking?

DETECTIVE 2: Oh, just the Los Angeles Police Department.

MARIA: Am I under arrest?

DETECTIVE 1: This is just a little get-acquainted session.

MARIA: I've heard about your little get-acquainted sessions. I want a lawyer.

DETECTIVE 2: Why don't you call Alice Greenfield? We could all have a little chitchat about civil liberties.

MARIA: Why should I talk to you?

DETECTIVE 2: For shits and giggles.

DETECTIVE 1: Are you the ringleader up the Ravine?

MARIA: I don't know what you're talking about.

DETECTIVE 1: We don't believe you.

DETECTIVE 2: Next you'll tell us there'll be a cathedral on Bunker Hill one day.

MARIA: There'll be a cathedral on Bunker Hill one day.

(A beat. They scoff.)

(More to herself) And a Mexican sheriff and mayor!

DETECTIVE 2: What? . . . What do you know about the marijuana we found growing behind the police academy?

DETECTIVE 1: Where did you get this little book by Karl Marx?

MARIA: What are you guys, the Red Squad or something?

DETECTIVE 2: We know most of you took the city's cash offer and haven't left the Ravine for eight fuckin' years!

DETECTIVE 1: Tell old lady Arechiga and the last families to get off the hill.

DETECTIVE 2: Do it fast and do it quiet.

DETECTIVE 1: Or else.

MARIA: Or else what?

DETECTIVE 2: The Punch and Judy show.

DETECTIVE 1: Who else you been talking to, Maria?

DETECTIVE 2: Names, now!

DETECTIVE 1: Spill!

MARIA: You want names? I'll give ya names . . .
Blackie
Bimbo
Bubbles
Captain Marvel

(The Detectives, disgusted, exit.)

Cakes
Chema
Blue Moon
B-19
El Dopey
Chavela
Chacha
Buttermilk Sky
El Beaver
Fili
El Mosco
Cisco
Chuy la Vaca
Fifty Cent Ernie
The Ice Man
Billy Goat
Shazam
Search Lights
Punky
Pipo
Pelonie

Pasty Cogan
Lefty
Las Changas
Somehow

(Manazar begins his following speech here. Maria overlaps, speaking in a hush:)

Fito
Kiko la butch
Hollywood
La Pocha
Jimmie Nico
Huero
Goofy
Froggy
Jazzbo
Cowboy
Clipper
Codo
Chino
Coyote
Two Nickel Donuts
Two Gun Brooks
Two Ton Tony Galento
Okie and
Arkie.

MANAZAR *(Overlapping)*: On May 8th 1959, it was eviction time, and there on national television in black and white, fourteen county sheriffs began forcibly removing the last family from the hill. I just stared, not believing my eyes. I got in my car and raced to the Ravine, but the cops wouldn't let me pass.

MARIA: Let me go! Let me go! Get your pinche hands off of me! *(Screams)* You can't do this! This is my house. I'm not going anywhere.

MANAZAR: Let her go, pig!

SHERIFF: Please, lady, you're going to have to cooperate with us. Get the handcuffs on her.

MARIA: Malditos, malditos. Noooo! I was born in this house. You have no right to do this. Don't lay a hand on the children!

SHERIFF: Stop kicking, lady, you're going to get hurt!

MARIA: ¡Sí se puede, sí se puede!

MANAZAR: Memory cannot be flattened. Memory is history singing in tune with the stars, and no sheriff's baton can reach that high.

MARIA: ¡Viva Zapata! We shall overcome this! No homes, no justice!

MANAZAR: And then the sheriffs moved in on Maria's mom.

(The Mother stands center stage holding a shotgun.)

MOTHER: We are not the Mulhollands. *(We hear the pump action of a shotgun)* We are not the Lankershims or the Van Nuys. *(We hear the pump action of a shotgun)* But you'll remember this name: Arechiga, *(The pump action of a shotgun)* Cabral, Casos y López . . . *(Shotgun)* Pérez, *(Shotgun)* Ramirez. *(Shotgun)* You took our sons to fight your war, and now you take our homes. *(Shotgun)* Our land. *(Shotgun)* I don't want to be buried in Boyle Heights . . . *(Shotgun)*

ALL *(A prayer)*: Sí, señor.

MOTHER: I don't want to be buried in Whittier or White Fence . . .

(Shotgun.)

ALL: Sí, señor.

MOTHER: When I die, take my ashes and scatter them in La Loma.

(Shotgun.)

ALL: Sí, señor.

MOTHER: La Bishop.

(Shotgun.)

ALL: Sí, señor.

MOTHER: Palo Verde.

(Shotgun.)

ALL: Sí, señor.

MOTHER: Mí casa no es tú casa. ¿Y sabes qué? Why don't you tell the pinche sheriff to build a stadium in his own goddamn backyard!

(We hear a bulldozer, siren and the sounds of the city.)

MANAZAR:
>Our backyard, a hand that touched
>a still wild river,
>home for paloma,
>coyote, and
>carrizales,
>the green smell of moss
>outside my window.
>Later, barricaded by boulevards,
>freeways
>clouds of high-octane smoke
>and a ceaseless roar.

Oh, by the way, the Ravine was named after Julián Chávez, a young farm worker from New Mexico. In the 1840s, he sold the land for eight hundred dollars. Today it's worth, ooh, chingado, one hundred, two hundred million? Huh, he shoulda hung on to it. And no city official who tore families out of the Ravine ever fathomed that a Mexican would be mayor of L.A. . . . .

(Manazar laughs and exits.
Back to Dodger Stadium—1981.)

VIN: We're at the top of the ninth, two outs and Valenzuela's been dominating these Astros, who remain scoreless thus far. We may be looking at a shutout for this amazing Mexican rookie. Yes the mariachis are tuning their instruments in the bleachers . . .

(Vin ad-libs as the mariachis play and sing:)

MARIACHIS:
    El Toro, El Toro es Fernando
    El Toro, El Toro es Fernando
    El Toro, El Toro es Fernando . . .

VIN: You can smell the carne asada and chicharrones from here. This crowd is loving this kid and the sombreros are at the ready. I've never seen an opening day quite this folkloric in all my life. But the Astros are threatening. Art Howe is on first base, the tying run at the plate. Here we go, after a long tense conference with Scioscia at the bag, here comes Fernando heading back to the mound, we're certainly gonna find out what this twenty-year-old muchacho's made of today. Taking the sign, the windup, the eyes to the back of the head, *strike one*—two strikes away from history!

(The Residents and Activists enter. The little houses descend from above onto the field.)

Fernando staring out to second base. Valenzuela once again absolutely transfixed on the center field area.

(The people talk to Fernando:)

MARIA: Fernando, La Effie Street was a sad and romantic sight. Shrines were built along both sides of the street. Each contained a sacred image. Little processions, the children wearing white veils. Working men all carrying a tallow candle. Beneath the lovely and fragile garments and the best clothing marched a small army of old, worn and broken shoes. They seemed to be singing some kind of lament. A song about how the Mexicans would come back to live in their homes.

(We hear the large crowd roar.)

VIN: They are chanting Fernando's name here in the upper decks, Koufax and Drysdale come to mind, Fernando looking in, here comes the wind up, the high kick, screw ball for *strike two!*

(We hear the large crowd roar.)

NICKY APODACA THE 3RD: Q'volé Fernando. My old man, Nicky Apodaca, Jr., brought me to opening day when I was thirteen years old, and today I bring my little daughter who is nine months old. Man, we love coming up here to Dodger Stadium: the crowd, the green grass, the mountains, it just takes my breath away every time. I met all kinds of people from all over L.A. I even made friends with an Oriental vato from Monterey Park—actually we met in the parking lot, after a fender bender, but chingao, it's all good.

OK OK OK, if I cut my finger, the blood comes out blue, Dodger blue! I swear to God. This stadium was the best thing that ever happened to L.A. and believe me, a lot of Chicanos feel the same way. One more thing, we hate the pinche Giants. ¡Que vivan los Dodgers!

BAND: ¡Viva!

ROZ: Can I say something here, Fernando? It's me Roz, Rosalind Wyman, the youngest City Councilperson in L.A. history—I still hold the record, sorry Alex—and I'll tell you something, here we are, all these years later, and some people are still angry about Chavez Ravine and that just rips my guts out, Fernando. But let me tell you, the first year the L.A. Dodgers won the playoffs, horns all over the city started blowing, Los Angeles came together for the first time: the Valley, the Eastside, the Westside, the Southside, the city had coalesced around something they had built, something they'd been a part of and that was a good thing for this town.

WILKINSON: The city of Los Angeles and the Red baiters smeared my good name, I was unemployable for quite a spell. Thank goodness for the Quaker fella in Pasadena who hired me as a janitor or my family would have starved to death. My whole life changed, turned upside down. It was the end of a dream, young man, the end of public housing in Los Angeles. I went to jail for a year. I was chased by the FBI for thirty-four years.

This document here is my death warrant, an internal FBI memo confirming a plot to assassinate me, sent to and initialed by director J. Edgar Hoover himself. The detective in charge of the Assassination Detail for the LAPD at that time was a young, ambitious cop named Darryl Gates.

My name is Frank Wilkinson and I am eighty-nine years old. And you know what, son? I outlived most of those dirty bastards.

MARIA: It's easy to romanticize the working-class residents of Chavez Ravine, but we should not. Many of us were immigrants or first-generation sons and daughters of immigrants. And what does the immigrant want? The immigrant *doesn't* want trouble, he wants to make it, he wants his little piece of land. My students often ask me, Professor Ruiz, then why was the fight for Chavez Ravine so important?

Look, I'm standing here on Bunker Hill—City Hall is there, the *L.A. Times*, Disney Hall going up over here, the federal courthouse there, the new cathedral just behind me and none other than the Department of Water and Power across the street. How did we ever have the audacity to take on this civic crucible?

It's true we lost, but what's important is that we helped create a culture of resistance. The struggle for Chavez Ravine prepared me for civil rights, the Farm Workers Union, my labor work with Bert Corona and the Chicana Movement. Chavez Ravine was huge for me. It made me the person I am today. So do me a favor, remember Chavez Ravine, eh?

HENRY: Hey, Fernando, let me tell you one more thing about Chavez Ravine, there was always a lot of talk about a buried treasure somewhere up here.

MARIA: Right, a conquistador hid his stolen gold in these hills . . .

HENRY: . . . like a myth right here under Dodger Stadium . . .

MARIA: . . . you mean Bishop, La Loma and Palo Verde . . .

HENRY: . . . I think there was a treasure, but the poor people never found it . . .

MARIA: . . . other people found it . . .

HENRY: . . . we never found it. Our only treasure was those umbilical chords that our grandmothers buried under our houses, like the one under second base.

MARIA: And no city official who ever removed families from that hill ever thought a Mexican would one day be mayor of L.A. Sí. Got the picture?

HENRY: Now go get them, Nando!

(Fernando pulls himself together for the final pitch of the game.)

VIN: Well, folks, we're down to what could be the final moments of the game. Valenzuela actually walked over to second base and touched the bag—perhaps it was some sort of Aztec ritual, I do not know. He's back on the hill and he wants to end this all right here, right now. Scioscia with the sign. The wind up, the high kick, the eyes rolling, the release . . . *Strike three!* It's a shutout for Fernando, this game is over, the mariachis are playing in the bleachers and little ol' ladies from Boyle Heights are dancing in the aisles. Throw your sombreros in the air! Drive home safely and so long from beautiful Chavez Ravine!

(We hear the crowd roar. The small homes around the field slowly begin to rise into the sky. Slow fade to black.)

END OF PLAY

WATER & POWER

Original story and stageplay by Richard Montoya for Culture Clash

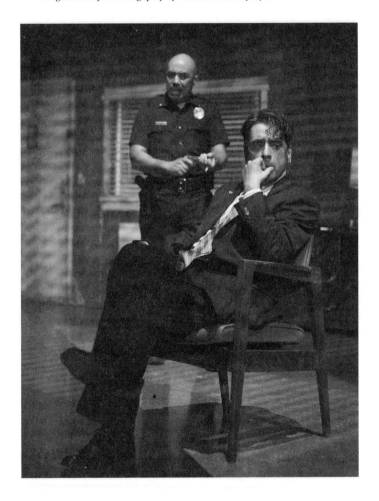

For Mr. August Wilson

ESSENTIAL NOIR

WATER & POWER IN THE SHADOWS OF L.A.

By Richard Montoya

Did the movies create noir or did the City of Angels? I have often wondered this as I walked the streets of L.A. at night, or even in the sunburnt light of day. I have felt the long shadows of a city in constant flux. A city quick to cement its history and its riverbanks. From the seedy motel rooms of Sunset Boulevard to the Dark Houses under the bridges where junkies go to die in East L.A. to the corridors of power—this is the world of *Water & Power*.

But it could be any large American city—there are shadows in all of them—and from these shadows strong forces emerge. Some grow stronger while others perish. The characters Water and Power will not perish if they can still hear the words of their father and the strength of his hand.

Water & Power is stage noir but, more importantly, it is a cautionary tale about emerging power in the U.S., and needs to take its place alongside the stories of other outsiders who found their way to power in the States: the Italian-, Jewish- and Irish-Americans.

PRODUCTION HISTORY

Water & Power was commissioned by Center Theatre Group's Mark Taper Forum (Michael Ritchie, Artistic Director; Charles Dillingham, Managing Director) and received its world premiere there in summer 2006. It was written by Richard Montoya for Culture Clash. It was directed by Lisa Peterson; the set design was by Rachel Hauck, the costume design was by Christopher Acebo, the lighting design was by Alexander V. Nichols, original music and sound design were by Paul James Prendergast, choreography was by Jennifer Sanchez; the dramaturg was John Glore, the fight director was Steve Rankin, the production stage manager was James T. McDermott and the stage manager was Susie Walsh. The performers were:

Actors	Understudies
Richard Montoya	Mateo Arias
Ric Salinas	Daniel Guzman
Herbert Siguenza	Bobby Plascencia
Dakin Matthews	Carl Weintraub
Moisés Arias	
Winston J. Rocha	
Emilio Rivera	

TIME

Before

PLACE

After

El agua que no vas a beber, déjala correr.
(The water you do not drink, let it run.)

—*Mexican saying*

Danger: High voltage power lines under-ground.

—*The DWP*

PROLOGUE

No pre-show music. The house lights slowly dim. The sound of a single drop of water becomes thunder and rain. Led Zeppelin's "The Rain Song" is heard. A shaft of bright light cuts a sharp contrast across the stage. A figure enters. It is Norte/Sur. Wheelchair bound, Norte/Sur is a Homeboy, a Vato from the street, a Veterano. He slowly wheels himself center stage, then makes a large, ceremonial circle with his chair. He is deliberate, methodical, he rushes for nobody or nothing.

The Dear Dancer is revealed standing upstage right or left in the shaft of light. He is a boy, shirtless, in white peasant pants, shakers around his ankles. He holds a shaker and wears antlers atop his head. He does not move except for an occasional flick of the wrist, allowing us to hear the shakers.

Norte/Sur stops slightly up-center, facing out. He reaches into the side bag of his chair, removing a black Piece Book, an art and poetry sketchbook favored by graffiti artists. He opens the Piece Book, then slowly and respectfully closes it. He speaks to the audience:

NORTE/SUR: It's been raining for seventeen days and nights in L.A. Raining real hard. Could be that the gods are pissed off about something. Yup, the Lords of Death are back in town. For sure. You have to be extra trucha with the Lords of Death, for they will cut you up just to see what you're made of inside, and you will thank them because they are charming. They can hide behind a badge or sit in the backseat with a shotgun. They wear pinstripes and broken promises. They can make trains jump the track, they know when its suppertime at your jefitas house. The Lords of Death can look at you from the other side of the mirror and you would never know.

The Lords of Death like to punish us when we reach too high. What goes up must come down. Day and night, good and evil, life and death. Smile now, cry later. Norte/Sur.

Water and Power, torn together in that space between the Thunder and the Lightning where so much can happen, or nothing at all. Somebody prays for rain, somebody prays for it to stop. Record rainfall could wash L.A. away. I think the Lords of Death are fucking with us right now. They like to throw us in the Dark House.

(Thunder. Deer Dancer darts off.)

Oddly enough, I'm looking for a Dark House right now. A place called the Motel Paradise. Yup, you know it, you've driven passed it a hundred times. It's one of those single-story, sad affairs that snake up and down the eastern edge of anywhere, the eastern edge of Sunset Boulevard.

That's the part of the boulee that you never wanna find yourself, on a dark and rainy night.

(Big thunder, or a shotgun blast. They sound the same on nights like this. Led Zeppelin's "When the Levee Breaks" slams in like a motherfucker. Norte/Sur quickly pulls his hoodie over his head and dashes off. Huge thunder.)

SCENE 1

Motel Paradise is revealed: a sad room complete with twin Patrick Nigel prints bolted to the wall. They have stood witness to years of unprotected sex.

One man is already in the room. A second man forces his way in. There is an altercation. The two struggle. A fight. Weapons are revealed as one man forces the other on the bed. Freeze. The men are face to face. One man points his LAPD revolver at the other.

WATER: Hi.

(Beat. They embrace, then a powerful push away. These are the Brothers Gilbert and Gabriel García, also known as Water and Power.)

POWER: You—need—to—get—the—fuck—out—of—here, NOW!

WATER: Why are you hiding in this shithole?

POWER: Don't ask.

(Water sees an AK-47 on the bed and a Mack 10 on the dresser.)

WATER: Oh Jesus, shit, why do you have so many goddamned guns?

POWER: Who made you Mr. Consent Decree?

WATER: You been drinking again?

POWER: Get the fuck out of here, Senator. The shit is about to hit the fan.

WATER: What sort of trouble are you in?

POWER: Big.

WATER: How big?

POWER: There's been a breakdown.

WATER: What kind of breakdown?

POWER: Just a breakdown. That's all I can tell you.

WATER: Call for backup.

POWER: I am backup.

WATER: Great.

POWER: How did you know I was here?

WATER: You called me, asshole.

POWER: The fuck I did.

WATER: I have a text message right here: "Motel Paradise, see your bro, room 13."

POWER: It wasn't me. I don't text. *(Slams a magazine into his AK-47 for punctuation)* It's gay.

WATER: Stop fucking around. I'm here already. What's up?

POWER: I'm in deep water.

WATER: How deep?

POWER: Over my head deep.

WATER: Yeah?

POWER: It's bad.

(A BlackBerry rings. Power draws his gun. Water carefully points to his coat pocket as an explanation.)

WATER: My BlackBerry. Easy. *(He looks at the call)* I gotta get this. Sober up, fucko. *(He answers)* Mister Speaker! Hey, no, perfect timing, sir. Couldn't be better. What do you mean what's in the Green Bill? Have you read my fucking Green Bill?

Power (Herbert Siguenza, background) over Water (Richard Montoya).

(Power is swigging from a bottle and lining up blow on the dresser.)

It doesn't "pole well"? Let me tell you something, Senator, this piece of fine legislation has real support, it's got coalition-building all over it. I've got the teachers, the nurses, the gay Latino firefighters. In fact, I'm talking to the police union right now.

(Power does a blast of cocaine. He sounds like a small steam engine.)

C'mon, Bob, co-sign this thing with me, the leadership always follows you and I swear to God we'll have green space—a million fucking trees—on forty acres of L.A. River on the Eastside. The Cesar Chavez River Walkway.

How about less asthma for Eastside third graders, huh? You don't give fuck-all about my third graders do you, Bob? Why should your kids west of the San Diego Freeway get to breathe better air? If you don't do this with me, I'm gonna have Daryl Hannah chain herself to that pine tree in front of your kids' preschool. You owe me, fucker! Gotta go, Bob. Later.

(He hangs up. Power does another huge blast of blow.)

What the hell are you doing, you Hoover vacuum-cleaner fuck?

POWER: Want a bump? C'mon, do a bump with your bro.

WATER: I can't do blow with you.

POWER: Since when?

WATER: I'm running a fairly important campaign at the moment fuck-stick.

(He finds asthma meds and other things on a bedside night-stand.)

Sweet, your inhaler is empty.

(He picks up a triple beam scale used to measure drugs and pre-cious gems. He reads a sticker on the scale:)

Oh Jesus, "Do not remove from Rampart Evidence Room."

(He wipes his prints off and discards it like a hot potato.)

POWER: It's OK, as long as you bring it back. It's like Netflix down there.

WATER *(Picking up a big black binder)*: LAPD Murder Book? *(He looks through the book)* Who are all the dead guys?

POWER *(Does a short blast)*: Monsters. I chase monsters, bro. And if I have become a monster, then maybe that makes me a better monster catcher.

(Water tosses the book onto the bed.)

WATER *(Resigned)*: Living the dream.

(Power does another blast of cocaine.)

POWER: You guys said, "More cops on the street," that's what it looks like.

WATER: That was a campaign speech, asshole.

POWER: That's the problem with you guys, you don't mean what you say.

WATER: I stand by every word.

POWER: Did you not say, "Get drugs off the street?"

WATER: Absolutely.

(Power smiles and does another blast.)

POWER: Well, I'm just doing my part, bro.

(Water lunges for the top of the dresser, shoving the cocaine to the floor.)

Hey! What the hell. Oh, man. That was the last of my shit.

WATER: Good.

POWER: I haven't seen you in months, and now you come crashing my party?

Fuck that, Gilbert.

WATER: I was gonna call, Gabe. Everything's been nonstop, 24/7.

POWER: Everything is everything. *(Takes a moment to breathe)* I saw my daughter today.

WATER: Yeah?

POWER: God, her mom's a cunt. There's this picture of them on the fireplace that I built. The new guy standing right there, holding my daughter, man, like she was his. A few years ago that was me, you know. I was photoshopped right out of the fucking picture. Invisible. And the day started with so much promise.

WATER: Is that what this is all about, bro? *(Places a brotherly hand on Power's shoulder. BlackBerry chirp)*
POWER: You gonna answer it?

(BlackBerry rings.)

WATER: Fu'uck. *(Beat. He answers)* Bob? What do you mean you've got to check with Washington first? Fuck the feds.

(Power is rifling through an old tool chest that reads DWP on it.)

East L.A. Machine politics, babe, it still works. Better than Chicago or any of the five boroughs. Yes. I'm getting very close to the governor so I can't let this thing get derailed by the slightest or it's dead in the water. *(Looking to his brother)* I'll be floating face up in the Pacific Narrows with my Tongva Indian ancestors. Do this for me and I'll get you a hundred Dodger tickets, third base line for the Crippled Children of Compton. You can be the Great White Hope, all hero and shit.

No need for name calling, Bob. No, I've been a Chicano since 1993, well I stopped in '95 but I recently joined up at COSTCO.

Uh-huh. Yes. Oh, thank you, Senator. You are a rock star. Bless you for your support, sir. Green space, it's so important man. One million trees, baby!

Thank you, dude. *(Hangs up his BlackBerry)* Oh yeah. That's how laws are made. Your brother is a stud. A proud progressive, but still a stud.

(Power slams his nightstick down on the dresser.)

Whoa!
POWER: Fuckers lose respect for the badge, gotta go about things in a different fashion know what I mean, bro?
WATER *(Softly)*: No . . .
POWER: People see a cop . . . sometimes they isolate you. You find yourself all alone, out there, sometimes you got no

choice but to bust a few bald cholo heads. *(Slams the night-stick again)*

WATER: Jesus. Was that the "to protect" or "to serve" part of your job?

(Another swift move with the baton. We feel its deadly force.)

POWER: I wanted to be a cop for all of Los Angeles, but they wouldn't let me, bro. *(He does a long shot of Cuervo)*

WATER: This shit is making you toxic, Gabe.

POWER: Me, toxic?

WATER: Uh-huh.

POWER: You would know. Toxic land deals with minority contractors used to be your main boogie . . .

WATER: Fuck you softly OK.

POWER: Don't be such a pussy.

WATER: Let's get the hell out of this shithole right now, grab a cup of coffee, sober up. Just you and me, like we used to.

POWER: Can't do.

WATER: Can do. I know a coupla detectives, robbery/homicide, connected guys, I'll make the call right now.

POWER: If you make that call my SWAT brothers are here inside three minutes, Tactical in four, Mental Assessment Response Team in five. Forensics before the sun comes up. They'll come hard for their own and they don't leave until they bust a nut. Like a hard rain.

WATER: Uh, yeah . . . *(His Blackberry chirps: duty calls)* Speak. Dude, I can't get away. Cover my ass on the "Green Space Bill" for one hour, be my laser. Buy me some time, you are my bulldog assistant, do it, possess the skill-set I taught you or you will be the Dog Catcher of Barstow. Go.

(He hangs up his BlackBerry. Power has slumped into an emotional state. He clutches his chest.)

Hey, hey now, what's going on over here . . .

POWER: My heart. Feel. *(He places Water's hand on his heart)*

WATER: Racing.

POWER: I know, huh.

WATER *(Taken aback when he notices)*: You got some blood on your badge, bro, let me hit that for you.

POWER: Shaving. Must have cut myself a little too close to the bone.

(Water cleans the blood with his kerchief.)

WATER: Yeah. Good to go.

POWER: Good to go. Who-ah!

(Power playfully punches Water in the gut.)

WATER *(Trying to calm him)*: Easy now. Gabe, sit down. Hey, do you remember, remember that time Dad told us to beat the crap outta each other?

POWER: When did he say that?

WATER: That time he made us box in front of his compadres.

POWER: Oh yeah, that time. That was brutal, man.

WATER: Nah, we got a little bloodied that's all.

POWER: I got bloodied, bro. *(Moves to a chair across from the bed)*

WATER: I was bigger than you then, Gabe.

POWER: Once upon a time.

WATER: On those Eastside streets, babe.

POWER: I could always dance though, bro. Dad learned me to bob-and-weave real good. That was the difference. Then I could go toe-to-toe with you.

WATER: You did beat the shit out of me that one time we fought in the Secret Circle.

*(We hear children playing in the distance.
A slow smile crosses Power's face. Water coaxes Power's grin.)*

You remember that, bro? It's a fond memory for you isn't it. Let me see that smile. What's up, carnal? What sort of trouble are you in, lieutenant? *(Places a tender kiss on his brother's cleanly shaven head)* There you go, bro, Gilbert and Gabriel. Gibby and Gabby. The twins. Together again. Remember those guys, bro?

POWER: Water and Power, baby.

WATER: Estrada Courts to the max.

POWER: Barrio Nuevo.

WATER: Wherever we went.

POWER: Whoever we met.

WATER: The Russians on Lorena Street. Bologna sandwiches from Angel's Market. Spam when we were good.

POWER: We're a long way from Costello Park, bro.

WATER: Dakota Street is just down the road.

POWER: Seems far, like way down there. *(Pointing off, then a deep breath)* Woosh. Weird.

WATER: Easy.

POWER *(With a sudden surge of energy, he rises from his chair)*: Peppers, City of Industry, 1978! Remember, bro? Whoo-hoo, whoo-hoo . . . Getting down at Rudy's Pasta House! *(Thrusts his hips, having a sad disco party in his head)* Montebello nights! Water and Power strutting to the Friday-night football games. Shit, even the brothers from Watts respected us.

WATER: That's because we respected the brothers from Watts.

POWER: I heard that, niggah!

WATER: No! Shhh.

POWER: Little Hazzard, Happy Valley, Maravilla, we went every-where, homes.

(Water starts to shine his shoes.)

WATER: Actually, we never went to Maravilla, it was too dangerous.

(We hear distant popping. Power crouches slightly with his fin-ger to his mouth like, "Talk quietly in the field.")

POWER *(In a whisper)*: Hear that, bro?

WATER: What?

POWER: Firing range at the academy, right on time.

WATER: Maybe it's some cholos down the street.

POWER: No. Above the lodge, Elysian Park.

WATER: How can you be certain?

POWER: Short blasts. Rata-tat-tat shit. Impatient cop action. Strictly 9-millimeter.

(Power climbs on a chair, draws his weapon and strikes his expert firing pose.)

WATER: Easy. Easy.

POWER: Hear that?

(We hear a distant train whistle.)

Union Station, right on time, too.

(Power checks his watch. We hear Ranchero music from a distant nightclub.)

WATER: You had to pick the loneliest mile on Sunset Boulevard.

POWER: It ain't so bad.

WATER: The Life of Riley over here.

(Far upstage of the action, a Mexican Popsicle Man wheels his cart slowly across the stage, with an occasional ring of the bell.)

POWER: Listen!

(We hear far-off Choir Voices.)

CHOIR VOICES: . . . agua que va El Señor Jesucristo . . .

POWER: The Mexican Evangelical storefronts.

(Water hears this.)

Damn, the city is working tonight.

WATER: Just like Dad used to say, bro.

(From offstage we hear the stern yet loving voice of Father.)

FATHER (*Offstage*): Boys! C'mon.

(*Dad's familiar whistle.*)

WATER: Breathe, brother. Breathe.

(*Power takes a deep breath and doubles over.*)

Good.

FATHER (*Offstage*): Let's go, boys.

(*Power crumples. Water helps him down from the chair.*)

WATER: You gotta calm down, lieutenant, pull it up. You've got to tell me what went down tonight, bro. Walk me through it, all of it.

POWER: I'm hanging on here, bro.

WATER: I'll hang with.

POWER: I may need a good lawyer.

WATER: You know I'm a lawyer, cabrón.

POWER: I said a good lawyer.

(*Water starts to clear the bed of weapons.*)

My brother, graduated from the People's Law School! Three-hundreth in your class. Passed the bar on his thir-teenth try. Perry Mason in the house. I got in an accident and my brother got me five hundred dollars!

WATER: OK.

POWER: Shit, all your Latino electeds have their law degrees, but they're escared to take the bar. That's chicken shit, but not my bro. You got balls, Gibby.

WATER: You gonna tell me what happened to you?

POWER: Can you handle it, bro?

WATER: Got to.

POWER: Because you were always kind of a pussy about shit like this.

WATER: I'm with you now, Gabe. And what ever it is we'll flip it. We have the skill-set. What would Pop say? Pop would say that every situation has pluses and minuses. Together we'll find the pluses.

POWER: Water and Power?

WATER: That's right. Dad's Pride and Joy.

POWER: Those brothers were blessed.

WATER: We're still blessed, bro.

POWER: You think?

WATER: Oh yeah.

POWER: You gonna back my play, Gibby?

WATER: Whatever it is, we'll handle it. OK? *(Flashes his confident smile for good measure)*

POWER: Don't leave me here, bro.

WATER: I couldn't do that.

POWER *(Awe)*: L.A. is full of ghosts.

(We hear thunder.)

WATER: Was that thunder or a gunshot?

POWER: They sound the same on bad nights.

WATER: C'mon, Gabe.

POWER: Ah, man, I think I fucked-up.

WATER: Can't be that bad, babe, right?

POWER: Right.

WATER: Good. Good, bro.

(Pause.)

POWER: I killed a man tonight.

(Water's smile evaporates.)

Killed him. Sure enough.

(Flashback to some thirty-two years earlier. Enter an eight-year-old Gilbert García ["Water"] and his father, Asunción García. Mr. García wears his Department of Water and Power

[DWP] overalls with his name tag and department logo. He places a chair just downstage of the previous motel scene. Little Water and Dad are sparring.

Water and Power remain in the motel in the shadows.)

SCENE 2

Asunción García, DWP reservoir and irrigation field man in Southern California, stands next to a simple wooden kitchen chair. Eight-year-old Gilbert is dressed in huge blue boxing shorts and matching boxing gloves. He has on boxing headgear and Converse sneakers. Father holds up his dukes as "Gibby" punches them like a little tough guy. A proud father fusses over his son as he removes his headgear.

FATHER: Did you knock the shit out of your brother like I told you, mijo?

(Gibby shrugs.)

Where is he?

GIBBY: In the room crying like a little pussy.

FATHER: Why is he crying?

GIBBY: Because I hit him.

FATHER: With a hook or an uppercut?

GIBBY: With a flurry of jabs! *(He executes the jabs)*

FATHER: Atta boy.

GIBBY *(Striking a Pachuco pose)*: Just call me Golden Gloves, ese!

(Father smacks him upside the head.)

Ouch.

FATHER: Don't get cocky, little man.

GIBBY: Yes, sir.

FATHER: Did you shine your black shoes like I told you at least?

GIBBY: Not yet, Pop.

FATHER: Chingow.

GIBBY: It was the final round, Dad, we had to finish.

FATHER: Como eres, Gilbert.

GIBBY: You're the one who always says don't leave a fight till it's over or until the fat lady sings.

FATHER: Don't tell me what I say.

GIBBY: And since we don't have a fat lady living with us . . .

FATHER: Ya! You talk too much.

GIBBY: Wull . . .

FATHER: ¿Cómo que wull? *(Yelling off)* GABBY!

GABBY *(Offstage)*: I don't feel good, Dad!

FATHER: Chihuahua, your brother is going to be late for his own damn funeral.

GIBBY: He's a good kid, Dad.

FATHER: Gilbert, your brother, how do I say it, well, he's slower than you. He doesn't use his cabeza.

GIBBY: Uh, uh, Dad, Gabby's really smart, I swear. He figured out how to make eight pieces from one Chicko Stick.

FATHER: Is that right?

GIBBY: Golly yeah, and you know what else? He knows how to fake with his left, then jab with the right and move his feets really fast.

FATHER *(Motions Gibby over to the chair, placing his son on his lap)*: Mijo, I'm gonna tell you something and I want you to listen extra good, OK?

GIBBY: Sure, Dad.

FATHER: Always, always no matters what, look after your brother, look after him real good. Never ever leave him alone somewheres. Where you go, he goes. Always watch his back, me entiendes?

(Gibby nods yes.)

Now repeat what I just said, cabrón.

GIBBY: OK. "Repeat what I just said, cabrón." *(That garners a slap upside the head)* Why do I always have to do the work?

FATHER: Because you were born first, mijo.

GIBBY: I know, I know. Eight minutes and fifty-nine seconds!

FATHER: And there was lightning, mijo . . .

(Gibby makes lightning sounds.)

. . . and there was thunder . . .

(Gibby makes big thunder sounds.)

And my little vatos were born between the . . .
FATHER AND GIBBY: . . . the lightning and thunder!
GIBBY: Yay!! Wait a minute. Dad?
FATHER: ¿Sí?
GIBBY: Am I supposed to look after Gabby or beat him up?
FATHER: Both.
GIBBY: At the same time?
FATHER: Shut up, mijo.
GIBBY: Wull, I'm sort of confused.
FATHER: Lookie, here's the plan: You and I will secretly tuff'n
   him up. And before you know it, he'll clobber you so hard
   like Archie Moore that you won't know what hit you.

Asunción García (Winston J. Rocha) counsels a young Water, Gibby (Moisés Arias).

(Father streaks a punch across Gibby's face in dramatic slow motion. Gibby turns his head like Archie Moore, expertly absorbing the blow. This boxing game is a great deal of fun and has a certain beauty to it. Gibby drops to the floor.)

GIBBY: I'm down for the count! Down for the count!

FATHER *(Lifting Gibby back to his feet)*: You will pick yourself up off that canvas and look your brother in the eye and you will have new respect for him! ¡Vale la pena! And then my boys will be the Twin Mirrors of Eastside Toughness. And people will have to respect you or else.

GIBBY: Why do they have to respect us, Dad? We're not rich, we're nobodies.

FATHER: Let me tell you something about respect, mijo.

GIBBY: Is this gonna take long?

FATHER: ¡Cállate!

GIBBY: Sorry.

FATHER: You know the little old white lady on the corner?

GIBBY: The smelly lady with eighty-four cats?

FATHER: No, the other one from the shursh.

GIBBY: The church?

FATHER: Sí, the shursh.

(Gibby rolls his eyes.)

See, I know sometimes she doesn't have enough to eat, but you know what? She carries herself así, con mucha dignidad. Always dressed to the nines. Everything in its place. Self respect, mijo. She has it. Respect yourself, Gilbert. Always.

GIBBY: OK, Dad.

FATHER: And one day, when you and your brother are all grown up, you can help that old lady.

GIBBY: Oh. Dad?

FATHER: ¿Sí?

GIBBY: How old is she?

FATHER: I don't know, como seventy-five or so.

GIBBY: Well, when we're grown up, won't she be dead already?

(Father considers the question and shakes his head. Bested by his son, he gets up.)

I'm just asking, Dad.

FATHER *(Exiting)*: You think you're so smart, cabrón.

(Gibby is left alone. He sits on the chair, kicking his legs the way kids do.)

GIBBY: Wull, you just said I was smart, Dad. *(He has yet another Gibby thought, and from his chair he quietly says to himself)* Oh brother, now I'm confused and full of rage.

(Lights shift back to the hotel room as Little Water exits running.)

SCENE 3

Motel Paradise. Water is seated at the end of the bed with his head buried in his hands. Power stands nearby, very still, smoking.

POWER: After I got off my shift I "borrowed" an unmarked cruiser from Parker Center Garage. I had put Dad's old DWP overalls in the trunk the day before. Waved at the city parking guy as I pulled out of the garage. Changed clothes under the Fourth Street bridge. I was methodical, bro, covered my tracks. I rolled back to the neighborhood, close to where we used to live, must have been about seven, quarter past. My Monster, Mr. Pelican Bay, released from prison early this morning, goes to his mom's house to have supper in East L.A., I know it will be like his first or second stop. I waited for him across the street in the unmarked car, just a few houses down from Dad's old house.

WATER: Oh Jesus . . . *(He moves off the bed and sits in a chair)*

POWER: Not much street traffic.

(In the shadows, we see a Mexican Vendor carrying a water-cooler bottle on his shoulder.)

VENDOR *(Distant)*: Agua . . . agua . . . agua . . .

POWER: I wait. I luck-out big time because the guy goes to see his jefita alone. A few more minutes, let him get settled in with Moms. I'm in the house like in nothing flat, this house, it's dark inside, just a few lights on, like that dark house under the bridge where the tecatos go to OD. The TV is blasting, novelas and shit, Mexican radio from next door covers me, I mean it's perfect, bro. Beautiful, seems fake almost, the little dining room separated from the kitchen. I luck-out again, Mom is back and forth with the tortillas and stuff, my guy hasn't seen a "home cooked" in ten to fifteen. He greazes down like a hungry animal. I'm hanging back in the shadows. *(Takes a long drag off his cigarette)* I wait for just the right moment, Mom's fussing over some wedding and quinceañera pictures in the back room. My guy gets off his cell phone, kicks off his black shoes, television, radio, perfect level, I tip-toe right behind the guy, I can smell the Three Flowers in his hair, I'm like this close. He's got a small four-leaf clover tattooed on the side of his neck, must be new, wasn't in his file jacket . . . *(Moves in behind Water at the chair, using Water as a sort of prop as he continues his story)* Food smelled good, bro. Real good. His cell phone rings, shit, he looks at the number, does not take the call—I catch another break. *(Pulls out his weapon, a beautiful little killing machine, with slow methodical movements)* Silencer. *(Places a lovely silencer on the end of the firearm)* I ask forgiveness for what I am about to do. *(Points his gun at the back of Water's head)* Everything stops, I can't hear the TV blasting anymore. My heart is pounding. Another shadow outside in the yard! *(Both men look off, over their shoulders—the Deer Dancer runs in the shadows, and then is gone like a vapor)* It passes. I gotta go now. Lift gun to back of head. *(Again, slowly raises his arm into position behind Water's head)* Pow. *(We hear an echo of a gun blast in the distance. Water moves his head in a fashion of a murder victim in super slow-motion)* Pow. Pow. *(Another echo for each gun blast in the distance)* I don't know how long his mother was standing there but she's watching from the kitchen doorway.

WATER: Goddamnit, no . . .

POWER: Oh yes. She was probably there the whole damn time, you know. At first I just shined her on, but she kept screaming for her baby. My Monster. She's screaming, but nothing is coming out, or maybe I just can't hear her, I dunno. She stares at me, Gilbert. Her son's brains splattered all over the JFK and Jesus velvet paintings. I lift my gun to her. *(Points his gun)* She looks at me, calm suddenly, not crying, not screaming. She makes the sign of the cross and then she does the same for me. *(Slowly makes the sign of the cross with his gun, the way the señora must have done for him)* Why would she do that, Gibby? My gun just fell to my side, I backed out slowly, I left her there standing silent in her kitchen doorway.

She saw it, Gilbert, she saw the whole thing. She looked deep into me, man, right through me. I've never seen that look before. She's gonna remember my face. She's gonna have me etched across her brain, like a laceration.

WATER: Oh, Gabby, Gabby, Gabby . . .

POWER: I dropped some stuff off at the Taylor Yards incinerator, threw Dad's overalls, Monster's cell phone in the fire. And that's it.

WATER: That's it?

POWER: Well, no. I mean PD is gonna be looking for me, and La Eme.

WATER: Well, opposites do attract, Gabriel.

POWER: Tonight they do. And they're gonna come hard.

WATER: Tell me, why did you clip the guy?

POWER: L.A. is not for everybody.

WATER: What the hell does that mean?

POWER: I had my reasons.

WATER: What possible reasons could you have to murder a man who had already served his time?

POWER: I did what I had to do. That's all I can say.

WATER: Oh God, you've been advising Homeland Security on L.A. prison gangs.

POWER: Affirmative.

WATER: Well you'll need to say a whole lot more, lieutenant.

POWER: Negative. No-go, pal. I'm not talking about this with you anymore.

WATER: Fuck this, I'm calling the LAPD negotiator right now.

POWER: The negotiator I know is also a sharpshooter. So that's not an option.

WATER: That's brilliant, Gabriel.

POWER: I'm serious as a heart attack, bro. I know too much. Other cops will want me out of the picture.

WATER (*Kicking the chair out of frustration*): Goddamnit, I knew it. Something was coming.

POWER: What?

WATER: Something would hit me here, hard. I would take some sort of blow, in the solar plexus. You used to knock the wind out of me. Just like that. I felt it earlier today, I swear to God I did. I did not know what to expect when I showed up here, but not this, not what I see now.

POWER: Gee, sorry, bro. Hey, I need to re-up. Where's my guy?

(*Norte/Sur bursts through the door in his wheelchair. Small thunder.*)

NORTE/SUR: Ese, Power, Pelican Bay is all over the house. Word got out quick, ese.

POWER: Which house?

NORTE/SUR: Your house, your father's old house. There's a shot-caller convention on the Eastside, ay.

POWER: Anybody follow you here?

NORTE/SUR: Yeah, three paisas and a border brother, but they're cool.

POWER: Don't fuck around. Who was that guy behind you just now?

NORTE/SUR: Some Jehovah's Witness, vato. Saving souls in the rain, business is brisk tonight apparently.

POWER: Who's at my house exactly?

NORTE/SUR: Real shooters, no spray-and-pray guys.

POWER (*More amazed and excited than angry*): You hear that, bro?

NORTE/SUR: And there's two Monterey Park dudes at the 7-11 by the crib.

POWER: Vatos from Monterey Park?

NORTE/SUR: No. Chinos, Asian cats. Fast and Furious vatos. Good cutters, expert knife guys.

POWER *(This is big)*: They're going multicultural on my ass, huh?

NORTE/SUR *(Reading almost businesslike from his Piece Book)*: Haters front to back. La Eme galore, ten percenters, they got it wired tight this time. And cops I ain't never seen before creepy crawling all over the ghetto. Bookoo jura. The barrio is going berserk tonight. *(Looks to Water)* What's up?

(Water nods.)

POWER: What did Chunky say?

NORTE/SUR: Couldn't get a hold of him at first.

POWER: Did you try his BlackBerry?

NORTE/SUR: Chale, all the homies have switched to Trios. Some sort of wireless promotion sweeping the hood. Luckily, Chunky still keeps an old-school pager.

POWER: Fascinating! And?

NORTE/SUR: He says no "get out of jail cards." "Get out of morgue cards," maybe.

POWER: That's kinda funny. Was he trying to be funny?

NORTE/SUR: Laughed my ass off.

WATER: And you are?

NORTE/SUR: Despensa, homes. Mister Norte/Sur.

WATER: Mister what?

NORTE/SUR: Norte/Sur. I'm the one who texted you.

WATER: How the fuck did you get my number?

NORTE/SUR: I googled you. That linked me to your L.A. field office, the jaina who answers the phone gave it to me. I told her I would financially contribute to your latest cause, as I have happily done on many occasions.

POWER: Why the fuck did you contact my brother?

NORTE/SUR: I had my reasons. I did what I had to do, ay. *(Turning his wheelchair to Water)* Yeah, I see your pictures in the paper all the time, you're skinny homes.

POWER: This is my guy.

WATER: This is your backup?

POWER: Shake his hand.

(Norte/Sur offers his hand, but Water doesn't take it.)

NORTE/SUR: I ain't trippin', ay. —Hey, man, who put the hat on the bed? It's bad luck, ay.

(He flings the police hat off. Water retrieves it.)

Ese, Power, this whole chingadrea is much more seriouser than I thought. Worser even than when that Latino CHP cop vato got wasted.

WATER *(Quiet horror)*: Oh God.

NORTE/SUR: The vato you offed was no soldier, Gabe, he was way up the food chain, you know.

POWER: OK! This is what I need: first, go to the last picnic table on the northwest corner of Elysian Park, under that table is a brown bag, get it.

NORTE/SUR: Simón.

POWER: Then release the pigeons on top of the roof at the Sir Palmer apartments.

NORTE/SUR: On Echo Park Avenue?

POWER: Simón. Then cross the street, put the bag under the boardwalk next to paddleboat number six.

NORTE/SUR: Got it.

POWER: After that, pick me up a Jamba Juice with a protein boost in it.

NORTE/SUR *(Repeating and taking note)*: Protein boost . . .

POWER: Then go to the carwash they're throwing for the dead homey.

NORTE/SUR: They're having a carwash for Mono?

POWER: No, for the homey that killed Mono.

NORTE/SUR: I can't go to Tripper's carwash, ay.

POWER: Go to Toker's carwash then.

NORTE/SUR: OK. Wait, what am I doing at the carwash again? It's raining cats and dogs out there.

*Power
(Herbert
Siguenza)
gives instruc-
tions to
Norte/Sur
(Ric Salinas).
Water
(Richard
Montoya)
looks on.*

POWER: Tell Chele to clean the inside of my car extra good, I want
    it smelling nice when they come for me. Have him put in
    some air-fresheners.

NORTE/SUR: Lemon lime or midnight cherry?

POWER: You choose.

NORTE/SUR: Cholo's choice. Done.

POWER: And find Fucker Joey.

NORTE/SUR: What on earth do you want with Fucker Joey?

POWER: Tell him I'm gonna need some Pico Rivera Muscle.

NORTE/SUR: Oh shit.

POWER: Yeah. Kique from Clover is gonna go ballistic.

WATER: Pico Rivera Muscle?

POWER: You got a point, bro, make that Atwater Village Muscle.

NORTE/SUR: Why not go with Frog Town Muscle?

POWER: Too close to Toonerville Muscle.

NORTE/SUR: They're out of commish que no?

POWER: No, they just dress nice now.

NORTE/SUR: Like the Vineland Boys.

POWER: Ask him to check on Diamond Bar Muscle.

NORTE/SUR: Won't that cause a conflict vis-à-vis the proximity to Canoga Park Muscle?

POWER: Fuck it, let them work it out.

NORTE/SUR: Cool. What about Los Feliz Muscle?

POWER: Never.

NORTE/SUR: Why not break a little taste off for the Ceder Block Piru Bloods?

WATER: Los Feliz Muscle?

NORTE/SUR: I'm gonna have to make a Muscle spread sheet.

POWER: Fuck it. Go to the L.A. River. Under the Sixth Street bridge you can wheel yourself through the tunnel leading all the way to the river bottom, find the homeless guy sleeping under a silver space blanket there, he looks like a miniature Disney Hall, ask him if Black Butch is out of the joint yet.

NORTE/SUR *(Writes down)*: Find the Miniature Frank Gehry.

POWER: Then find White Butch and get thirteen Dodger tickets, lower loge only, then go to Home Depot on San Fernando Road and get me some plastic tarpaulin. Go.

(Norte/Sur begins to shove off.)

Hold up. Call Casper from a landline, tell him, no, better yet ask him nicely as a favor, to give me a freeway shooting on the Harbor Freeway in about an hour. Nobody gets killed though.

NORTE/SUR *(Takes careful note)*: Victimless freeway shooting for cover.

POWER: After that go to Venice.

NORTE/SUR: Chale, can't go there, ay. I got beef with that Shore Line Crips set.

POWER: Get out to Malibu as quick as you can.

NORTE/SUR: Malibu? I'm on the bus, homes!

POWER (*His look is unsympathetic*): Then call fucking Rafas and ask him to give you a ride on his Harley! No excuses tonight Norte/Sur!

NORTE/SUR: Copy that.

POWER: Be sure to hit Tajunga Canyon before they close the gate. At the top of the trail is a waterfall, say three Hail Marys, one for each of us in the room here.

WATER: I don't want his prayers.

NORTE/SUR (*Taking another note*): Water not cooperating. This is gonna take some time, ay, and handicapped service is limited on rainy days.

POWER: OK, forget Malibu. Hit Tajunga Canyon, tell the Nazi Lowriders I need my guns back tonight, period.

NORTE/SUR: And things were going so well with the Aryan Brotherhood. Anything else?

POWER: Double back to the Original Shull in Boyle Heights, ask the rabbi for all his sharp instruments.

NORTE/SUR (*Takes a final careful note*): No brisses in East L.A. tonight.

(*There is a noise outside. Power pulls up a side arm.*)

POWER: What the fuck was that?

(*Norte/Sur looks out of the curtain. A Barefooted Guy streaks by dropping something.*)

NORTE/SUR: Calm down, ese. It's only the barefooted Guatemalans delivering the *L.A. Times.*

POWER: They still got delivery boys in L.A.?

NORTE/SUR: Yeah, even though circulation is down. Most of the homies have switched to the *New York Times.*

POWER: Stealth bastards. They look hungry, must be on some good yay-yo. You'll need to hump like them if we plan to see tomorrow.

(*Norte/Sur throws Power a tied-up bundle.*)

What's this?

NORTE/SUR: Mota laced with a touch of X to help you cope till I get back.

POWER: Who's it from?

NORTE/SUR: My homeboy Puppet, with warm regards.

POWER: Which Puppet?

NORTE/SUR: My Puppet.

POWER: And what Puppet is that exactly?

NORTE/SUR: You know, ese, Puppet ese vato loco homeboy Puppet.

POWER: I didn't know you had a Puppet, Norte/Sur.

WATER: What does it matter which fucking Puppet it is?

POWER: Actually it does matter, bro, I mean there are a lot of Puppets in L.A., man.

NORTE/SUR: Here we go again.

POWER: I mean there's Big Puppet, Little Puppet, Medium Puppet, Super-Sized Puppet, Puppet with Curly Fries, Economy Puppet, Puppet Master . . .

NORTE/SUR: Don't get all crazy, ay.

POWER: Well I know a lot of Puppets. So again I ask Norte/Sur, which fucking Puppet?

NORTE/SUR: And for the last time I'm telling you, my Puppet.

POWER: Put something on it. Put something on it, homes. Cholo up, dog.

NORTE/SUR: Cholo up? Fuck you, you know that.

POWER: Hustle it up so you can get back here and shave my head, nigga . . .

(Norte/Sur wheels over to Water.)

NORTE/SUR (Cautiously): Ni modo. Real good to see you here with your carnal, ese, Mister Water. I've heard nothing but wonderful things about you from your fucked-up brother over there. Could I bother you for an autograph in my Piece Book?

POWER: Save it for the book fair.

(Power stands by the door.)

NORTE/SUR (*Heading for the door, he looks at Power*): Almost forgot to tell you, three of the rooms are occupied here. (*A read from his Piece Book*) We got an old Cowboy in room five, he's waiting for a kidney or some sort of shit from Mary Queen of Angels Hospital. There's a butch ruca down the hall with her two kids, she's waiting for her old lady to get released from Chino in about an hour. Five souls in all. Everybody waiting for something in L.A. tonight.

POWER: Save it for the poetry slam.

NORTE/SUR: Water and Power in the same room, damn, this must be bad.

POWER: Go!

NORTE/SUR: Gone.

(*Power shuts the door and Norte/Sur is gone. Thunder.*)

WATER: What the fuck was that? Who is that guy?

POWER: Somebody I trust.

WATER: He shouldn't be here.

POWER: He's my biographer.

WATER: Your what?

POWER: He's a writer.

WATER: Bullshit, he's a banger and he brings you drugs.

POWER: He's the one thing I've done right in L.A. I love that cholo like a brother.

WATER: I am your brother, Gabe.

POWER: I love him like you then.

WATER: Fuck that. (*Grabs the dope and pockets it*)

POWER: At first I didn't like him, but after I shot him, I did.

WATER: You shot MapQuest?

POWER: Twice. Vato's got a lot of heart. I figured if he survived my bullets, then maybe I'm supposed to look after him. We've been through a lot. He's in my car.

WATER: What car?

POWER: He rides shotgun. You're either in my car or you're not. You're not in my car, homes.

WATER: When did you start talking like this, lieutenant?

POWER: Don't trip. He's my guardian angel.

WATER: You're a regular Father Boyle.

POWER: Like I said I trust him.

WATER: I'll be in your fucked-up car if that's what you want, Gabe.

POWER: I don't want you in my car.

WATER *(Whips out his BlackBerry)*: I gotta go talk to a guy.

POWER: What guy?

WATER: The only guy I know that can fix your mess.

POWER: I don't know your guy. I can handle it my way.

WATER: You're way don't work, bro.

POWER: It worked every time I saved your ass.

WATER: Why do you always have to be the "fuck-up brother"?

POWER: At least I'm not the "sell-out brother."

WATER: I have never sold out.

POWER: You believe your own bullshit?

WATER: I believe what Dad expected of us. And, this is not what he wanted, Gabe.

POWER: I honestly don't remember what that was anymore.

WATER: He wanted us to be those men, Gabe.

POWER: What men?

WATER: Those big guys, man. Standing tall in their fine black shoes. Goddamnit, Gabe. Straight shooters, bro. Walking the line. Spit-shined Garcías. The pride of East Los ese, champions of the little guy. Warriors groomed like gallos by Henry and the Old Man, handpicked from a crowded field by the powerful Berman Brothers themselves, with full blessings from The Machine. The people who helped you get into the academy. Richard. Gloria . . .

Do you remember them, lieutenant? Dad's Eastside superstars who would never ever forget the people in the housing projects. Yet tonight the García Brothers do not hear you poor people. We do not protect you and we sure in the fuck do not serve you because the bros are in this fucked-up room of yours and the shiny black shoes our father broke his back to give us are soiled and scuffed. And we will be way off the mark now. Thanks once again to your major lack of judgment, lieutenant. *(Heads for the door)*

POWER: Gilbert?

WATER *(His patience has run out)*: What?

POWER: Save your guy for a rainy day.

(Distant thunder.)

WATER: It's that rainy day.

(Lightning, then thunder, and Water is gone. Power remains in the shadows of the motel room as his father and a younger version of himself enter.)

SCENE 4

On another part of the stage Father waits for his other son. Little Gabby ("Power") enters. He is shirtless and wears Converse sneakers, red boxing shorts and matching huge, red boxing gloves and protective headgear. He's got the beginnings of a shiner. Mexican radio faintly plays in the air.

GABBY *(With a whine)*: Dad? Dad?

FATHER: ¿Sí mijo?

GABBY: I feel like shit, Dad.

FATHER: ¿Qué paso slugger? ¿Por qué 'stas llorando?

GABBY *(Sort of crying in the comic way kids do)*: Gilbert says I'm stupider than him. Is it true, Pop?

FATHER: C'mon, mijo. No mames. Mira, let's just say that Gilbert got the brains but you got the bolas.

GABBY: But my testies are small, Dad.

FATHER: They'll grow. *(Puts a kerchief to Gabby's nose)* Blow.

(Gabby blows.)

Again, mijo. Are you keeping up your dukes at least?

GABBY: Yeah, but Gilbert swings real fast, that fucker.

FATHER: Oh with the language.

GABBY: Sorry, Dad.

FATHER: You guys talk like midget truck drivers. What's wrong with you little cabrones?

GABBY *(Shrugging)*: I dunno.

FATHER: You have to protect yourself, Son. Mira, when your brother comes in with his quick jabs, surprise him with a left hook. Just like . . .

GABBY: Archie Moore!

FATHER: ¡Correcto! And you know what? He'll never expect it. And I'll give you a silver dollar when you knock him on his nalgas.

(Gabby likes the idea and laughs.)

And then I'll take you up to the reservoir with me.

GABBY: OK. I'll shine my shoes extra good!

FATHER: Excellent idea, mijo.

GABBY: That would be the best day I ever had in the whole wide world.

FATHER: What does it say on my shirt right here?

(As Gabby reads, he points with an index finger the way kids do.)

GABBY: The Department of Water and Power, City of Los Angeles.

FATHER: Es todo, mijo. See, your brother is my Water, and you are my Power. ¿Ves?

GABBY: Maybe I should be Water, Dad?

FATHER: No, no, mijo, you are my Power.

GABBY: But I don't wanna be Power, I wanna be Water!

FATHER: No, mijo, Gibby is already mi Aguita, and you are my Poder.

GABBY: But Gibby gets everything.

FATHER: Lookie here, little vato.

GABBY: Can I be the Gas Company?

FATHER: No.

GABBY: Can I be the Fire Department then?

FATHER: Ya, Gabby, ya . . .

GABBY: Maybe I don't wanna be a utility company.

(Father sits Gabby down on his knee.)

FATHER: You are Power and you should be really, really happy with that.

GABBY: Why?

FATHER: Because.

GABBY: Because why?

FATHER: Porque under the city right now, there are these big turbines, see . . .

GABBY: What's a turbine?

FATHER: Like a giant propeller.

GABBY: How big is it, Pop?

FATHER: Bigger than our house.

GABBY: Nooooo.

FATHER: Oh síííííí.

GABBY: Nooooo.

FATHER: Uh-huh, and the rushing waters turn the giant turbines and that's how we make the power that runs the city. And if you listen carefully, you can hear those turbines spinning under the earth. They never stop, mijo, always moving like an octopus, feeding the city because she never stops eating like a monster. Listen carefully, mijo.

(Gabby takes an impatient beat, his head moving like an inquisitive puppy as his Father makes arm motions to help Gabby imagine.)

GABBY: Can't hear a thing, Pop.

FATHER: Get on the floor there, put your ear on the ground just like an Indian. Go on, Son.

(Gabby happily squirms on the floor.)

Cálmate.

(Gabby settles down.)

Listen real hard, mijo. Listen real close.

GABBY: I CAN'T HEAR A THING!!!

(Father goes down on one knee to calm Gabby and get him to listen more carefully.)

FATHER: Shhh.

GABBY: Wait a sec, wait a gosh-darn second, Pop, hold on.

(Gabby is really paying attention now.)

FATHER: Listen, mijo, listen.

(We hear the lowest, deepest rumble like that of a tremor, but more harmonic, churning as it moves through the house, and then is gone. Gabby jumps up like cat.)

GABBY: I heard it! I heard it! Dad, I heard it, I heard the monster.

(Gabby takes quick jabs at Father's raised hands. A quick celebration and then an embrace.)

FATHER: Did you feel it, mijo? Did you?

GABBY: I did, I did! I swear.

(Gabby is nearly trembling.)

FATHER: That is the Power, mijo, that is what you are to me.

(Gabby raises both arms showing Cheerios-sized muscles.)

(Whispering) You are Power.

GABBY *(Trembling as though he is possessed)*: I! AM! POWER!!!

FATHER: You will be a sanjero like Mister Mulholland! Controlling the water valves of the Mother Ditch, La Sanja Madre en Chinatown. You must never be what I am, mijo.

GABBY: A Mexican?

FATHER: A Mexican you will always be, with your head held high. A poor Mexican you will never be, I will make sure of it.

GABBY: But I wanna be just like you, Pop.

(Father pours himself a tequila. The bitter drink barely holds down the pain and hurt of a man who wanted more from life.)

FATHER: I dig ditches, boy! But you and Gilbert will be the men who decide where the water and the power come and go in this desert pueblo. One day if you're lucky, you will run the DWP!

GABBY: The Department of White People!!!

FATHER *(Taps Gabby upside the back of the head)*: Here, drink this, quickly.

(He offers Gabby a small shot of tequila. Gabby drinks it with a sour lemon face.)

Shake it off, mijo.

(Gabby shakes his head wildly.)

Now go clobber your brother in the head when he's not looking. ¡Ándale!

GABBY *(Calling offstage)*: Gilbert, hurry up, Dad wants us to rule Greater Los Angeles for the poor people and I don't want to be late!

(Gabby exits. Father looks out:)

FATHER: Mis pinches morros . . .

(Father proudly grabs his lunchbox and exits for work.)

SCENE 5

Norte/Sur wheels his way to the stage. He stops several feet in front of Power but Power does not see him. Norte/Sur slowly punches the air.

NORTE/SUR (*Putting up a closed fist*): Water. (*He brings up another closed fist*) Power. Water for life. Power for progress. (*He punctuates these words with gentle punches straight ahead*) Water/Power. (*He opens his Piece Book*) This is my Piece Book. I keep all sorts of things in here. I did the cover myself. These are my poems, little stories, drawings and articles of interest. Oh, here goes my drawing of Snoopy in a lowrider. Pocahontas on a stripper pole. Yeah, gots all kinds of crazy stuff in here. Here's Victory Outreach bitch with some big ol' titties.

I kinda keep a record of the things people want to forget.

Here's a newspaper picture of the night I got shot by Officer García, Mister Power. That's my carnal right there, you can't really see me but those are my legs sticking out. If you look real close, you can see my Lucky Lugz, ay, my lucky shoes. I always wore them Lucky Lugz when I ran the streets. Every homeboy and homegirl needs a little luck running those streets out there.

I had a homeboy named Lucky, but he's dead already. When we were shorties together, tiny locos, we used to run up Chavez Ravine all the time. Dodger Stadium and stuff. It just goes back and forth like that. Up and down.

You're probably wondering why I call my shoes Lucky Lugz if I had them on both times I got shot. Well, I'm still alive, ain't I?

See, some people might feel lucky to have the best table at the finest restaurant in town. That would depend on who's picking up the tab.

(*He wheels off.*)

SCENE 6

The Water Grill Restaurant. Two modern chairs and a sleek steel table are set.

Enter the Fixer, an elegant man of a certain age, an omnipotent figure, the man behind the most powerful of the city, resplendent in an all-white suit. He is an Anglo-Saxon Westsider who is worldly and incredibly street savvy. The Water Grill is open in the wee hours of the night for this most valued and powerful customer. El Ministro is dressed in a black suit. He stiffly waits just upstage of the Fixer. El Ministro will attend to every need of his boss, the Fixer, including, but not limited to, filling glasses, running interference and securing all perimeters. El Ministro wears iPod earphones in his ears, the chords trailing inside his jacket.

Water enters and takes a seat. El Ministro raises his hand slightly and a Busboy enters. The Busboy is the Deer Dancer dressed impeccably in a white busboy/waiter coat and pants, barefoot with antlers atop his head. He fills water glasses with precision, places a napkin on the Fixer only, then exits.

El Ministro stands a few feet upstage never taking his eyes off his boss.

FIXER: I like fusion. Do you like fusion? I'm ravenous. Thirsty too.

(With a languid and unhurried lift of the Fixer's hand, El Ministro delivers a martini with three olives. The Fixer takes an unhurried taste.)

Ah, perfection. It's not easy getting a dry martini in this town after midnight. The vermouth is a little bruised but it will suffice. Don't you like having the Water Grill to yourself in the wee hours of the rainy morning?

(After a beat. He fixes on Water.)

Agua y Poder.

(The Fixer has a way of elongating and enjoying important syllables of certain words. It can be unnerving.)

Water, Power. Power, Water. Lefty-loosey and righty-tighty. Tell me, how are they? Out of the womb best friends. ¡Los Carnales! Gosh, when was the last time I saw you? I remember, private box, Staples Center. Am I right?

The Fixer (Dakin Matthews) toys with Water (Richard Montoya).

Who were you with that night? Ah yes! The Orange County Sheriff and the Southgate City Councilman if I'm not mistaken. Lord what a posse. Before they headed to the Big House, no?

Those men did not respect their constituents.

A certain justice has been meted out by the people. A valuable lesson for all Chicanos who want to swim in the upper waters with the Great White Sharks.

(He puts a fatherly arm around Water) Funny thing, you know, I was saying to an SC graduate ethics class just this morning how essential it is in our sometimes, unfortunate business to protect the sacred public trust. Trust. It is a precious commodity amigo. FYI: if you trust me order the watercress salad, it is divine.

WATER: No thank you.

(The Busboy enters to take their order.)

FIXER: Two watercress enseladas, por favor.

(The Busboy exits.)

So, how's tricks? What can I do for my go-getter, do-gooder Brothers García? What does it say there in front of where your daddy used to work? "Water for Life, Power for Progress." Does it still say that? I just love that. Makes me feel safe somehow. L.A. can still be a scary town you know.

WATER: Whoever this gentleman standing behind you is, I need him to leave us for a few moments, please.

FIXER: He can't hear a thing. Relax.

WATER: I can't. I cannot relax.

(The Fixer looks over his shoulder to El Ministro. He removes his earphones.)

EL MINISTRO: ¿Sí jefe?

FIXER: Oh, don't call me that, it embarrasses me so. *(Lets out a fake laugh)*

EL MINISTRO: Forgive me, sir.

FIXER: What on earth are you listening to?

EL MINISTRO: The Notorious B.I.G.

FIXER: Ooh, I love them. Hum a few bars . . .

EL MINISTRO *(Kicks out a few beatboxes)*: "Somebody's gotta die . . ."

FIXER *(Joins in)*: "If I go, you gotta go."

EL MINISTRO: "Somebody's got to die. . ."

FIXER: "Let the gunshots flow!"

EL MINISTRO: "Somebody's gotta die. . ."

FIXER *(Raises both arms in the "raise the roof" fashion)*: "Throw your signs in the air, and wave 'em like you just don't care . . ."

(El Ministro obliges the Fixer and waves his arms, but always with cool.)

I love that! *(With one "pleased with himself" clap of the hand)* Woo! So much raw power and truth in the rap game. Just breaking down the knowledge fool. Thank you for your authentic self, "G." I tell you, Gilbert, this fella rolls correct or he don't roll at all.

EL MINISTRO: Palabra. *(Taps his heart two times in a Pimp/Playa way)*

FIXER: Found him on Jimmy Crack Corner, and now look at him. One love, playa. You know who gave me my street cred, don't you? My Negritude.

(Water shakes his head no.)

A certain Mister Tupac Shakur. Whom I met at the Playboy Mansion with his personal bodyguard, a moonlighting LAPD sergeant.

(Water knows this.)

Your brother. Who you need to keep alive. Oh, but what fun back in the day. You need to have more fun, Mr. Waterman.

WATER: Can we talk now, please?

(Fixer raises his hand as if to say, "Hush."
The Busboy enters with a bread basket. He places one roll carefully at each setting. Just before he exits El Ministro grabs a roll out of the basket for himself.)

Here's the deal . . .

FIXER: No. Here's the dealio, Senator García, and please listen oh so carefully, boo, the city doesn't need two more snot-nosed Mexican kids sharing a prison cell with our good friends the sheriff and the Hispanic councilman. La Pinta—prison—would be a very unpleasant place for a former star prosecutor and his cop brother. Norteños and Sureños fighting over the bros.

(The Fixer butters his roll.)

Yellow mellow butter, feeling good.

WATER: Before you apply your notorious corn-holing technique
let me say . . .

FIXER *(Calm)*: Shut, the, fuck, up. Please. *(Takes a bite of his roll)*
I'm sooooo intense tonight. I was confused for so long,
I thought when the Prison Gangs said no more drive-bys,
they meant "drive-thrus." I haven't had a Happy Meal since
1996. The Cripps and Bloods truce might still be holding
thanks to our good friend Tom Hayden, but Water and
Power may have fucked it all up for good. And here's the
unfortunate kicker for you and your carnal: four teams of
shooters from Imperial Beach to Soledad all have the green
light on Señor Super Poder.

And you know what happens when power lines hit the
ground.

(Distant thunder is heard.)

Oh, here comes the watercress. Yummy for my tummy.

(The Busboy moves in and out.)

Thank you, boo.

*(Water's BlackBerry chirps. He looks at the time and shuts it
off.)*

Take the call.

(Water silences the BlackBerry.)

Eat. You'll need it. Break bread like the good Lord said.

WATER: I have never asked you for anything. And tonight I need
a favor.

FIXER: And I need a prison on the Eastside. Does not mean I'm
going to get a prison on the Eastside.

WATER: Gloria will never allow that to happen.

FIXER: I need condos on your L.A. River Green Space, Mister Agua. I need live/work lofts, gated communities, gringo hipsters walking little dogs, storefront galleries with crappy art, a Coffee Bean would be sa-weet! IKEA, East L.A.!

WATER: We are not having this conversation.

FIXER: We most certainly are.

WATER: Oh, I cannot . . . look, that land is going green.

FIXER: Didn't you get enough Greenpeace pussy during the "Heal the Bay" era?

WATER: My green bill is well on its way to the governor, sir.

FIXER: There are sundry ways a bill can die from committee to Terminator.

WATER: That land has been promised to the people. I gave my word.

FIXER: Nothing is concrete in L.A., except the river.

WATER: I made a promise.

FIXER: The men looking for your carnal have a promise, too.

WATER: My gosh, is this is a shakedown, sir?

FIXER: Heavens no, I'm trying to square-deal ya here, amigo.

WATER: Well then for God sake ask anything else of me. I am prepared to offer you anything else. Just please, please, please, help me make my brother's safety a reality.

FIXER: Is there even a contexto for reality here? I mean step through this slowly with me, Senator: top ranking cop bivouacked at seedy motel with side-kick crippled cholo. Well-dressed assassins on Officer García's trail. Cops on Officer García's trail. Prison gang, who's name—so feared—I dare not repeat it at this table, donning war bonnets as we speak. Might I suggest we bow our heads and pray to my good friend Cardinal Mahoney that nobody find Officer Garcia before I can work my miracle.

WATER: I came here to seek your good council because of the tremendous amount of respect I have for you. Not to bargain with you.

FIXER: *You don't fuck with La Eme!!* You don't fuck with La Eme, boo-boo. If you wanna walk across hot coals with Tony Robbins—passé but OK. Rolling brownouts in unincorporated sections of the San Fernando Valley just for kicks—cool! Five Tijuana whores and your own private narco traficante—you got it! Lunch at the Getty with the stolen statues from Rome—done! I can make the bells ring three times at any firehouse in Southern California and all that happy shit if you desire, but don't come asking me to help the poor bastard who kills a top soldier from the other team as an independent contractor. My gosh! I've got no wiggle room here, Gibs. PD brass got their blue panties in a bunch in record time on this one. La Eme won't come to the table unless I let them go tea bags on my forehead and I'm just getting too old for that shit. El Hermano has fucked-up big time. He may in fact already reside in that special place juuuust outside my reach.

WATER: Nothing is out of your reach.

FIXER: I can't reach the salt. Pass it. Soup to nuts, my boy, soup to nuts. It's a package deal. *(Pours wine)* Drink your fine South African Riesling, counselor, after all, Chinese children are dying of thirst in Little Italy tonight. *(He drinks)* Salvation of the soul, protection of the body.

(Water checks the time. He adjusts himself in his chair then proceeds carefully.)

WATER: Did you ever see a mezuzah in an East Los Angeles doorway? I have. In Boyle Heights. And it struck me, you know, one culture stepping into the footprints of another. And all these Mexican families moving into these Eastside homes protected by this wonderful little thing up there, in the doorway. I had no idea what it was at first. But one of Fred Ross's old-time volunteers explained it to me. And I never forgot. You worked with Fred once upon a time. Way back when. When he and Saul trained a kid named César Chávez. You were there. And now the Cesar Chavez River Walkway will honor all of that. It is a beautiful piece of legislation. Essential. This bill is my mezuzah for the Eastside.

FIXER: Have I heard you tell that story before?

WATER *(A professional smile)*: Lest we forget where we came from.

FIXER: Don't sit here and act like you haven't sucked on the perky titties of entitlement, Gilbert. Your brother has exploited every pink nipple of opportunity ever presented to you. 'Tis your right, as American as Daddy cashing in his GI Bill.

WATER: OK . . .

FIXER: So let's be clear, this is why we find ourselves at this table tonight. Everything is on the table, amigo. You and I are the modern long knives, and we must continue to carve up the Eastside. And I need one more slice of that pie.

WATER: I am a humble public servant . . .

FIXER: Bullshit. Kill your bill in committee, Senator.

WATER: Absolutely not.

(Water rises from his chair. El Ministro keeps a close eye on him.)

FIXER: You're tougher than the mothers of East L.A.

WATER: My people want clean air, too.

FIXER: As evidenced by what? Ooh! Idea: How 'bout I get the construction companies who have contributed to your many campaigns to build a computer center for the Chicanitos? The Cesar Chavez Education Center, between a Pinkberry and a Forever 21!

WATER: It won't wash. Political suicide.

FIXER: Come what may, your constituents will forgive you.

WATER: Chicanos don't forgive. It's not in our DNA.

FIXER: Look, boo, the Brothers García have managed to piss off some very powerful people.

WATER: One of the brothers.

FIXER: We don't discern where one brother leaves off and the other begins, after all, I'm just a stupid white guy from Brentwood so what do I know?

WATER: Why don't you save your "just a white guy from Brentwood" routine for your clients at the Arch Diocese.

FIXER *(Looks calmly at Water)*: Come here. *(Using his index finger in that wagging way)* Come. Lean in.

(Water leans in slightly over the Fixer's shoulder.)

Let me tell you what this white guy knows that you may not. And I can only say this once, so follow the bouncing ball as best you can, Gilbert. The bad-ass hombre your brother assassinated in East Los Angeles earlier this evening was carrying a contract for murder of a high profile target. That "contract" was signed, sealed and approved by a commission of men, hombres whose very existence I know scarcely about. And I know a lot. I know this: the contract—due to the death of bad-ass hombre—killed by the hand of your brother is now null and void, nobody can carry it out. Having said that, there is this caveat, the new improved contract transfers to Power.

WATER: I don't follow.

FIXER: Neither did I. I had to look it up. Real spicky stuff, archaic rules going back to your old country. In effect, your brother, by his actions, so egregious, exchanged his name for the original on the contract.

WATER: Who was the original target?

FIXER *(Pointing his elegant finger in Water's face)*: You.

(Water tries not to lose it.)

An overzealous, ambitious prosecutor named Gilbert García sent a nobody street thug named Escobar to prison twelve years ago for a crime he did not commit. Officer García handled the police reports naturally. Mr. Nobody became Mr. Somebody who was released yesterday. Mr. Somebody had the green light to pull off the first known hit on a sitting member of the California State Senate. Your brother stopped history. *(He whistles with his fingers in a playful, sick way)* Contrails of corruption every which way. Your hermano saved your life. And now you must save his. My condos.

WATER: Not possible.

FIXER: This is L.A., boychick, anything is possible. For example: I ask PD to stand down while this fellow and his brother from Culiacán . . .

EL MINISTRO: Matamoros.

FIXER: I stand corrected. Matamoros. He and his brother will be at the Motel Paradise in forty-two minutes to pick up all unauthorized LAPD weapons and sweep the place of various narcotics. The brothers will then plant those weapons on an expendable homeboy in the city of . . . Carson! Sometime between now and let's say sunrise.

EL MINISTRO *(Moves close to Water)*: Tell your coked-out-queer-cop-degenerate brother not to shoot us, we shoot back, ese. Send the crippled cholo to the Taco Delta stand, the one with the steam rising up to the sky across from the wetback nightclub. We'll follow the cholo back to your carnal. Tell wheelchair vato not be a hero, I've got spotters all over the area. Bookoo backup, you know what I'm saying? They don't fuck around, ese. Te lo juro. Have I made myself clear?

(Water nods.)

Very good. Nice tie.

FIXER: Ah, brothers helping brothers, qué casualidad, qué curioso. Let me know when our ribbon cutting ceremony can commence on that lush waterway we forgivingly call the L.A. River.

Gilbert, I cannot stress enough how important it is that everything outlined this evening proceed in a timely fashion. Any deviation could be most unpleasant. Origami my friend, origami. All things must fold perfectly into place. Senator?

(A long beat.)

WATER: OK.

FIXER: Make the call, Gilbert. God's not looking. Green space dies. Power lives.

WATER *(Hits speed-dial on his BlackBerry)*: Hey, guy, uh, shit, listen, we've hit a brick wall, and before it hits the press let's let some people know that they have found toxins on the land, and some sort of Indian burial ground as well. Let's leak some stuff to the press about Bob, I gotta Swift Boat him before he does me. Chumash, I think. I have to kill the bill. Calm down, calm down. We're walking away. The green space is dead. It's a brown field. I got to walk away. Go.

(Water sits back at the table and gulps down some white wine.)

FIXER: All in all I'd say a very productive evening. Good work, son.

WATER: Fuck the whores of this town.

FIXER *(Brightly with friendly finger pointing)*: But you are one of us. Oh goodness, look at the time.

You know Rabbi Learner says we must all endeavor to be happy, it is our responsibility, takes real effort though. I don't like a young man who does not dream. The city still needs your dreams, kid. She hungers for them.

(Water drinks directly from the wine bottle.)

Your mezuzah story. The late, great, Honorable Edward R. Roybal told that story much better, rest in peace. *(He crosses himself)* He told it much better because it was his story. Not yours. Alas, the hour is late, we forget things.

Excuse me. I've been on these old tires all day. I usually enjoy a foot massage in tepid water about this time but my masseuse has retired for the night sadly.

(The Busboy enters with a small wash basin. Water rises from his chair as El Ministro moves the table away.)

Would you wash my feet in warm salted water, Water?

WATER: That's hilarious.

FIXER: I need for you to wash my feet in warm salted water.

WATER: The fuck you say . . .

(The Busboy places a towel on the floor for the Fixer, then pours warm salted water into the basin.)

Water (Richard Montoya) washes the feet of the Fixer (Dakin Matthews) as the Busboy (Moisés Arias) helps.

FIXER: Water and Power. Power and Water, they thought they were real princes of the city, the dukes of Earl, but they're still just snot-nosed Mexican kids from the Eastside dripping down Daddy's leg.

(El Ministro hangs quiet and menacingly in the shadows. The Fixer methodically places his feet in the basin.)

Ah, nothing more soothing in the world. Come. Don't be shy or embarrassed, I had to do this a hundred times for Condoleeza before I got the hang of it. She's got the prettiest little black toes.

(Silence. Then the sound of water as the Busboy scoops water with his hands and washes the Fixers feet.)

Just listen to that water. That's it. Come closer, Water, come to the water, man.

(El Ministro moves in, gently forces Water toward the basin and on his knees.)

I have always maintained, contrary to popular belief and medical certainty, that water is, in fact, thicker than blood.

(El Ministro carefully removes Water's jacket. Water reaches into the basin and begins to wash the Fixer's feet. The Busboy backs away.)

Good Hispanic. Good Hispanic. Who would have thunk you'd have the touch? Easy there. Oh, you're feeling me now, dawg.

(Water looks at the Busboy. He turns away.)

Good Hispanic. Barack Obama has beautiful feet! God I love this town. How does it go? "I love L.A. . . ."
    Mountain lion spotted in Eagle Rock. We live in the "wild kingdom," kid!

(All walk offstage as the Fixer continues laughing and singing.)

SCENE 7

Back at Motel Paradise. Power is pointing his gun into the mirror, sort of posing for Norte/Sur, who is hunched over his Piece Book, drawing fast. The radio is on.

POWER: Just like this, calm like a bomb.

NORTE/SUR: Hold still, man, almost done. Raise your arm just a bit, homes.

POWER: Any higher and it's not what I did. It will be your version of what I did. Not what I really did.

NORTE/SUR: You're talking to the Picasso of the Barrio, homes. Got it.

(Norte/Sur closes his Piece Book. Power relaxes his pose. A beat.)

POWER: It's real quiet. Damn. I hate when it gets this quiet.

NORTE/SUR *(Looks at his watch)*: How long's your carnal been gone?

POWER: A few hours.

NORTE/SUR: How much did you tell him?

POWER: Not everything. Turn the radio up, man.

(Norte/Sur turns up the radio. We hear the Dramatics' "In the Rain.")

Ah, man, I love this jam. Damn. Oh yeah. Must be the Huggie Boy show.

(Power dances in the center of the motel room, really feeling it, taking in the slow jam. He lifts his arms, dancing like a homeboy.)

Ah yeah, feel it, homes.

NORTE/SUR: I remember this dance, ay, its been a while but I remember dancing with the jainas. Sha!

(From his chair Norte/Sur starts to dance using his arms: the cop and the cholo are dancing to the oldie.)

POWER: Do it right or don't do it at all, homeboy.

NORTE/SUR: Órale.

(Power goes behind Norte/Sur's wheelchair and gently lifts him from behind, holding him up. Power provides the legs and feet for the crippled cholo.)

POWER: There it is right there. You got it, bro.

NORTE/SUR: Don't let your bro hear you call me bro.

POWER: Don't trip. Just feel the music, man.

NORTE/SUR: I remember dancing just like this.

POWER: Yeah?

NORTE/SUR: Not with a cop right behind me but something like this.

POWER: Been a long time since I danced like this.

NORTE/SUR: Is it hard to dance when killers are looking for you?

POWER: It's the best time to dance.

NORTE/SUR: I gotta write that one down, ese.

POWER: Don't write, just dance. Feel the jam.

(Norte/Sur and Power dance, closely, tenderly. A long beat.)

NORTE/SUR: Hey, man, is that your night stick in my ass or has it just been a long time since you danced with a cholo?

POWER: Shut the fuck up, man!

(Power sort of tosses Norte/Sur gently onto the bed. Norte/Sur reaches for his Piece Book and pulls his chair close to him. Power keeps moving to the jam.)

NORTE/SUR: Hey, vato, if anything happens to you, you know like something bad, and you die and shit, don't hang around like Patrick Swayze did in that movie.

POWER: I'll be long gone, trust me.

NORTE/SUR: I'll see to it that even the homies come by to pay their respects to Power, know what I mean?

POWER: You would do that for me?

NORTE/SUR: Homey love. For sure. *(He makes his way back into his chair, but one of his legs needs some help)* Help me with my left foot, ese?

POWER: Daniel Day Lewis over here.

NORTE/SUR: Gracias, homey.

POWER: So, which homeboys, which ones will come to my wake?

NORTE/SUR: Uh, I don't know, I'd have to check it out, you know, see which vatos are available, I'm sure I could dig up somebody.

POWER (*Liking the idea*): Hey, get the hardcore vatos from White Fence, Cuatro Flats or Maravilla, OGs, veteranos from the old school. No youngsters.

NORTE/SUR: I dunno, ese, the older OGs are kinda busy with funerals and shit.

POWER: So which homies for sure?

NORTE/SUR: Well, I know at least one fake-ass cholo from Silverlake or West L.A. who might be willing to come. He wears a Von Dutch hat backwards but I'll make sure he takes it off when he comes to the wake.

(*Power fixes that visual in his head for a moment.*)

POWER: No hipsters at my funeral. And that's an order.

NORTE/SUR: I'll find someone. Come hell or high water.

POWER: Just forget it.

NORTE/SUR: Maybe I could get Edward James Olmos to come, I helped him sweep the streets after the L.A. Riots, he owes me.

(*Power slowly points his gun at Norte/Sur. Norte/Sur takes a careful note.*)

No Edward James Olmos.

SCENE 8

Norte/Sur exits the motel. The Deer Dancer moves slowly through the hotel room. Power moves about with his AK-47. He doesn't see the Deer Dancer. Norte/Sur speaks to the audience from an aisle off the stage.

NORTE/SUR: You see the Deer Dancer there? If you see him, you are one of the lucky ones. He is our protection, a lucky charm, a talisman. I first saw him at MacArthur Park in L.A., dancing with the elders, so I know he comes from a long line of Deer Dancers. His people came from across the Rio Yaqui, a familia known as the Clan of the Wolf. Even on these mean streets of L.A., one whispers those words: "Clan of the Wolf." Los Fadiceos. They wore baggie black pants, black shoes, white tees and black shirts buttoned only at the top like the homies do. They were the first known cholos. Like gangsters.

    This little vato came from all that.

    The Deer Dancer must return to MacArthur Park and dance ceremony all night, if he stumbles or falls, if the cops kick his ass, if he stops dancing—then nothing can keep the Lords of Death at bay. He was taught early on that for some, death in the big city is imminent, and every little Deer Dancer knows that the dance ends in death, but he must continue on the Red Road regardless. He must dance so that his tribe can live. From his death there is life. After winter, spring; summer, fall.

    You never get something for nothing.

(Norte/Sur exits.)

SCENE 9

Motel Paradise. Four A.M. Water enters.

POWER: Bagpipes. I want bagpipes. You be sure I have them.
WATER: What?
POWER: Yeah. We play them across the street when we bury cops.
WATER: We don't have time for this, man.
POWER: I've lost a lot of brothers already. The politicians change, you guys come and go, but the bagpipes remain.

(Points toward the cathedral) There. *(Pointing to his head)* Here. Bagpipes. Damn, I hate the feeling of power they give me. So real you know?

WATER: We'll talk in the car, let's go.

POWER: Rows and rows of cops, sheriffs from all over the country. Standing at attention in the cathedral courtyard for hours in the hot sun. Nobody moving, out of reverence for a fallen brother. Patrol cars lined up from here to Chinatown. Engine ladders crossed, the flag hanging over Temple and Grand Avenue.

Carefully fold the flag that was draped over the coffin, pass it to the widow.

She is weary of our remembrance faces.

Sometimes the child of a fallen officer is so young they think every cop is their father. What do you say to that, bro? What do you tell that child?

So I ask my God Cop in my best white voice: What do you want from me? And I make my little deals with him. He wants me to take my grief and turn it into power. That power is the bullets coming out of my sidearm. It's the baton crashing down on the next cleanly shaven head. My God is righteous, bro. And righteous are the peacekeepers. I am a monster, but he forgives me because I am a monster built of dead cops and bagpipes. They built this dark house. One cop funeral at a time.

WATER: You don't have to justify your bagpipe bullshit to me, bro. I made the deal.

POWER: I didn't ask you to make a fucking deal. What did you give up?

WATER: A lot.

POWER: You stupid fuck. You didn't have to do that.

WATER: Oh I did.

POWER: Why are you always trying to be the good guy?

WATER: I've heard the bagpipes.

POWER: The smart brother?

WATER: I heard them at the cathedral.

POWER: Why the fuck are you always trying to save the goddamned world, Gil?

WATER: We were taught to save the goddamned world, Gabe. Do you remember that? That is what we were taught. And I have heard your bagpipes, bro, and they weren't for one of your cops, no, bagpipes mixed with the voices of farm workers. Bagpipes for César, Gabe.

POWER: César who?

WATER: Chávez, you idiot.

POWER: Fuck César.

WATER: Never say that again, Gabe. We made a promise to César and that is what I gave up tonight for you.

POWER: For you!

WATER: For you, bro!

POWER: Then you got played.

(The brothers start to push each other around.)

Fuck César, fuck Dad and fuck all promises made to anybody anywhere! *(Raises his pistol toward his brother)* And fuck your "De Colores."

WATER: Gabe . . .

POWER: Your bagpipes are not my bagpipes.

WATER: Gabby, man, put the gun down, bro. Listen to me, please.

POWER: I can't hear you, the bagpipes drown you out.

WATER: Put the gun down.

POWER: You want to hear "De Colores"? Fine, you sing it. Remind me of that tune, hum a few bars, c'mon, bitch, sing it! Sing it!

(Power slams the magazine into his gun. Water goes to his knees. Turbine sounds begin.)

Sing it, motherfucker, sing your goddamn song, César!

(Power cocks his gun. Water tries to plead with his brother, but struggles to find the words, to make a sound.)

WATER: Put, the gun down. Brother, please.

The García Brothers: Power (Herbert Siguenza, left) overpowers Water (Richard Montoya).

(Power takes aim.)

"De colores, de colores se visten los campos in la primav-
era. . ."

POWER: Yeah, sing it!

WATER: "De colores, de colores. . ."

POWER: Next verse, keep going, come on. Sing, César, sing!

WATER: ". . . los pajarillos. . ."

POWER: Sing! Sing!

WATER: That's all I know! I don't remember all the words.

POWER: You phony Hispanic fuck.

*(Power laughs wildly. Water seizes the moment and tackles
Power. The gun falls to the floor. The brothers wrestle, more
struggle. Turbines can be heard. The wrestling turns into an
all-out fistfight and a struggle for the loaded gun. Punches are
thrown. The brothers go down. Suddenly the lights go out.
Silence. Then:)*

Quiet. Quiet, Gibby.

WATER: Huh?

POWER: Hear that?

WATER: What?

*(A surge of turbine blares, then grinds to a halt.)
From the shadows we see Norte/Sur.)*

SCENE 10: THE DARK HOUSE

Norte/Sur wheels across the stage in darkness.

NORTE/SUR: The Dark House. This Dark House shit is for real,
dog. I'm very, very serious right now. Maybe because I'm
afraid of the dark myself, don't tell nobody, it's private
information. Let me ask you this: Have you ever been in a
place so dark that you can't tell if you're alone in space or
surrounded by monsters?

I've been in the Dark House before. Yeah, there was a cholo carnival in the hood, and my homey had just OD'd on the Zipper, so I went into the funhouse so nobody would see me cry. It was so dark in there, man, I couldn't find my way out for two hours. I was real scared. Those Lords of Death were reaching for me, smiling all happy through sad clown faces in the blackness. Endless. Like a spooky ice scream truck song that never stops.

I read somewhere that the Maya got so tripped-out in the pitch black jungles of the Yucatán, that they left without a trace. Well, the bros have been kicked to the Dark House by the Lords of Death.

Ambitious vatos, smart guys, hopefully they can figure out what the Maya could not.

(As Norte/Sur wheels away we hear the spooky voice of a child:)

CHILD *(Voice-over; a hushed echo)*: Power, come out and play-yay. Power, come out and play-yay. . .

SCENE 11

Back at the motel. The brothers are still in the dark.

POWER: Gibby? Gibby?
WATER: What?
POWER: You OK?
WATER: Fuck off.

(Huge thunder, then lightning.)

WATER AND POWER: Woah!!!
WATER: How the hell was there just lightning after the thunder?
POWER: Because that was the thunder after the last lightning from before.
WATER: Sounds about right.

POWER: You stuck me pretty good, cabrón.

WATER: Should have taken your fucking head off, man.

(Lightning.)

Damn, stop.

POWER: You escared?

WATER: Yeah.

POWER: You always hated thunderstorms since we were little.

WATER: Yep.

POWER: Remember that time when we were camping and the tent got flooded and there were bears and stuff?

WATER: Nope. You obviously have our childhood mixed-up with somebody else's.

POWER: Yeah, maybe I saw it on *Scooby Doo.*

(Beat.)

WATER: You could have told me my name was on the contract? You're a real jerk, you know that?

POWER: Was that really all you knew of "De Colores"?

WATER: Yeah, I'm a phony fuck, remember?

POWER: Sing it again. Maybe it will come back to you.

WATER: It won't.

POWER: Sí se puede.

WATER: Stop.

POWER: Please, bro, I'm begging on my knees.

WATER: You're not on your knees, you're sitting on your fat ass.

POWER: C'mon

WATER: All right. "La Gallina con el pío, pío, pío. . ." There's a bunch more píos and a Flock of Seagulls . . . "and she's buying a stairway to heaven. . ."

(We make out the shadow of Norte/Sur who has entered the motel room.)

NORTE/SUR: "¡Y por eso los grandes amores, / De muchos colores / Me gustan a mí!"

(Thunder. The lights flicker on.)

Am I the only motherfucker up in here that knows the words to "De Colores"? While you two were rolling around in here I wheeled myself up to Lilac Terrace. I got a good view from up there, coyotes howling and everything.

WATER: And?

NORTE/SUR: Well, word on the street is this: No contract on Power. The homies are standing down. Nobody's tirando blows against you now.

POWER: I'm not buying it.

NORTE/SUR: Te lo juro, homey.

WATER: I told you it's done, it's handled. With my guy.

(Sounds of helicopters. Power swings into action.)

POWER: It's never done. I don't know your guy, I don't trust your guy.

(Norte/Sur lays out new weapons, mostly small handguns, on the dresser. He begins to load them.)

WATER: Gabe, Gabe?

POWER: No. They're coming here, man, and they're gonna take me out, they don't miss.

NORTE/SUR: Maybe you should get out of here right now, Water, man. Take this and go.

(Norte/Sur hands a weapon to Water. Power intercepts.)

POWER: No. Just go, bro, go, you can't help me now.

WATER: I did help you. I'm part of the deal now.

POWER: There is no deal. It's a setup! This ain't your game, Gilbert. I told you, no code, no rules. I'm out, man. It's that simple.

WATER: It's not going down like that.

POWER: The men who are coming here are going to kill me.

WATER: La Eme isn't coming here, bro.

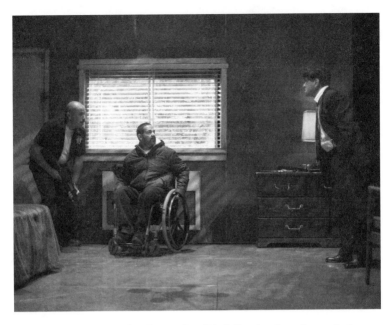

Power (Herbert Siguenza) and Norte/Sur (Ric Salinas) make a plan against Water's (Richard Montoya) wishes.

POWER: I'm not talking about La Eme.

WATER: You got it wrong, bro. I'm taking you home. LAPD is part of the fucking package.

POWER: Does "contagious fire" mean anything to you?

WATER: My guy's got LAPD in check.

POWER: L.A.'s better off without me.

WATER: They're going to arrest another soldier for the murder. No. We're walking. That's the deal, that's the promise. See those guys in the parking lot?

NORTE/SUR: The vatos in the Crown Vic?

WATER: No, the black Escalade.

NORTE/SUR: When did they roll up?

WATER: Just now. Those are my guys, we're golden.

POWER *(Peeks out the window)*: Traffic Division is closing down part of Sunset.

WATER: Your city is working, that's all.

POWER: Norte/Sur?

NORTE/SUR: Sounds like it could be, but I just don't know for sures. Difficult to be certain.

POWER: What should I do, homey?

WATER: Hey, I'm right here and I'm telling you what to do, homey.

POWER: Give us just a moment, bro. Please?

NORTE/SUR *(Moving past Water toward Power)*: Despensa homes.

WATER: Right. I'm not in your car.

(We hear a Harley Davidson drive by in the distance.)

NORTE/SUR *(More of a question to himself)*: That sounded like Rafas.

(Power crouches close to Norte/Sur. They hold hands in a soul handshake way. It is a quiet, intimate moment. Water looks away.)

POWER: What do I do?

NORTE/SUR: This is for sure some critical shit right here, Gabe. Maybe Water has it like that with his fixer, vato.

POWER: Maybe, huh?

NORTE/SUR: What's your plan B, ay?

POWER *(Grave)*: A pair of dice.

NORTE/SUR *(Leans in for some very private, very scary counsel)*: I heard some other foos were gonna die tonight for sure. Word had come down from the pen early, you know. They were gonna hit some black dudes in the Avenues that had nothing to do with this pedo. Blame it on the mayates again and shit. It ain't right, homey.

POWER: Right.

NORTE/SUR: Right. You messed with the Chain of Command, vato. And unless I'm very wrong, or if Water's vato doesn't have the right power—

POWER: The worst may be yet to come.

NORTE/SUR: Let me ask you this then: What does your Spidey Sense tell you?

POWER: To be ready for anything.

NORTE/SUR: Then ask your brother to put something on it.

WATER: I'm right here Norte/Sur, talk to me.

NORTE/SUR: For the safety of your carnal, for the brothers, put something on it.

WATER: I already put a million trees on it, so fuck you, Norte/ Sur.

NORTE/SUR: Good point. *(He looks back to Power)* I'm gonna have to go with your carnal on this one, ay. You must accept Water's terms. Either that, or go out in a blaze of glory.

POWER *(Leans into Norte/Sur)*: He's been telling me what to do my whole life, man, I just thought tonight it would be my turn to call the shots. The shot-caller.

NORTE/SUR: I hear you, bro, but then again why switch up now, of all nights you know?

POWER: Yeah.

NORTE/SUR: And the sooner the better, so we can end this desmadre.

WATER: It's over. It's over, guys. We're leaving all weapons behind. I'm gonna pack you up myself, bro. Norte/Sur, please roll out to the parking lot and tell black Escalade we're coming out in two minutes. You're the signal they're waiting for.

NORTE/SUR: Simón.

WATER: And ask them how fast they can get to Cedar's emergency room just in case . . .

(Just before Norte/Sur exits, he faces Power, who is seated at the edge of the bed.)

NORTE/SUR: This feels right. *(Begins to move out)* Stay up, foo.

POWER: Stay down, dawg.

(They touch knuckles.)

WATER: Go!

NORTE/SUR: Gone.

(Norte/Sur wheels out to the parking lot. The brothers are left together.)

WATER: Gabe? Gabe?

(Beat.)

POWER: Let's do it then.

(Water starts gathering Power's things, then moves into the bathroom. Power remains frozen on the bed.)

I'm sorry, bro. Sorry about all this.

(Water keeps packing his brother's things.)

WATER: We'll get through it, lieutenant, you'll see. We'll take a vacation together, go away for a while, you know. And this long night will be behind us soon enough, bro. Shit, Dad might even have been proud of us.

POWER: You think?

WATER: Golly yeah, proud of his Water and Power, man.

(Water and Power recede into the shadows of the motel. Power begins to quietly lay out black tarpaulin on the motel bed.
Father and a young Gabriel enter downstage singing "De Colores." The two are dressed nicely. They stand in front of the old DWP building on Cahuenga Boulevard.)

FATHER AND SON: "Y por eso los grandes amores, / De muchos colores / Me gustan a mí."

FATHER: Sing it, mijo!

(Gabby belts out the last verse con gusto.)

GABBY: "¡Y por eso los grandes amores, / De muchos colores / Me gustan a mí!"

FATHER: ¡Qué bueno mijo! The girls are gonna love it when you sing that song, mijo.

GABBY: They all like Gilbert, Dad, I have bad luck with girls.

FATHER: I thought you were playing stink-finger with the little gavachita down the street?

GABBY *(Shakes his head no in shame, looking down)*: She dumped me, man.

FATHER: Where's your confianza, my lil' Power man?

GABBY: I dunno.

FATHER: Lookie here, lil' vato, here is what we'll do. I'll be your sponsor.

GABBY: My sponsor?

FATHER: Sure, why not, mijo, we'll iron your brand-new chinos perfectly, like mine. And then, you can borrow my Sir Guy jacket. What you wanna do is carry it like a vato, a real gentleman. Never worn, always carried on your arm, así. *(He carefully wraps his jacket over his forearm, cool like that)*

GABBY: Wow, that's sharp, Dad. Te ves muy cool.

FATHER: No matters if your parents are on relief—man, your stuff better look sharp! No excuses. And make sure those French Toes are spit-shined but good. *(He does a cool pose, showing off his chinos, jacket, shoes)*

GABBY: Ooh.

FATHER: Here, you try.

(Gabby drapes the Sir Guy jacket over his little arm and poses.)

GABBY: Órale.

(Father and son do the secret handshake.)

FATHER: Excellent, mijo. Never worn, always carried: chinos, jacket, shoes—the Holy Trinity.

(Father does a nifty move, running his hand through his hair. He holds his hand out, palm up, and lightly leans back. Gabby smells the Three Flowers in his Father's hand. He eyes his Father's shiny hair. He smiles to the heavens, eyes closed. This is Gabby's best day in the whole wide world.)

GABBY: Hee-hee . . .

Gabriel, Power (Herbert Siguenza, left) says good-bye to his younger self,
Gabby (Moisés Arias).

FATHER: Now go practice in the mirror. Ándale.

(Little Gabby runs from this moment, directly into Motel
Paradise—he is face to face with his grown-up self. Power sits
on the edge of the bed, on the tarpaulin he has just laid down.)

WATER *(From the bathroom, off)*: Hey, the water just went out.

GABBY *(Speaking to his older self)*: Dad says never wear your Sir
Guy jacket, just carry it like this.

POWER: Neat. Let's not tell Gilbert, OK.

GABBY: OK.

POWER: Hey, you wanna get some chocolate cake later?

(Little Gabby nods yes. Power and his younger self do a lovely
little hand motion. They are totally in sync, it's as if looking in
a mirror.)

WATER *(From off)*: You talking to yourself?
GABBY AND POWER: Yeah.
GABBY: Is there a monster *under* the bed?

(Power nods no.)

Is there a monster *on* the bed?
POWER: The lady in the doorway tonight, why did she look at me like that?

(Little Gabby shrugs.)

Did we kill Mom when we were born?
GABBY: Dad says we're never supposed to talk about that.
POWER: Oh. OK.

(Power slowly puts his gun to his head. Gabby runs off.)

WATER *(From off)*: You say something, bro?
POWER *(To his brother)*: Sorry what I said about César.

(Click. White light.
In the instant that Power pulls back the hammer of the gun, white light is on him at the edge of the bed. These are not out-side lights coming through the window or people closing in on him, this is Power closing in on Power.
Water comes running in from the bathroom.)

WATER: Gabby! No, Gabby. No. Norte/Sur! Officer down! Officer down! Move it! Move it!
(Water cradles his brother; quietly) Gabby!

(Time passes. It is five A.M., Motel Paradise. We hear the Notorious B.I.G. version of the Dramatics' classic "In the Rain." Water continues to hold his brother. He closes Power's eyes.
The bed moves upstage into darkness.

El Ministro quickly sweeps the room of weapons and furniture. The Deer Dancer appears. He wears only the antlers, white peasant pants and ankle shakers. He carries another shaker. At first the Deer Dancer's movements are fluid and slow. His dance becomes more frenetic, an offering for the life of Power. The dance becomes ever faster. The Deer Dancer must dance with all his might to keep the Lords of Death at bay. The Lords of Death are receiving Power—Deer Dancer is their receipt of him, he leaps for his life. When the offering is done, he exits.)
The sound of rain.)

SCENE 12: A BOX OF RAIN

Norte/Sur wheels himself onstage. He slowly looks up, arms outstretched, palms up. It rains down on him. This Box of Rain exists only for Norte/Sur. Downpour. He smells the rain, feels the ceremony. He looks up to the sky.

NORTE/SUR: I like the sound of the helicopters. I like the way they feel.

The helicopters in the hood, ghetto birds flying low to the ground, sometimes so low I can feel the wind of their blades.

The power of their blades. Sometimes it's the only breeze that day. I can smell the jet fuel. It's the only time I can feel the bones in my dead legs.

(Norte/Sur is cleansed. He exits. The rain stops. The stage is clean.
A man in Rose Hills overalls enters and mops the pool of water on the stage.
An indentation in the floor suggests Power's grave.)

Ese Power!

SCENE 13: AFTER THE STORM

*Rose Hills Cemetery. One month later. Bagpipes play for Power.
(Finally.) Bagpipes flood the theater. Water enters wearing a sport
coat and sunglasses. He holds a single rose. He places it on Power's
grave. The bagpipes subside. Norte/Sur enters. He joins Water at
the graveside.*

NORTE/SUR: Hey.

WATER: Hey. Found the place all right?

NORTE/SUR: Took eighteen buses to get here. A new record for me.
Man, that last Cavalry hill over there was a motherfucker.

WATER: Thanks for coming.

NORTE/SUR: So, how you doing?

WATER: I haven't seen you since that time at Trader Joe's . . .

NORTE/SUR: Whole Foods, ese. I saw you at Whole Foods not
Trader Joe's. The aisles are wider at Whole Foods, I take
note of that stuff.

WATER: I stand corrected.

NORTE/SUR: Full disclosure, you know.

WATER: Due diligence, my man. How are you?

NORTE/SUR: Real good, real good, Senator. We had a carwash for
your brother, you know. All the homies and homegirls
washed a lot of cop cars and lowriders that day, it was
weird, man, a bunch of cops and cholos together at that
Chevron on Beverly and Atlantic, you know?

WATER: I know exactly where that is.

NORTE/SUR: Very, very tense situation, but hardly no pedo.

WATER: Good. Good.

NORTE/SUR: Damn, been over a month, still seems like yesterday. I really, really miss your carnal.

WATER: I know you do Norte/Sur.

NORTE/SUR: I miss his, his noise you know? Vato made a lot of
noise.

WATER: He did.

NORTE/SUR: I brought these flowers for him. They look kinda
fucked-up, but at least I didn't steal them off another grave
like the Armenians do.

WATER: Never say that again.

NORTE/SUR *(Looks around the cemetery)*: Gosh darn, takes a grip of water to make these cemeteries green. We're still in a desert, right?

WATER: It's still a desert. *(Enough chit-chat)* I'm having trouble with something, maybe you could help me out, Norte/Sur. I'm having trouble picturing you and my brother together. Hanging out and stuff.

NORTE/SUR: Yeah, we used to play . . . shoot-'em-up-bang-bang . . .

WATER: He told me about that. What else Norte/Sur? What else can you tell me?

NORTE/SUR: Let me say this about your brother: He's the only vato that ever encouraged me to write. He got me in a chingón screenwriting class at Universal Studios for Latino writers, taught by a real Jewish guy.

WATER: No kidding.

NORTE/SUR: Oh yeah, I even hung out with Brian Grazer and Opie. Yeah. I gave them their street cred and they got me an expert adviser gig on a Tom Cruise gang movie. I gotta go to Scientology once a week, but it ain't so bad.

WATER: I like the poem you read at my brother's funeral.

NORTE/SUR: Yeah?

WATER: It had an elliptical quality.

NORTE/SUR: I get that from my mother, she got seizures real bad, rolling on the floor and everything.

WATER: That's not what I meant . . .

NORTE/SUR: I'm just bullshitting you, man, I know what it means. You think I write in circles.

WATER: Beautiful circles. Where's your sketchbook now?

NORTE/SUR: My Piece Book? Never leaves my side.

WATER: Can I see it?

(Norte/Sur offers the book. Water quickly finds his brother's name.)

My brother's name is all over this thing.

NORTE/SUR: Well, yeah, he was my road dawg, ay.

WATER: I'm going to have to ask you if I can hang on to your book.

NORTE/SUR: Why?

WATER: I have to protect my brother.

NORTE/SUR: And yourself, eh?

WATER: Nothing personal, Norte/Sur, I just don't know what's in here. Could be full of all kinds of stuff.

NORTE/SUR: I don't lie, ese. I used to lie plenty, but not since I started going to Kaballa. My therapist thought it might be good for me.

(Water stares out. A long beat.)

WATER: They say there's only seven people you can trust in L.A.

NORTE/SUR: You already know two of them.

WATER *(Staring out)*: Rose Hills Cemetery. Feels lonely up here.

NORTE/SUR: Go home, Senator, take a long shower, eat fresh field greens with organic balsamic vinegar and try to learn what the gringos and Jews already know about power.

WATER: And what is that, oh great wise cholo?

NORTE/SUR: One: To have power and not use it. Two: If you do have it, spread it around. You Hispanics are still in your infancy with pinche power and it makes me sick. "I got it, so you can't have none."

WATER: Anything else?

NORTE/SUR: You should learn to respect the Four Directions like the Indian elder does. You might want to get all spiritual and shit like me. I'm enlisted like a motherfucker.

WATER: I will take that under advisement.

NORTE/SUR: I could teach you.

WATER: That's OK.

NORTE/SUR: Did the mayor call you yet?

(Water shakes his head no.)

He will. Underneath those expensive suits beats the heart of a homey who got kicked out of Cathedral High.

WATER: All rivers reach the sea.

    So, what are your plans, Norte/Sur?

NORTE/SUR: I got an ol' lady now.

WATER: Is that so?

NORTE/SUR: She's in a chair, too, but we can still bone.

WATER: I'm happy for you.

NORTE/SUR: She was Miss Montebello 1989, ay.

WATER: Royalty, eh?

NORTE/SUR: Oh yeah. She's still got some of the crown lodged in her brain, but she ain't retarded or nothing. After I see her I gotta go back to the hood and make things right with some little homies I know. It's my duty to tell them of the cautionary tale and destructive nature of water and power. Youngsters gotta learn, got to recognize, that the cold heart of Hispanic ambition can leave your soul as dry as the Owens Valley.

WATER: Do me a favor, Mr. Norte/Sur, be sure to tell your little homies that being a cholo ain't all that. Don't get all romantic about jumping them into the life—do not have them cholo up. And you tell them that no good ever comes from a dead cop.

NORTE/SUR: Agreed. I'd like to show them that Piece Book there.

WATER: Absolutely not.

NORTE/SUR: I would show them the pages of Gibby and Gabby, and they would know that the carnales were blessed. That the bros outsmarted the Lords of Death, but that there was a price to pay.

(Water, overcome, leans down to the grave.)

There was a price to pay.

WATER *(Silent)*: Yeah.

NORTE/SUR: You were your carnal's backup.

WATER: And for that I can feel proud?

NORTE/SUR: Where I come from backup is paramount.

(A beat.)

WATER: Gangbanger philosophy.

Norte/Sur (Ric Salinas) and Water (Richard Montoya, right) pay their respects to Power.

NORTE/SUR: L.A. gangs will never die, Senator, ever. The City of Angels needs her soldiers, she hungers for them. Even if they're gangsters in suits and ties.

(Water can only look away.)

Are you mad at him?

WATER *(Laughing slightly through his tears)*: When did he decide to do it, Norte/Sur? At what moment?

NORTE/SUR: For my money, he did it the moment he figured out that all the bad things he did would go with him. The fallout, the bad press. He set you up, bro. Your fixer vato called him when Escobar got out and was gunning for you. Your vato played it beautifully, except Power wouldn't let you get played like that. That's how the Eastside rolls, ese.

WATER (*Quiet realization*): Na . . .

NORTE/SUR: Look, you went up in the polls, got your César Chavez River Green Space chingadera passed. Everybody still loves the García Brothers, homes. Even his fellow officers posted a nice obituary on the bulletin board up at the firing range.
True Blue Vato. He kept his promise to you, to your pops, to his city. Some good came from this dead cop. And it's all carefully noted in those pages. Nothing to fear in my Piece Book, ese.

(*Water offers the Piece Book back to Norte/Sur, reaching over the grave.*)

Nah, it belongs to you now. Learn more about your bro, ay. He's in there. All of him.

(*Water keeps the Piece Book.*)

WATER: Hey, why don't we do your little Four Directions thing now.

NORTE/SUR: Órale, Water, I'll do the in-and-out fast-food version.

(*We hear a flock of Canadian geese. As Norte/Sur reaches for his eagle feather:*)

Nice ducks.

WATER: Canada geese.

NORTE/SUR: Canadian geese in East L.A.?

WATER: Technically we're in Whittier.

NORTE/SUR: Even worser. OK, let's do this. First, we face the north, no, let's do the south first.

(*The guys are clumsy in their initial effort as Water goes to his knees.*)

You don't have to get on your knees, ay.

OK, toward our ancestors, our brothers and sisters from across the border, el otro lado.

Next we must face the, uh, west, yeah, where the sun sets and we give thanks for the end of the day, that no harm will come to any homey . . .

WATER: Or cop . . .

NORTE/SUR: Simón. To the north, where we see a traffic jam on the Pomona freeway. It is in el norte where Deer Dancer lives as well.

And finally we turn to the east where Grandmother lives right behind the King Taco. Grandmother Moon, she will see her sons shine again. We must humble ourselves to her. Ho.

WATER: Ho.

NORTE/SUR: That's it, that's all I know. *(He puts away his feather)*

WATER: Can I drop you off somewhere?

NORTE/SUR: Think I'll hang out here with your carnal just a taste longer.

WATER: OK, well, uh, look, let me know if you need a letter of recommendation or anything like that.

NORTE/SUR: Let me know if you need one.

WATER: I gotta bail.

(Water heads off, but is stopped in his tracks. He has found an amazing drawing of The Twins in the Piece Book: Power, resplendent in his lovely uniform; Water in his usual impeccable suit; each brother is crouched down like a homeboy.)

NORTE/SUR: The Garcías are the Eastside.

WATER: They were once.

NORTE/SUR: Nah, Water and Power forever, homes.

(Water looks away a final time.)

Let him rest now, loco.

(Water slowly turns to Norte/Sur, holding the open book and the drawing over his heart.)

Con safos.

WATER: Con safos. Thank you, bro.

(Norte/Sur nods. The men touch their hearts. Then Water is gone.
Norte/Sur is center stage. He motions for somebody to join him. The young Deer Dancer/Homeboy enters. This time the Deer Dancer wears antlers, black bandana, black Pendleton, baggie khakis and shiny black shoes. Norte/Sur motions for the Deer Dancer to stand directly in front of him. He motions for him to remove his antlers, black shirt, bandana and black shoes. The black shoes go into Norte/Sur's side bag. The rest of the garb is placed gently on the Grave of Power.

Norte/Sur is ending a few cycles here: the gangbanging and ambitious Hispanic cycle both come to a momentary end with his actions.

The Deer Dancer has a little boy shirt on and is now barefoot. He looks like what he is, just a boy. He moves a few reluctant feet away from Norte/Sur. Norte/Sur produces a baseball. He tosses the ball to the Deer Dancer. A beat, the Deer Dancer looks back, unsure.)

NORTE/SUR: Go on. Play. Be a kid.

(The Deer Dancer tears off through the house like any kid would. We hear him squeal with a child's delight and then laugh. Norte/Sur watches the kid scram, a satisfying smile crosses his face.
The "Rain Song" reprises.
Norte/Sur does a lovely little twirl with his wheelchair. His dance. His closing of this ceremonial circle.
The lights slowly fade to black.
Curtain call music: "I'm Your Puppet."
P.S.:)

There is a street in East L.A.,
A street that separates the city from the county,
The cops from the sheriffs.
Garfield High from Roosevelt High,

And there were two little brothers
Who danced beautifully between those two worlds
Under the eye of a loving father,
Where a mother needed to be
In that fateful hour . . .
Water and Power.

END OF PLAY

ZORRO IN HELL!

To the True Chicano—
Prince of California, Our Hamlet of the west—
Fernando Sanchez,
Loving Son of Chunky and Chicano Park, San Diego, Califas.
C/S

GET YOUR Z ON!

By Tony Taccone

Zorro. Just say the name and images flood your mind: the dev-ilishly simple mask, the dashing black cape, the fiercely rear-ing steed . . . moonlit assignations with smitten señoritas and a righteous demand for justice from a sneering Gobernador . . . narrow escapes, swashbuckling battles and always, finally, the triumph of Good over Evil. Whether you were introduced to the story via the spooky manliness of Tyrone Power or the easy superficiality of Guy Williams or the more recent gyrations of Antonio Banderas, whether you got hooked by the comic book or the Halloween costume, the ability of the story to win us over is nothing short of astonishing.

Take, for example, the experience of the three fearless comedians who comprise Culture Clash. Blessed with laser-sharp wit and acerbic tongues, Richard Montoya, Ric Salinas and Herbert Siguenza relished the opportunity to turn their formidable satiric talents to the task of tearing apart the myth of the legendary Masked Man, a persona thought to be an insult to Chicano culture. How hard could it be? After all, Zorro was no more than a silly icon of pulp fiction, a Spanish dandy liv-ing behind a mask, a man armed with a simplistic ideology and a bad costume, responsible for more kitsch merchandise and cheap dialogue than virtually any other superhero. Any ten year old could see through this. The opportunity to expose the banality of the myth in light of real racial suffering, real class struggle, real political analysis . . . it was not going to be hard.

And so it was nothing short of shocking that when in the course of creating *Zorro in Hell!*, the story began to exert its almost inexorable power. The process began as you might expect: research took us through the original fiction of Johnston McCully, the era of fascinating and strange silent films, the sanitized, squeaky-clean, Disneyfied version of the 1950s television show, and the various ensuing incarnations that are presently on display at your local video store. We all laughed . . . a lot. Everywhere you looked there were innumerable comic possibilities: Jewish guys dressed up to look like Indians, ingenues who would swoon upon hearing the sounds of Zorro's approaching horse, fat friars, fat gentry, skinny peasants (more Jewish guys mixed with some Italian guys) who signified their poverty by looking permanently downcast until the miraculous arrival of the Masked Man . . . and then (simultaneously!) their eyes would pop out of their heads as they rallied to overthrow El Gobernador and his crooked cronies. This was going to be big fun . . .

Yet after the laughter subsided, we began to ask ourselves some compelling questions: Why does this story work for more than one generation? What aspects of hero worship appeal to our very nature? In spite of the transparency of the mask, what is the lure of dual identity? Why does Zorro have an ambiguous sexual identity? Even if the political analysis contained in the story is reductive and naive, why does it feel reaffirming? Given the precarious state of the planet, do we need Zorro?

It was by asking these questions that *Zorro in Hell!* started to take real shape. In fact, the journey of the central character mirrors that of the one taken by CC during the course of the rehearsal process. The plot centers around a cynical, disaffected writer who has armed himself with some bad jokes and a lazy political swagger that inoculates him from his own creativity and prevents him from taking any revolutionary action. While trying to write a new play (a critique of Zorro from the Chicano perspective), he encounters a Two-Hundred-Year-Old Woman and her band of crazy cohorts (including an ornery old footman claiming to be "the first Chicano," two gay cowboys, a grizzly-bear therapist named Kyle and the ghost of Joaquín Murietta). Taken together, they form a small, guerrilla army dedicated to the resurrection of the authentic spirit of Zorro. The Old Woman's mission is to find a leader who has the courage to stand up against injustice, who will ignite a massive revolt against a society that has become politically and culturally dormant. To that end she tests the young writer, cajoles him, teases him, argues, persuades and finally forces him out of his self-inflicted funk . . . until he is, at last, jarred into action . . . his soul and spirit revitalized, ready to retake control over his own life and to unleash his new-found energy onto the slumbering world. His target: none other than California's own "Gobernator," Arnold Schwarzenegger.

Crazy? Damn straight. Funny? It better be.

But behind the surreal high jinks and the rapid-fire jokes, behind the outrageous comic personas and the anachronistic asides, all of which bear the singular stamp of Culture Clash, one can hear the emergence of a new voice: the genuine voice of Zorro. But this incarnation of the Masked Man is different from those of his predecessors. With his frail psychic makeup, his mixed-race heritage and his virtually permanent state of confusion he is more akin to Everyman. He stumbles into his calling because circumstances beyond his control determine that he has no other choice. It is not some high-born gift of intelligence, power or grace that endows him with heroic attributes, but his simple humanity. The Zorro concocted by Culture Clash is a professional Fool who is drafted by the people to remind us of how we are all connected, of how we can achieve empathy through laughter, of how vulnerable we all are. This is a Zorro who needs help, one whose abilities are fulfilled only if all of us join in the struggle, if we all, in fact, become Zorro.

And so it was, over the course of a two-year development process, that *Zorro in Hell!* morphed from a cheeky satire to a bold piece of agitprop. Like the reluctant hero of the play, the

Clashers overcame their personal and collective cynicism to describe a world where progressive change is possible, where anger is channeled into celebratory song, where the comfort of passivity is transformed into the spirit of activism. *Zorro in Hell!* is a comic tonic, a rallying cry for the formation of an army of Fools, for a mass movement of enlightened clowns, so that the world may learn to laugh in harmony, in peace, in love . . . Hasta la Victoria Siempre! Get Your Z On!

Tony Taccone is artistic director of Berkeley Repertory Theatre, where he has staged more than thirty-five shows—including world premieres by Culture Clash, Rinde Eckert, David Edgar, Danny Hoch, Geoff Hoyle, Quincy Long and Itamar Moses. He directed Sarah Jones' Tony Award—winning *Bridge & Tunnel* and returned to Broadway in 2009 with Carrie Fisher's *Wishful Drinking*. He commissioned Tony Kushner's *Angels in America*, co-directed its world premiere, and has collaborated with Kushner on seven projects including *Brundibar* and the premiere of *Tiny Kushner*. Two of Taccone's recent shows transferred to London, and two scripts that he penned will have their premieres in 2011.

This article first appeared in the Winter/Spring 2007 edition (TF 30) of *TheatreForum*, Jim Carmody, John Rouse, Adele Edling Shank, Theodore Shank, eds. www.TheatreForum.org

PRODUCTION HISTORY

Zorro in Hell! was commissioned and produced by Zorro Productions, Inc., Berkeley Repertory Theatre (Tony Taccone, Artistic Director) and La Jolla Playhouse (Des McAnuff, Artistic Director). It received its world premiere at Berkeley Repertory Theatre on March 17, 2006. It was directed by Tony Taccone; the set design was by Christopher Acebo, the costume design was by Christal Weatherly, the lighting design was by Alexander V. Nichols, the sound design was by Robbin E. Broad, original music was by Vincent Christopher Montoya and the fight direction was by Dave Maier; the dramaturg was Shirley Fishman, the movement director was MaryBeth Cavanaugh and the stage manger was Kimberly Mark Webb. The cast was:

Actors

Richard Montoya
Ric Salinas
Herbert Siguenza
Joseph Kamal
Sharon Lockwood
Vincent Christopher Montoya

A NOTE ABOUT MUSIC

Pre-show music is an eclectic mix of Smithsonian Folkways American Roots collection; antiquated border music; Los Lobos's *La Pistola y el Corazón* and *Just Another Band from East L.A.*; Johnny Cash's "Folsom Prison Blues"; Odetta; Woody Guthrie (*Sacco and Venzetti*); NorCal indy bands, such as Spearhead, Seventy, Love Dogs; Socal indy bands, such as Quetzal, Ozo; Balinese, Cajun, Chinese railroad hymns; Moroccan, Chilean/Andean; Jerry Garcia's "Friend of the Devil"; Robert Johnson and a Gregorian chant or two.

When the actors are in places, Manu Chao's "Clandestino" will always be heard with increased volume; it will fade out before the upcoming announcement.

| ACT ONE |

The house lights are up. Over a loudspeaker the audience hears a Voice in Spanish and English.

VOICE 1 *(Making an announcement)*:
Damas y Caballeros bienvenidos al Teatro Alta California.
Ladies and gentlemen, welcome to El Teatro Alta Californio.
En este momento apáguen sus telefonos celulares y old-school pagers. At this time we ask that you silence all cell phones and firearms.
Otra vez, por favor, apague sus telephones. Once again, silence all cell phones or you will be whipped at intermission.
Gracias! Y ahora, disfruten *Zorro en el Infierno*. Enjoy Culture Clash.

(House lights out.
A single guitar is heard.
The curtain rises. The lights slowly come up.
The guitar is augmented by layered sounds of distant thunder, Arabic wails, Indian chants and drums as deep as the Continental Divide itself: a sonic culture clash.

Upstage, looming over everything, is a huge California Bear Republic flag.

A Man seated downstage center, wearing a mask, faces the audience.

The Man is strapped into a straightjacket and seated in a metal chair. He is fitted with a hockey mask and plastic spit guard. He sits upright. A Nurse enters and tends to him. The guitar and occasional distant thunder continue under his poem.)

MAN:

They seek him here,
they seek him there,
they seek him everywhere,
is he in Heaven,
is he in Hell,
that damned elusive
Pimpernel!

(With one hand the Nurse removes the hockey mask and spit guard to reveal the Man's Zorro mask. She exits.)

I wear the mask. I submit to the mask.

(Two men—Agents 1 and 2—enter upstage in the shadows.)

The self, less important than the masses. The mask as political weapon, self-sacrifice. The Zapatistas, of course.

VOICES *(Over loudspeaker)*: ¡Todos somos Marcos!

MAN: I googled myself last night. The news is not so good. Zorro porn sites, chat rooms . . . I am the Walmart fucking Price Slasher for Chrissakes! I am a downloadable ring tone.

(We hear ring tone 1: a horse whinny and a whip crack.)

One match, one man, one woman can ignite a revolution or recall a sitting governor. Heroes stand up for an entire community and the people get inspired!

Government Agents (Joseph Kamal, left; Ric Salinas, right) interrogate the Writer (Richard Montoya).

VOICE 1 *(Over loudspeaker)*: I am Spartacus!

VOICE 2 *(Over loudspeaker)*: No, I am Spartacus!

MAN: No, Che Guevara said right after he got off his motorcycle, "When your land is invaded, when values and culture are threatened by outsiders, there is no resort but to fight and die." Fight and die. *That* is love.

AGENT 1 *(Moving out of the shadows)*: Now who the fuck are you?

MAN: "I am Inigo Montoya. You killed my father, prepare to die . . ."

AGENT 2 *(Following Agent 1)*: Why did you threaten the governor?

MAN: Because I am bicultural, bicurious and bipolar.

AGENT 1: Threats against elected officials are reported to Homeland Security.

MAN: Let's combine FEMA with MENSA so that more *pendejos* can run the country.

AGENT 2: Why did you spray a large black "Z" on the capitol dome in Sacramento?

MAN: I make a mark! *(A large Nike logo appears on an upstage wall)* Not that mark. I saw a dead fox by the side of the road.

Tawny and beautiful with streaks of amber and blood red, once proud and free, reduced to suburban road kill. I picked up el fox, and buried him, properly, facing east like the Indian taught me.

(The Nurse enters with more meds.)

NURSE: Indians are alcoholics. Calm now, take your meds.

MAN: "Mine eyes have seen the glory . . ."

NURSE: Shhh. *(She stuffs the meds in his mouth)*

MAN: I have a memory of the land, the memory tastes of rolling hills, endless vistas, natural rock outcroppings. Redwoods standing witness to the wild salmon's journey north from the bays to the rivers and deltas, snaking up the valleys to the snows of the upper pass. All of it lovely, essential, vital. Tierra. California! Worth dying for, que no? "Give me liberty or death," right, just like Tupac said!

My California, she is now an endless series of subdivisions and strip malls choking what little there is of natural habitats and there is no open land nowhere for the fox to roam.

AGENT 1: I'm still heart sore over the plight of the spotted owl.

AGENT 2: Bioterrorist, tree-hugging, Green Peace pussy. NPR listener!!!

AGENT 1: You're in it up to your mask, fella.

MAN: I will be the wounded grizzly, the dead fox on the side of the road who will not get away unless I light the fire with my single match. I will be the drunken Indian stripped of his tribal collectivism. I am a West Virginia coal miner darkened by sadness, working my ribbon of coal.

AGENT 1: Who the fuck are you?

MAN: I am Zorro. I must be Zorro. I will be a mujahadeen Zorro. A Chicano jihadist who will wage war against the Narcos and Tea-Baggers!

(We see a huge slide image of Sarah Palin with a rifle. Loud shotgun sound.)

SARAH *(Voice-over)*: We shoot wild wolvés in Alaska.

MAN: Sangre will be spilled, death to the governor of this Bear Republic of Cal-ee-forn-I-A!

AGENT 2: Say that again and you'll be "waterboarding" in Guantanamo with the rest of the sand-niggers. *(Removes a nine-inch chrome syringe from his pocket)* This may pinch a bit. *(He injects the Man in the side of the neck)*

MAN: Inoculay-shun . . .

AGENT 2: It's a clean needle, I think.

MAN: I can see the Killing Floor from my porch.

(Lights shift. We see only the head of the Man as he feels the effects of the narcotic.)

I am Zorro . . . Though I wasn't always Zorro. There was a time when I was a nooorrrmaalll Chicano . . .

AGENT 2: Normal Chicano?

AGENT 1: Now there's an oxymoron I can live with.

AGENT 2: Start singing, start from the beginning. Slowly.

MAN *(Very slowly)*: My journey started some time ago . . .

AGENT 2: Not that slowly!

MAN: I forget when exactly, but these are the events as I can best recollect . . . *(Spanish guitar. The Agents back out slowly)* Was I here, or was I there? Was I in Heaven or was I in Hell? *California!!!*

(The Man flees. The bear flag becomes a flurry of video images: historic, post-modern, pop-culture icons of Taco Bell to Speedy Gonzales to the Taliban, to hundreds more. This transition continues as night falls. Crickets. Calm.

The Man reemerges. He is now The Writer, wearing a backpack, drab, black, L.A.-writer-type clothes, a disheveled suit and tie perhaps. He moves slowly across stage.

The Two-Hundred-Year-Old Woman, carrying a shotgun, enters.)

TWO-HUNDRED-YEAR-OLD WOMAN: Who goes there, friend or foe?

WRITER: Writer.

TWO-HUNDRED-YEAR-OLD WOMAN: Writer?

WRITER: Why, yes, ma'am, from Los Angeles.

(Huge shotgun blast!)

Whoa!!!!!!!!

TWO-HUNDRED-YEAR-OLD WOMAN: Dang, I missed.

WRITER: I'm the one who called. I'm writing the Zorro play.

TWO-HUNDRED-YEAR-OLD WOMAN: Oh yeah.

(Another shotgun blast.)

Oops, didn't mean that one.

WRITER: That's exactly what Dick Cheney said.

TWO-HUNDRED-YEAR-OLD WOMAN: Zorro writer, eh? I did shoot a writer back in '38 for his flowery prose and pecadillos.

WRITER: I assure you, ma'am, I am unarmed.

TWO-HUNDRED-YEAR-OLD WOMAN: Don't be so sure 'bout that, the pen is mightier than the sword.

WRITER: Then take my Sharpie and give me the shotgun.

TWO-HUNDRED-YEAR-OLD WOMAN: So you've come to conduct your important Zorro research you say?

WRITER: If you don't shoot me.

TWO-HUNDRED-YEAR-OLD WOMAN: What Gómez-Peña calls reverse anthropological excavations.

WRITER: I guess. I'm not sure where I'm at frankly. You're not listed on MapQuest, there are no signs back up the road. Where am I, lady?

TWO-HUNDRED-YEAR-OLD WOMAN: Well, son, you've arrived at the oldest, most authentic living archive of early Californ-i-o history.

WRITER: I don't see nothin'.

TWO-HUNDRED-YEAR-OLD WOMAN: Well then, let me be the first to welcome you to the El Camino Real Inn.

WRITER: What inn?

TWO-HUNDRED-YEAR-OLD WOMAN: This inn!

(Walls move from all sides to form an Adobe lobby, leading into El Camino Real Inn.)

WRITER: By the saints!

TWO-HUNDRED-YEAR-OLD WOMAN: Step on up to the reservation desk so we can get you checked in.

(A huge, dusty, two-hundred-year-old reservation book sits atop the reservation desk.)

Many a writer have stayed at the inn here, sonny.

WRITER: Writers, ay?

TWO-HUNDRED-YEAR-OLD WOMAN: I've made literary legends from schoolboys, pubescences to Pulitzers—that's my motto! And I'll do what I can for you.

WRITER: Well, I'll only be a few days. I'm gonna drink like Hemmingway and then go my way.

TWO-HUNDRED-YEAR-OLD WOMAN: I'll do what I can for ya, just don't muck it all up. The Zorro legend is not to be trifled with.

WRITER: Legend? See, I don't plan to work that hard, ma'am.

TWO-HUNDRED-YEAR-OLD WOMAN: No?

WRITER: Nah, I only took the gig because I'm broke.

TWO-HUNDRED-YEAR-OLD WOMAN: No shame in that.

WRITER: See, being Latino with one leg shorter than the other qualified me for this Other Voices grant last year. But I spent all that money doing research, so I'm thinking I could write something lazy and folkloric for the subscribers, you know, keep everybody happy.

TWO-HUNDRED-YEAR-OLD WOMAN: A lethario with no shame.

WRITER: Yeah, plus I'm "crazy busy" at Starbucks all day writing spec scripts for reality TV shows, so . . .

TWO-HUNDRED-YEAR-OLD WOMAN: You should know I take great umbrage to deadbeat poets. I ran Ginsberg and his flock of naked boys outta here in '58.

WRITER: Quaint.

TWO-HUNDRED-YEAR-OLD WOMAN *(Pointing to the reservation book)*: Put your John Henry there next to John Hancock's name . . .

WRITER: Is that Hancock's signature?

TWO-HUNDRED-YEAR-OLD WOMAN: Scout's honor.

WRITER: How long have you been running the inn, ma'am?

TWO-HUNDRED-YEAR-OLD WOMAN: Well, let's see, Daddy bought the land from a Spanish monk named Junipero . . .

WRITER: Serra?

TWO-HUNDRED-YEAR-OLD WOMAN: Yup. Right after the Seventeenth Mission was built just down the road. It was a mixed-use, mixed-race compound for a while.

WRITER: I see.

TWO-HUNDRED-YEAR-OLD WOMAN: Ma started the first Montessori school in the Wild West. She was a founding member of the Native Daughters of California.

WRITER: Founding member, is that possible?

TWO-HUNDRED-YEAR-OLD WOMAN: Young man, in California, anything is possible.

WRITER: Naive.

TWO-HUNDRED-YEAR-OLD WOMAN: That's what I thought till I felt my first earthquake. The San Andreas Fault shifting 'neath my feet. Large tectonic plates of land, butting up against each other, rumbling and undulating like a wild bull. Great friction and more temptation per square foot than any place in the world.

WRITER: When was that?

TWO-HUNDRED-YEAR-OLD WOMAN: Right after I penned the "purple mountain majesties" and "amber waves of grain" crap.

WRITER: Ol' Sister Christian's been around around the block a few times. How old are you, lady?

TWO-HUNDRED-YEAR-OLD WOMAN: None of your bee's wax.

(The Writer takes notes.)

WRITER: Member of AARP.

TWO-HUNDRED-YEAR-OLD WOMAN: The notion of rugged individualism was the unwritten contract of California.

WRITER: Have greed and gun will travel.

TWO-HUNDRED-YEAR-OLD WOMAN: You're smarter than you look, son.

WRITER: That's 'cause I went to Cal Arts for thirteen years.

TWO-HUNDRED-YEAR-OLD WOMAN: Lookie here, boy, General Fremont and his men kill De Haro—yet, Fremont gets a town and schools named after him while De Haro gets one lousy street in the Castro. Good S&M shops down there though . . .

WRITER: Who's a villain and who's a hero.

TWO-HUNDRED-YEAR-OLD WOMAN: Ah, now that is the essential question. Not to mention our collective need and desire to create heroes.

WRITER: And destroy them?

TWO-HUNDRED-YEAR-OLD WOMAN: A Mexican discovers gold . . .

WRITER: And John Sutter gets the credit.

TWO-HUNDRED-YEAR-OLD WOMAN: The Chinese build the railroad . . .

WRITER: Amtrack gets the credit.

TWO-HUNDRED-YEAR-OLD WOMAN: Culture Clash writes *Chavez Ravine* and . . .

WRITER: Ry Cooder get's the credit!

TWO-HUNDRED-YEAR-OLD WOMAN: Intellectual territories.

WRITER: "Don't fence me in."

TWO-HUNDRED-YEAR-OLD WOMAN: One man's paradise is one man's hell, all depending on how you look at it. What side of history you fall on, the business end or . . .

WRITER AND TWO-HUNDRED-YEAR-OLD WOMAN: Or who writes the history end.

TWO-HUNDRED-YEAR-OLD WOMAN: The pen *is* mightier than the sword.

WRITER: I see.

TWO-HUNDRED-YEAR-OLD WOMAN: One more essential question.

WRITER: Shoot.

(The old woman reaches for the shotgun.)

I mean ask away.

TWO-HUNDRED-YEAR-OLD WOMAN: Cash or credit?

WRITER: Discover card.

TWO-HUNDRED-YEAR-OLD WOMAN (*Snags the card*): I'll be needing that for your incidentals just in case you get eaten by the bear.

WRITER: Right. Ha ha ha . . . The bear. Oh, you're good. (*Signs his name. Starts reading other names from the book*) Oscar Wilde? Eugene O'Neill, August Wilson, Whitman and Neruda stayed here?

TWO-HUNDRED-YEAR-OLD WOMAN: Yes, sir. And I'm gonna tell you like I told them: Just 'cause you got no talent don't mean you can't write.

WRITER: You told them that?

TWO-HUNDRED-YEAR-OLD WOMAN: Pert near.

WRITER: Harsh.

TWO-HUNDRED-YEAR-OLD WOMAN: They come here looking for inspiration.

WRITER: Well, now therein lies my other dilemma, Zorro does not inspire me. (*He reaches for a large book on the reservation desk*) Victorian pornography: Now this inspires me.

TWO-HUNDRED-YEAR-OLD WOMAN: Eugene had the same problem. He sat right there with a terrible case of writer's block, wholly uninspired.

WRITER: Eugene?

TWO-HUNDRED-YEAR-OLD WOMAN: Wrote the *The Iceman Cometh* right there.

WRITER: As in O'Neill?

TWO-HUNDRED-YEAR-OLD WOMAN: Oh yeah, 'cept that wasn't the title then. He called his opus *The Iceman Goeth.*

WRITER: *Iceman A'Goeth?*

TWO-HUNDRED-YEAR-OLD WOMAN: I straightened him out. I'm the one that changed the title and he made a fortune. I dramaturged the fuck outta that play.

(*The old woman rings the desk bell like the devil.*)

Don Ringo! Don Ringo, we have an alleged writer out here, needs his room key! Don Ringo! (*Facing Writer*) I'm tired of ghost writing for you all and not getting my propers. I've got a big bone to pick with Ferlinghetti!

WRITER *(Reading another title)*: *The Call of the Wild!?*
TWO-HUNDRED-YEAR-OLD WOMAN: Jack London was a bully and a braggart! After I bested him at Scrabble in the parlor, I eighty-sixed he and Ambrose and I'll do the same to you. Don Ringo! *(The old woman rings the desk bell like the devil)*

(Don Ringo, an old man in a dusty, early Californio outfit, enters with the help of an old wooden cane with an Indian head topper.)

DON RINGO: I'm coming, señora, I'm coming.
TWO-HUNDRED-YEAR-OLD WOMAN: Ride like furry, Don Ringo.
DON RINGO: Can't you see I'm running, I'm running as fast as I can!
TWO-HUNDRED-YEAR-OLD WOMAN: This is Don Ringo, his pa was a Spanish cattleman, his mother was a Yaqui Indian named Ramona . . .
DON RINGO *(Striking a Pachuco pose)*: I'm the first Chicano!
WRITER: I thought Machete was the first Chicano?
TWO-HUNDRED-YEAR-OLD WOMAN: Nope. That title belongs exclusively to Don Ringo.
DON RINGO: I'll take your bags, sir.

(Don Ringo reaches down, then rights himself face to face with the Writer.)

I am the first Chicano, ese! *(Striking another Pachuco pose)*
TWO-HUNDRED-YEAR-OLD WOMAN: We know that already, Don Ringo. *(She rings the bell again for good measure)*
DON RINGO: Don't make me go *Good, Bad and the Ugly* on you.

(We hear the Sergio Leone classic tag.)

TWO-HUNDRED-YEAR-OLD WOMAN: Never mind him, Writer, he's prone to dramatics on account of the encroaching land developers.
WRITER: Land developers?

(Don Ringo starts to exit.)

TWO-HUNDRED-YEAR-OLD WOMAN: Let's have a nip, shall we? Come join me at my mini adobe wet bar.

WRITER: Mini adobe wet bar?

(Don Ringo slams an adobe bucket of ice and two shot glasses on the reservation desk.)

DON RINGO: Mini adobe wet bar!

(The Writer looks through hundreds of dusty books and documents.)

WRITER: First editions galore: *Cannery Row*, Saroyan, Monroe Doctrine, Nathaniel West, defense argument for the Scottsboro Boys with handwritten notes in the margin, "The ballad of Sacco and Venzetti"?

TWO-HUNDRED-YEAR-OLD WOMAN: Helped Woody with the second verse is all I did.

WRITER: The Treaty of Guadalupe Hidalgo and *The Communist Manifesto*?

TWO-HUNDRED-YEAR-OLD WOMAN: Writ the same year and . . .

(He opens the red book.)

WRITER: . . . autographed by the authors themselves: "Thank you for your rewrites. Love and kisses, Karl"? "P.S., I sent your suggestions regarding Ana on to Leo"?

Your collection is amazing, ma'am. Shouldn't these rare titles be in a university with the scholars and academics?

TWO-HUNDRED-YEAR-OLD WOMAN: Academics are shit.

WRITER: Yes, ma'am.

TWO-HUNDRED-YEAR-OLD WOMAN *(Grabbing a sword from the wall)*: To be disemboweled on sight!

WRITER: Disemboweling academics is legal but only at Brown and CUNY College.

(The Two-Hundred-Year-Old Woman punctuates her points with elegant sword movements.)

TWO-HUNDRED-YEAR-OLD WOMAN: This is the oldest, most thorough living archive of early Californio history. And I am the keeper of the sacred Zorro myth and legend.

(The old woman pulls a lever.)

Wallah!

(Dramatic music. In an instant, all manner of Zorro paraphernalia falls down from above as new walls are revealed. Every Zorro penknife, lunchbox, movie poster, action figure, whip, mask and other costume pieces ever created are revealed.)

WRITER: Look at all this Zorro crap! Did you get it all on zBay? Ha! My God, a Zorro dildo! I haven't seen one of these since the seventies!

DON RINGO *(With the crack of a whip)*: Put that down!

WRITER: Son of a bitch, Don Ringo! *(He drops the dildo)*

DON RINGO: Never touch the Zorro dildo . . .

(The old woman smiles and hands him a drink.)

TWO-HUNDRED-YEAR-OLD WOMAN: Laudanum. Good for what ails ya.

(The Writer sniffs.)

WRITER: Smells like snizzle.

TWO-HUNDRED-YEAR-OLD WOMAN: Don't spoil my jag, son, drink up.

WRITER: What's in it?

TWO-HUNDRED-YEAR-OLD WOMAN: A tincture of opium.

WRITER: Sweet.

(They drink. Don Ringo pours more.)

TWO-HUNDRED-YEAR-OLD WOMAN: President Lincoln was very fond of the stuff. It's terribly addictive.

WRITER: Nah—may I have a venti?

(Don Ringo pours. The Writer starts to read more book titles:)

The Curse of Capistrano?

TWO-HUNDRED-YEAR-OLD WOMAN: First printing. Written by the genius himself, Johnston McCulley, 1919.

WRITER: Genius?

DON RINGO: Simón.

WRITER: Don't you mean the gringo, pulp-fiction hack who concocted the Zorro myth that burdens me now?

DON RINGO: Johnston McCulley was no hack, and for you to suggest so is *puro pedo ese.*

WRITER: Ah, the first Chicano apologist, are you related to Richard Rodriguez?

DON RINGO: Your inability to comprehend the Zorro myth based on true facts will be your undoing, muchacho.

WRITER: Let my undoing begin! Keep pouring, Don Ringo.

TWO-HUNDRED-YEAR-OLD WOMAN: See, like you, ol' Johnston walked into this very inn, desperate, yearning, for inspiration. It was then I gave him the story of the Scarlet Pimpernel. *(Hands the Writer another book)*

WRITER: So Johnston reads the novel and steals the duel identity idea and sets it in early California? You know, I may be a playwright without health insurance, but your boy McCulley was a plagiarist.

DON RINGO: Blasphemy!

TWO-HUNDRED-YEAR-OLD WOMAN: That's OK, Don Ringo. Our relatively young and untested writer reminds me of Dougie when he arrived here.

WRITER: Dougie?

DON RINGO: Fairbanks, Senior, pendejo.

TWO-HUNDRED-YEAR-OLD WOMAN: Dougie arrived in 1920 with his new bride Mary Pickford. He was exhausted and nervous about his fleeting career. We made love for hours at a time.

WRITER: You made love to Fairbanks?

TWO-HUNDRED-YEAR-OLD WOMAN: No, Pickford. She was a hottie!

(Don Ringo rolls his eyes.)

I shared with her my favorite book, *The Curse of Capistrano*. She takes the book to Dougie. It brings him out of his funk faster than a Hemlock Woolly Beetle boring through Muir Woods.

WRITER: You don't say.

"Pickford was a hottie! We started the first ever lesbian women's drum circle!" Two-Hundred-Year-Old Woman (Sharon Lockwood) and Don Ringo (Herbert Siguenza).

TWO-HUNDRED-YEAR-OLD WOMAN: In those pages he finds the perfect avenue for his well-endowed physical attributes.

(Don Ringo clears his throat.)

Dougie exits stage left straightaway for Hollywood to make his picture . . . Mary stays behind and we start the first ever Lesbian Women's Drum Circle.

(We hear echoes of the Drum Circle.)

WRITER: So, *Curse* was filmed here?

TWO-HUNDRED-YEAR-OLD WOMAN: The Holy Grail of all the Zorro pictures, the Rosetta stone, the original, the genesis.

WRITER: *The Mark of Zorro?*

TWO-HUNDRED-YEAR-OLD WOMAN: I'm talking about lights! Camera! Action!

DON RINGO: Check this out, loco!

(With a dramatic lifting of her arms, the lights and sound shift. A large antique film projector is heard. Lights flicker in an old-time silent movie way. We see a live re-creation of the "Cantina" scene from the silent film The Mark of Zorro. *Enter the puffed-up Sergeant Gonzales. He boastfully poses with his sword. The title card reads: "WHERE IS THE MONKEY THEY CALL ZORRO, I FEAR HIM NOT!" Zorro appears heroically in a window or on a ledge. The next title reads: "I AM ZORRO AT YOUR SERVICE." The men face off for the classic duel. After a missed punch, the Sergeant is frustrated, his blade gets stuck in the wall.*

Title card: "DEATH TO THE GOVERNOR." A smiling Indian enters and nails an "EMINENT DOMAIN" notice on the inn wall. Zorro chases him off.

The Sergeant reveals a "Z" on his chest. Title card: "I AM THE DEFENDER FOR JUSTICE AND EQUALITY, PROTECTOR OF THE POOR AND CHAMPION OF THE OPPRESSED!" The Sergeant and Zorro exit dueling.

The lights shift. Back at the inn the old woman grabs the notice off the wall.)

TWO-HUNDRED-YEAR-OLD WOMAN: Another eviction notice, curses!

DON RINGO: Qué gacho.

WRITER: Who was that Indian man in the Hawaiian shirt?

DON RINGO: He's a lawyer named Trader Joe.

WRITER: Was he part of the movie or was he real?

TWO-HUNDRED-YEAR-OLD WOMAN: What movie?

DON RINGO: Oooo weee oooo oooo.

WRITER: Wait a minute . . .

TWO-HUNDRED-YEAR-OLD WOMAN: Damn Injun lawyer claims this is sacred Injun land.

WRITER: Then this land must rightfully go back to the Native Americans.

TWO-HUNDRED-YEAR-OLD WOMAN: So they can build another cheesy goddamned casino?

WRITER: Haven't they earned the right to build a cheesy casino if they want to? As long as there's a sweatlodge in the back, and maybe a golden stripper pole, I see no problem.

TWO-HUNDRED-YEAR-OLD WOMAN: It's just a ruse, boy, a smokescreen, the Injuns are being used yet again to hide the State's greedy and unjust eminent domain laws.

DON RINGO: Thieves in pinstripes and fountain pens!

WRITER: OK, I now understand: I'm trapped in a college production of a Tony Kushner play.

DON RINGO: It's no joke damnit, they've all been trying to steal her land for centuries!

WRITER: Who's stealing the land? Don Ringo!

DON RINGO: Spaniards, Mexicans, Home Depot, Pixar, the Scientologists . . .

WRITER: I'm all tore up about your land being stolen and all, but I must retire to my room and smoke a big fat doober.

DON RINGO: We don't allow ganja at the inn.

TWO-HUNDRED-YEAR-OLD WOMAN: It's OK, Don Ringo, I'll waive the no marijuana rule for one night. I did as much for the outlaws Cheech and Chong.

(There is a coyote howl. The Writer takes note and heads for his room.)

WRITER: I stand by what I said before the movie.

TWO-HUNDRED-YEAR-OLD WOMAN: What movie?

DON RINGO: Ooooo weeeee.

WRITER: Who are you people?!

DON RINGO (*Striking a Pachuco pose; dramatically*): I am the first Chicano!

WRITER: Look, Lerch, you just can't call Zorro literature.

TWO-HUNDRED-YEAR-OLD WOMAN: Says who?

WRITER: Says me. Now, Fenimore Cooper, he was a great American Romantic writer.

TWO-HUNDRED-YEAR-OLD WOMAN: Piss-poor in the sack though.

(*Coyote howl.*)

WRITER: McCulley had no regard for accurate history, man, he lazily crisscrossed important facts, leaving Zorro to exist in a sort of historical vacuum.

TWO-HUNDRED-YEAR-OLD WOMAN: But he existed on paper, man, he existed in the hearts and minds of people. Castañeda validated that aesthetic with *Don Juan*.

WRITER: Did you sleep with Carlos Castañeda?

TWO-HUNDRED-YEAR-OLD WOMAN: No, but I had a threesome with Lewis and Clark.

DON RINGO: Great fiction writers that they were.

(*A double coyote howl.*)

WRITER: *Westward Ho* has new meaning for me now.

(*Don Ringo grabs the Writer around the collar.*)

DON RINGO: Another comment like that and I will challenge you to a duel behind the Pottery Barn near the Crate and Barrel!

WRITER: Easy, Don Bingo.

DON RINGO: Let me knock him off his Hispanic high horse, Doña.

TWO-HUNDRED-YEAR-OLD WOMAN: That won't be necessary, Don Ringo. I hear his wits sharpening like blades already. *(Don Ringo backs off)*

WRITER: With all respect and sexual trysts aside, ma'am, it's still all bullshit.

DON RINGO: Ya 'estuvo, ese. Enough.

(Don Ringo makes a slow move toward the Writer.)

TWO-HUNDRED-YEAR-OLD WOMAN: Let him be, Don Ringo . . .

WRITER: Look, McCulley was no better than the early California Boosters who sold the golden state like snail oil.

DON RINGO: And what was wrong with that?

WRITER: Nothing, if you're OK with colorful banditos, Sleepy Mexicans, spitfire señoritas with mid-Atlantic accents, moonlit patios and tequila coolers flowing endlessly.

DON RINGO: Ah, those were the days!

WRITER: Ah yes, those were the days, and all of it, a fabrication. Because what was actually going down was a one-two punch of discrimination and romanticization. This allowed the dominant society to effectively freeze Mexicans in time and space. Historic stereotypes set in amber. Cultural cryogenics they call it!

TWO-HUNDRED-YEAR-OLD WOMAN: I call it romance with a capital "R"! Where is your joie de vivir for goodness sakes? I remember a time when you Chicanos had a strong sense of romance and adventure, you were a rebellious people. That was long before you started raising your children on cheap meats and forty-two-ounce Big Gulps. What ever happened to romance, Don Ringo?

DON RINGO: It's locked away in a cold-storage unit on the outskirts of Nebraska.

WRITER: Thank you, Juan Steinbeck. I didn't come here to debate you kind old folks, look, whatever. Good night, ma'am.

(A beat.)

TWO-HUNDRED-YEAR-OLD WOMAN: Johnston McCulley never got the respect he deserved as a writer.

WRITER: Neither have I, lady.

DON RINGO: Buenas noches, failed sitcom writer.

WRITER: What did you just call me?

DON RINGO: I said, Good evening, sire.

WRITER: You just keep the laudanum flowing up to my room, and turn down the bed as quick as you can, and place a mint on my pillow if you please!

DON RINGO: Watch your back, little *puto*.

WRITER: What?

DON RINGO *(In his face)*: I am the first Chicano, ese!

WRITER *(In his face)*: Yes, that has been established!

TWO-HUNDRED-YEAR-OLD WOMAN *(Like a den mother)*: Boys.

WRITER: Just to refresh your memory, Don Chewey Baca, the deal with the, uh, yeah, the Spanish thing, right, they sort of wiped-out languages, they wiped-out ceremony and religion. We're talking about killing the Indians, OK. So complete was their destruction, so brutal was their raping, so paranoid was their fear of the Godless savages that the barbaric baton is passed on to the Mexicans who follow suit. So, by the time the Yankees come around, a culture of death and dominance is firmly rooted. No, I take that back, the gringos actually take it up a notch, they take the liquidation of the Indians to the next awesome level. Our very own American Holocaust, the native savages baptized in Hidalgo blood, and we are given this benevolent Spanish Dandy to pacify us?

TWO-HUNDRED-YEAR-OLD WOMAN: Every generation creates its own heroes, son.

DON RINGO: There is no crime in that.

WRITER: Crime no, but when we elect those heroes to govern us, then, well . . . let's just call it a creative malaise, a lull in the collective imagination of America. I'm missing *Project Runway*.

I will consider your rhetorical questions regarding romance first thing mañana! Safe to say I won this round.

TWO-HUNDRED-YEAR-OLD WOMAN: I yield nothing to you, young man.

WRITER: Thank you for the show. Boney nocheys, Don Rickles.

(The Writer exits.)

DON RINGO: Pinche metrosexual.

TWO-HUNDRED-YEAR-OLD WOMAN *(Pointing off to the Writer)*: What do you think of our writer, Don Ringo?

DON RINGO: I don't like him.

TWO-HUNDRED-YEAR-OLD WOMAN: I see potential.

DON RINGO: I see disaster.

(El Músico, in a black Oakland Raiders poncho and wide-brimmed hat, gives us a flourish on his Spanish guitar à la Pulp Fiction. The Writer is unpacking in his room. There is a knock at his window. He opens the window.)

WRITER: Yes?

WHISKEY: Hola, amigo.

WRITER: Hola, who the hell are you?

WHISKEY: My name's Whiskey Pete. Put your hands up.

WRITER: Why?

WHISKEY *(Brandishing a gun)*: Put 'em up I said!

WRITER: Don't shoot, I'm just a writer.

WHISKEY: They shoot writers, don't they? Hold this.

(The Writer holds Whiskey's gun.)

WRITER: I'm gonna have to ask you to leave.

WHISKEY *(Yelling out the window)*: Coast is clear, Mexican Jack!

(Whiskey grabs his gun back. Another man appears in the window.)

WRITER: Who's he?

JACK: I'm Mexican Jack, keep your hands where I can see them. Hold this for me.

(The Writer holds Jack's gun as he climbs in the room.)

WRITER: I demand to know what you guys are doing here.

JACK: We ain't here to turn down your bed, no siree. Hey give us back our guns!

(Whiskey and Jack grab their guns back.)

WHISKEY *(Excited and slow)*: We, just robbed a stagecoach!

WRITER: A stagecoach? What stagecoach? There are no stage-coaches anymore.

WHISKEY: For your information, mister writer boy, we robbed the coach to save the old lady's inn here, and we gotta hide the loot in this room.

WRITER: Why my room?

JACK: Your room has the safe.

WRITER: What safe?

WHISKEY: The safe behind this here painting of the dogs play-ing poker, partner.

(Jack and Whiskey jump on the bed and move to the painting.)

Whiskey (Ric Salinas, left) with his better half, Jack (Herbert Siguenza).

WRITER: This here makes no sense.

(There is rustling in the scrub just outside the window.)

WHISKEY: What was that?

(Guns are drawn.)

WRITER: Look, this is all very quaint, I commend you on your Old Navy outfits. I'm gonna have to ask you fellers to . . .

JACK: Shhhhhh!

WHISKEY *(In a stage whisper)*: Shut the fuck up, tenderfoot!

JACK: Who is it?

WHISKEY: Well, it's either the posse come to string us up, or, it's that masked fella.

WRITER: The who?

WHISKEY: The one they call El Zorro.

JACK: You think?

WHISKEY: He's come to help us save the old lady's inn.

WRITER: Guys, Whiskey Pete, Mexican Jack, I hate to be the one to break it to you but your "masked feller" does not exist.

JACK: The hell you say.

WRITER: Somebody made him up, like the Tooth Fairy.

WHISKEY: Are you saying he's like a ghost?

JACK: Or a shadow-cloud specter perhaps, caught somewhere betwixt myth and reality.

WHISKEY: Fact versus fiction, a matrix of sorts, eh? I believe Nietzsche talked about that shit you know.

WRITER: Nietzsche?

(Coyote howl.)

WHISKEY: I hear tell the masked fella leaves a mark, with his sword, he carves a large "S" wherever he goes.

JACK: I do believe it is a "Z," Whiskey Pete.

WHISKEY: I beg to differ, amigo, it's an "S," I do opine.

JACK: Then what do you call this smarty pants?

(Jack turns around to reveal a "Z" on the seat of his pants.)

Like a dog leaving his mark, claiming his territory, saying:
"I was here." "I exist."

WHISKEY: Kinda existential, ain't it?

WRITER: Gentlemen, I just went through all this at the old folks
home—Zorro is a fabrication.

WHISKEY: Fabrication?

WRITER: Mildly intriguing at best.

WHISKEY: Intriguing?

(Whiskey closes in on the Writer.)

WRITER: Maybe.

WHISKEY: Do I intrigue you?

WRITER: Uh.

WHISKEY: Do you find me intriguing?

WRITER: Well . . .

WHISKEY: Am I here to intrigue you?

WRITER: You're scaring me, good fella.

(Jack closes in from the other side.)

JACK: Just because you haven't seen The Masked One don't
mean he doesn't exist. For once you lay eyes on him, it
burns torpid lacerations against your brain, the silhouette
against the full moon, the imposing figure cut out of the
night with his cape, his brown eyes burning behind the mysterious mask, the boots made of Corinthian leather . . .

WHISKEY: Don't forget his whip!

JACK: Or the sword made of Toledo steel.

WRITER: Sounds like you fancy The Masked One.

JACK: I fear him as much as I fancy him.

WHISKEY: I fancy pretty fellas myself.

WRITER: OK, guys . . .

JACK: Go on, tell 'em, tell 'em 'bout that feller you met over in
Frisco, Whiskey.

WRITER: Good night then . . .

(Whiskey and Jack waltz with music around the tiny room.)

WHISKEY *(Wistful)*: Well, we danced all night we did. *(Sings:)*

> De camptown ladies sing this song
> Doo-da doo-da . . .
> De camptown racetrack's five miles long
> Oh, de doo-da day!

(Wistful again) And later that night, I put my mouth on his privates, and in the morn he made me a cup of coffee with foamed milk on top. That man is known as the Cappuccino Cowboy.

(Whiskey and Jack make cappuccino foam sounds.)

JACK AND WHISKEY: Ha ha ha ha ha ha . . .
WRITER: Help!
WHISKEY: One day, when the law of the land permits, I'm gonna marry me that fella. And we'll keep a little cabin up at the Russian River or a cottage in Ptown.
WRITER: This is all wrong!

(The Writer sits on his bed, head in hands.)

JACK: I've got no quarrel with you dancing with other fellas, just sounds a little queer is all. Complicated and such. On one hand you're a manly, outdoorsy type, rough 'round the edges, and on the other hand . . .
WHISKEY: . . . I'm in touch with something deep down inside.

(A horse whinnies just outside the window. They point the pistols in that direction.)

JACK: Quickly, the loot.
WHISKEY: We got to put the money in the safe now, so turn around.
WRITER: Why?

JACK: OK, close your eyes then.

WRITER: Again I ask why?

WHISKEY: So you don't see the combination, stupid!

(The Writer closes his eyes.)

JACK: What's the combination, Whiskey?

WHISKEY: Thirty-five right, twenty-one left, eleven right.

WRITER: I can hear you.

(The safe opens. They put the loot inside and shut it.)

JACK: OK, you can open your eyes now.

(Jack and Whiskey start exiting through the window.)

Can we count on you to join the Legion of Caballeros and help the old gal?

WHISKEY: And save California?

WRITER: Nah, not today. No, I'm gonna write a play, masturbate, and drink a 2001 Coppola Shiraz from Trader Joe's.

JACK: You know Trader Joe?

WHISKEY: How 'bout Two Buck Chuck?

WRITER: Uh . . .

WHISKEY: I say you're yella, a yella playwright is all you are.

WRITER: I ain't yeller.

WHISKEY: Yes you are. Now dance, yella writer, dance! Dance!
(Starts shooting)

WRITER: I'm dancing, I'm dancing!

(The Writer does some spazzy moves. The highwaymen laugh up a storm.)

WHISKEY: Dance!! Damn ya, dance! Get your freak on! He's a regular Lola Montès.

JACK: Look, boy, the old lady used to own six thousand acres. That land has dwindled down to seventeen hundred square feet. Everybody that comes through here just takes.

(Whiskey gets real close to the yella Writer.)

WHISKEY: Are you a giver or a taker?

WRITER: I'm trying to take so that I may give back to my *comunidad.*

JACK: You're no different than the church, or the 49ers, or the Oakland Raiders. You're just a taker.

WRITER: I'm a writer.

JACK: Taker!

WRITER: Giver!

JACK: Faker!

WHISKEY: Lose your land, you lose yourself.

JACK: We got to save the inn. Now or never, sink or swim, ride or die, saddle up, yella feller.

WRITER: I ain't yeller I says.

JACK: Let's ride then!

(Jack dives out the window and onto his horse.)

WHISKEY: You know, the great writer Thoreau once wrote . . .

JACK *(Popping his head back in)*: C'mon, Whiskey, this is no time to be literary!

(Jack disappears and we hear his horse gallop away.

Whiskey approaches the Writer with a menacing glare, and then plants a big wet one on his kisser. Whiskey then jumps out the window and runs away.

The Writer is dazed. He closes the window and sits down to start writing.

We are now with Whiskey, Jack and the Two-Hundred-Year-Old Woman just in front of the inn.)

TWO-HUNDRED-YEAR-OLD WOMAN: Ten for you and ten for Whiskey.

WHISKEY: Thank you, Doña.

JACK: You know, ma'am, we've been working without an Equity contract now for thirty years.

TWO-HUNDRED-YEAR-OLD WOMAN: You Lort C actors are all alike.

JACK: Just trying to do the best we can.

WHISKEY: Bringing authenticity to our roles and such.

TWO-HUNDRED-YEAR-OLD WOMAN: Put a lid on it, Whiskey.

WHISKEY: Yes, ma'am.

TWO-HUNDRED-YEAR-OLD WOMAN: Our writer amigo didn't believe you guys for a single moment. You were supposed to inspire him, not put your mouth on him!

WHISKEY: Got a little swept up in the moment is all, ma'am.

TWO-HUNDRED-YEAR-OLD WOMAN: Next time stick to the plan.

WHISKEY: Yes, ma'am.

JACK: He might be tougher to crack than Jack Kerouac.

WHISKEY: Did you sleep with ol' Rambling Jack, ma'am?

(A coyote howls.)

JACK *(To Whiskey)*: I guess she did.

(Back in the Writer's room. He is putting a clean sheet of cerulean bond paper into an old typewriter.)

WRITER: Control . . . Alt . . . Where's the delete button? How can I write without a send button? Oh well, I should write something Sam Shepardy: *Curse of the Chicano Class.*

(Coyote howl. The Writer decides to test the howls of conquered writers:)

Isabel Allende?

(Howl.)

Joan Didion?

(Howl.)

Anthony Bourdain . . .

(No howl.)

Ishi the last California Indian?

(Howl.)

The Cleveland Indians?

(A wolf pack of howls. He shrugs and gets to work. The Writer flexes his writing fingers.)

Title: *Brokeback Vato!* No, uh, *Y tu Zorro También*, uh, *Amores Caballos . . .* I got it, *Zorro in Hell!* Sounds like crap . . . shit!

(The Writer lights a joint and takes a big hit.
The lights shift.
Psychedelic whirls bounce off a descending ceiling fan. We hear The Doors' "The End." The Writer moves in slow-motion tae kwondo fashion. He paints his face with camouflage paint, which looks like a mask. The Writer uses his bed as a riverboat, taking an oar from under the bed. The lights go up and down to signify the passing of time. A Vietcong soldier in peasant hat and rifle runs by. Helicopter sounds, machine guns, mosquitoes, crickets. The Two-Hundred-Year-Old Woman crosses as The Madhatter. A bald, shirtless Brando appears in the window.)

BRANDO: Are you my assassin? The horror, the horror. Never get off the boat. Fucking A right! Never get off the boat!

(Lights up and down as the Writer puts a pillowcase over his head, extending his arms outward to appear as the now famous image of the Abu Ghraib tortured prisoner.
Lights up and down as the Writer is handed pills through a bedroom window by a Bear Claw.
Lights up and down as the Writer tenderly caresses his nipples. He is handed Zorro pajamas. He puts his hands in the pant's pockets.)

A VOICE: Psst! Psst! *Señor!* You should not touch yourself.
WRITER: I wasn't going to touch, wait a minute . . .

(The Writer looks behind him, and a Sleepy Mexican statue has just come to life. Soft guitar music.)

Who the hell are you?
PANCHO THE STATUE: My name is Pancho, Junior. I am the Sleepy Mexican in the Zorro movies. I'm the guy with the big sombrero sleeping next to a cactus or against the church door. That is me.
WRITER: You're a member in good standing of a drug cartel?
PANCHO THE STATUE: No, señor!
WRITER: You are a member in good standing of a drug cartel?
PANCHO THE STATUE: No, señor!
WRITER: You are a Hollywood actor?
PANCHO THE STATUE: Yes, sir. *Sí, cómo no.* Look, I have a Screen Actors Guild card, *mira no más.* I come from a long line of unionized Sleepy Mexicans. My father, Pancho, Senior, was the first Sleepy Mexican in the original silent movie with Douglas Fairbanks. I made my movie debut in the Tyrone Power movie. Remember when El Zorro rides gallantly into town, kicking up dust in our faces and then marks the wanted poster with a "Z"? Well, I was the Little Sleepy Mexican next to my papá, the Big Sleepy Mexican. My papá is retired now and he gave me his famous sombrero. The Smithsonian called me, saying they wanted the sombrero for their museum. I say, "No way, José. This sombrero stays with the familia in Glendale, California. Gracias pero, no gracias." My son will be in the new Antonio Banderas movie.

(Pancho the Statue falls asleep.)

WRITER: Hey, hey, hey!
PANCHO THE STATUE: You see, there will always be work for Sleepy Mexicans, because there will always be Zorro movies. So you see, *señor,* for my familia and me, Zorro lives! Oh sí. Zorro *vive!*

WRITER: Wait a minute, wait a minute, what do you know? I mean, you are a sad Mexican stereotype who feeds the insatiable media machine and I have no idea why I'm even having a conversation with you, you're a freakin' adobe statue.

PANCHO THE STATUE: No, señor. You are the one who is sad, for you merely see a Sleepy Mexican, but I sleep with one eye open, ever vigilant, always alert for the moment when the sleeping giant will rise up and take back her land.

WRITER: And how do you propose to take back America, Sleepy Mexican?

PANCHO THE STATUE: With my switchblade!

(Pancho opens a pathetic blade.)

WRITER: Great, a stereotype on top of a stereotype.

PANCHO THE STATUE: *Cómo que no,* I will disembowel the dominant culture, reversing el Manifest Destiny.

WRITER: You are a wise Latina!

PANCHO THE STATUE: One day, California will once again, become Mexico.

WRITER: It already is Pancho. Ever been to East L.A.?

PANCHO THE STATUE: You have jokes, señor, very funny, remind me to laugh. You thought I was Esleepy Mexican but I am Esleepy giant. *¿Como te llamas?*

WRITER *(Looking at his watch)*: Its about ten P.M.

PANCHO THE STATUE: *¿No sabes español Pinche pocho?*

WRITER: Yo sabo Nacho Libre.

PANCHO THE STATUE: No, no, no, you are not ready to be El Zorro.

WRITER: I never said I wanted to be El Zorro!

PANCHO THE STATUE: You no wanna be Zorro? OK, put on my magic sombrero, it will make you invisible.

WRITER: Invisible?

PANCHO THE STATUE: Oh yes, sí como El Harry Potter. All the Sleepy Mexicans are invisible in the movie.

WRITER: What movie?

PANCHO THE STATUE: This movie, boiy! Keep one eye open!

(Pancho quickly places the sombrero on the Writer and shoves him into action. The Writer sits onstage in the classic Sleepy Mexican position far stage right. Lights! Camera! Action! A movie projector light flickers. We hear a song:)

CALIFORNIO CHORUS:
> We ride, through the night
> For justice
> By day we sleep
> We ride, on the wings
> Of angels
> To fight tyranny and
> Evil-doers . . .
> We ride!

(Diego, a handsome dandy in period dress, enters. All the characters in this "movie" speak with Mid-Atlantic accents and "act" real good!)

DIEGO: Mamá? Papá? I'm home from Spain!

(Friar Felipe enters.)

FRIAR FELIPE: Diego, my boy, you have returned from "Eth-paña!
DIEGO: Friar Felipe
FRIAR FELIPE: My, how "han-thom" and "dith-stinguished" you look, muchacho. You are taller and whiter than before.
DIEGO: And you, dear Friar, are as fat and dark as ever.
FRIAR FELIPE: Give me a hug muchacho! Look at you.

(The men embrace. Friar Felipe helps himself to a reacharound, grabbing Diego's firm buttocks. Don De La Vega enters, he clears his throat and the men quickly separate.)

DIEGO: Papá!
DON DE LA VEGA: Diego, my son! You have returned from fencing school in "Eth-paña."

DIEGO: Top of my class, Father. Some things never change.

DON DE LA VEGA: There are many changes, my son.

DIEGO: Changes? What sort of changes, Papá?

DON DE LA VEGA: I am no longer El Gobernador.

DIEGO: What?

DON DE LA VEGA: I was recalled, by an Austrian.

DIEGO *(Anglo accent)*: *Puta madre.*

(Friar Felipe crosses himself.)

DON DE LA VEGA: Diego, there is more bad news. Your Uncle Ramón was killed.

DIEGO: My dear Uncle Ramón? Oh dear, what did you do with his outfits?

DON DE LA VEGA: A golden arrow pierced his skull.

DIEGO: My God, a golden arrow pierced his skull?

DON DE LA VEGA: Clean through, my son.

FRIAR FELIPE: May God have mercy on his soul.

DIEGO: I feel faint.

Oh dear. Who was it, Father, who killed Uncle Ramón?

DON DE LA VEGA: The evil Don del Oro!

(Guitar stab: tan tan tan . . .)

FRIAR FELIPE: Don del Oro . . .

(Guitar stab: tan tan tan . . .)

The very leader of the savage, soulless, unbaptised Yaqui Indians.

DON DE LA VEGA: Your Uncle Ramón was going to lead the Legion of Caballeros to deliver California gold to Presidente Benito Juarez in Mexico City. You must lead the men. Things could get violent, my son.

DIEGO: Does the Californio only know his brand of makeesmo? Must he lust for blood as his Aztec ancestors did?

DON DE LA VEGA: We must act swiftly before Don del Oro strikes again.

(Guitar stab: tan tan tan . . .)

DIEGO: Could not these disputes be settled on the fandango dance floor?

(Diego executes a fancy fandango jig.)

DON DE LA VEGA: What? You must lead the men into battle, my son.

FRIAR FELIPE: Atta boy, Dieguito.

DIEGO: Very well, then I shall wear my French cuffs, they will flutter in the wind like the swallows returning to Capistrano.

FRIAR FELIPE *(To Don de la Vega)*: Did he say "swallows"?

DON DE LA VEGA: I heard "swallows."

DIEGO: I must take a bath in lotions of carnations and crushed lily musk to remove the dust and fatigue of travel.

FRIAR FELIPE: Good idea, Dieguito.

DON DE LA VEGA: Don't encourage the boy, Friar, he doesn't need a bath, he needs a wife! *(Turning to Diego)* Son, have you seen Lupita yet? She has been obediently waiting for your return.

DIEGO: Oh, Papá, the weaker sex can be so tiresome. Where's my Sleepy Mexican?

(Don de la Vega looks to Friar Felipe.)

FRIAR FELIPE: Don't look at me. I never touched him when he was an altar boy. ¡Nunca!

(Friar Felipe and Don de la Vega exit, leaving Diego onstage as he looks for his Sleepy Mexican. The Sleepy Mexican is right in front of him, but Diego doesn't see him until he takes his "magic" sombrero off.)

DIEGO: Sleepy Mexican! Where are you? Oh, there you are. Draw my bath at once and press my black tights and cape.

(Diego exits followed by a confused Writer/Sleepy Mexican. On another part of the stage we see the beautiful Lupita praying near a cross.)

LUPITA: Heavenly Father, I do not want to marry Diego de la Vega, for he dresses better than me and he fancies the decorative arts. Give me a man, Father, a man with *sangre* in his veins, a man like Zorro.

(Bernardo, the mute servant, appears.)

Bernardo, the mute Indian servant, what is it?

(Bernardo mimes and whistles as Lupita tries to interpret.)

A stranger? No. The raccoons have returned to Capistrano? The prices have been slashed at the Mercado? A man on a horse? What is it Bernardo?!

(Zorro appears with a strum of a guitar.)

ZORRO: Enough, Bernardo.

(A disgusted Bernardo whistles and points to Zorro and exits.)

At your service, señorita.
LUPITA: Ah, señor Zorro, what are you doing here?
ZORRO: I have come to give you a ride on my big horse.
LUPITA: Tornado?
ZORRO: Sure, him, too.

(Lupita slowly looks up to Heaven, hands in prayer position.)

LUPITA: Thank you God. *(Back to Zorro)* You must go before you are caught by the Gobernator.
ZORRO: Adíos, Señorita Lupita. *Mi amor.*

(He tenderly kisses her hand and is gone.)

LUPITA: Call me mañana, we can fandango after brunch.

(Big guitar flourish.
Later that night, El Zorro pays El Gobernator a visit. He
must make his way past a Guard first. The Guard is quickly dis-
patched. El Gobernator enters.)

EL GOBERNATOR: Who goes there?

(El Gobernator wears a Kaiser Helmet, monocle, thick mus-
tache and short riding whip.
Zorro puts the sword toward El Gobernator's throat.)

By the saints! ZORRO! NO! You are back? I thought you
had vanished for good.

ZORRO: Vanish? Me? Why no Señor Gobernator, it is you who
will disappear after you resign and reappoint Don Alejandro de la Vega as your successor.

"Not a "Z" on my fresh adobe walls, I just had them painted!" Zorro (Joseph
Kamal) taunts El Gobernator (Herbert Siguenza).

EL GOBERNATOR: Over my large, dead body!

ZORRO: That can be arranged.

(Zorro swishes his sword close to the Gobernator, making his pants fall down.)

Is that a cactus in your pants or are you feliz to see me? Your final act as Gobernator will be to sign this letter, returning the land to the poor.

EL GOBERNATOR: Very well, where's my pen, I had it here . . .

(El Gobernator finds his rapier.)

On guard!

(They sword fight, holding for dramatic beats.)

ZORRO: Do you fandango, Gobernator?

EL GOBERNATOR: I beg your pardon?

ZORRO: Do you fandango in the dark, alone?

EL GOBERNATOR: I did once in Vienna, why do you ask such questions?

ZORRO: Because a man who does not fandango in the dark alone may not be a man at all.

EL GOBERNATOR: I am confused, El Zorro.

ZORRO: Maybe this will help you understand.

(Zorro makes a "Z" on the wall.)

EL GOBERNATOR: My God, not on my fresh adobe walls, I just had them painted!

ZORRO: That is my mark to remind you I was here.

EL GOBERNATOR: I think I would have remembered.

(Zorro is gone.)

Zorro's a monster! An animal! He's history's first graffiti artist! Guards! Guards! Guards!

(The movie sequence ends. The film projector disappears. Back in the Writer's room, the Writer is in bed in his Zorro pajamas. Seated in a chair next to the bed is a grizzly bear named Kyle.)

KYLE: Zora Neale Hurston writes that in African culture, the rabbit, the bear, the lion, the buzzard, the fox are all cultural heroes from the animal world. But they're tricksters, shape-shifters.

WRITER: There's a grizzly bear in my room. OK.

KYLE: Robin Hood, another sort of nocturnal animal, another archetype folk hero who stole from the rich and gave to the poor.

WRITER: There's a grizzly bear in my room and he's talking.

(Offering to Kyle.)

Laudanum?

KYLE: No thank you.

WRITER: How long was I out?

KYLE: Five days.

WRITER: I must have knocked out after the movie.

KYLE: What movie?

DON RINGO *(Offstage)*: Oooooweeeeoooooo . . .

KYLE : The old lady thought you might have some issues you'd like to discuss, perhaps I can help get your creative mojo going?

WRITER: Am I in bear-apy?

KYLE: I guess you could call me your bear-a-pist.

WRITER: What's your name?

KYLE: My name is Kyle.

WRITER: Kyle the Grizzly Bear therapist, here's what's going on, uh, spellcheck on my computer changes the word "Chicano" to "chicanery."

KYLE: What's really bothering you?

WRITER: Narcos. Arizona. Killer drug cartels. Tea-Baggers. Post-Radical America! Plus I'm OCD and ADD, and I feel like I'm invisible.

The Writer (Richard Montoya) in therapy with Kyle the Bear, Ph.D. (Ric Salinas).

KYLE: Ah, the Sleepy Mexican complex!

WRITER: That's helpful, Doctor Kyle. Yes, see I'm afraid that I may be stuck, failing, unlettered, a hack no better than Johnston McCulley really. Don Ringo may be right, maybe I'm just a wannabe shit-com writer, relegated to writing for the not-for-profit theater. I've got a duffle bag full of rejection notices from the *George Lopez Show* and all that rejection fuels my radical Chicano-ness out there, but in here, right here, I have a sneaky suspicion that the Sleepy Mexican is more awake, more alive than me.

KYLE: We all go through periods of creative lulls, peaks, valleys. For example, my ideas are basically based off another bear's ideas. At some point I simply had to embrace this. Nothing is authentic.

WRITER: Nietzsche!

KYLE: Yes, he was saying that every man's idea is based on another man's idea, i.e., the Bible, the Talmud, the Koran, *A Million Little Pieces.*

WRITER: Nietzsche said God is dead. I know this for sure because I googled God.

KYLE: He may not have meant that God is dead, as in there in no God.

WRITER: That's sort of what I've been trying to tell the old horny lady downstairs. Zorro is not real, he is a myth!

KYLE: But when do myths become real?

WRITER: When they're on the History Channel?

KYLE: When people believe in them.

WRITER: Were you a Ritalin bear?

KYLE: I was a latchkey bear.

WRITER: Oh.

KYLE: See, the old lady believes, so, for her the hero is real. She draws her strength from that and maybe you should, too.

WRITER: Gee, you're smarter than the average bear.

KYLE: I have two degrees from Cal.

WRITER: Go bears! Kyle, you know they say it's hard out there for a pimp, but I think it's harder for a pimpernel.

KYLE: You just got to keep it real, Boo-boo.

WRITER: You're a bomb-ass bear.

KYLE: So, in your mind I exist.

WRITER: Well, you're sitting here, aren't ya?

KYLE: Am I?

WRITER: An existential bear.

KYLE: Scratch my back.

WRITER: I bear-ly know you . . .

KYLE: My back itches, therefore it must be scratched.

(Kyle rises, the Writer scratches.)

Oh yeah, right there, haven't been able to reach that spot in years, ah yeah right there . . .

WRITER: Ah, such a cute bear, such a good bear, such a smarty-pants bear.

KYLE: I would appreciate it if you did not infantilize me.

WRITER: Yet my culture has been romanticized for centuries. See?

KYLE: Borges talked about the Latin lover-outlaw, and America's desire to string him up by his balls. Hollywood simply took it to the lowest common denominator.

WRITER: Borges sucks, he's Argentinian.

KYLE *(Looking off into the distance)*: I have a memory of the land. My California is now an endless series of subdivisions and strip malls. Nowhere for the fox to roam. Zorro is the fox.

WRITER: You're losing me, Yogi.

KYLE: Get up!

WRITER: Huh?

KYLE: I said, on your feet!

(Kyle grabs a single sword off the wall.)

The sword . . .

WRITER *(Concerned)*: Uh-huh . . .

(Kyle uses his bear paws as he refers to his own bear face.)

KYLE: The Face! Individuality.

(Kyle reaches for a Zorro mask that fits him perfectly.)

The mask! Communality. Like the shtetels of Eastern Europe. What my Rabbi calls "Universal concerns for the whole."

WRITER: Jews always get it right.

KYLE: Why do you think kids from Brooklyn to Boyle Heights would steal away for hours at the double-feature matinee on Saturdays? Zorro spoke to us.

WRITER: Did you have a bear mitzvah?

KYLE: I should kill you for that.

(Kyle has the Writer up against the wall with the tip of the sword at his throat.)

WRITER: Whoa, back up, pal. Hey, that smarts.

KYLE: Yes, it should smart plenty, you need to hurt, fella. You've gotten soft and undisciplined.

WRITER: Do these Zorro pajamas make me look fat?

KYLE: Zorro's self-sacrifice for the good of the community speaks to the old lady, it speaks to us.

WRITER: Yeah but . . .

KYLE: Yeah but what?

WRITER: Zorro doesn't speak to me, bro. As a kid he didn't mean shit to me either!
Come on, he's a Spaniard!? And you're a freaking bear-man!

KYLE: Bear-American, thank you very much. You're half Spanish, do you hate half of yourself?

WRITER: Only the bad half.

KYLE: Zorro may have been the first radical Chicano.

WRITER: How dare you say "Zorro" and "Chicano" in the same bear breath.

(Kyle gives out a huge bear roar. He pins the Writer down, thrashing him.)

Help, Doña!

(Lights shift as Don Ringo enters cracking a whip, followed by the Two-Hundred-Year-Old Woman.)

DON RINGO: Down, oso, down!

(Whip sounds.)

TWO-HUNDRED-YEAR-OLD WOMAN: Well now, that's the spirit. Looks like everybody is getting on just fine, a little rough-housing is always good for stimulating the mind. Faulkner was such a fucker that way.

(Coyote howl.)

KYLE: I couldn't crack him, señora. May I eat the Chicano bastard? Chicano!

TWO-HUNDRED-YEAR-OLD WOMAN: Stand down, Kyle. There'll be no snacks till I read me some pages.

WRITER: I got to get out of this "looking glass."

(The Writer grabs his backpack and starts packing his things.)

DON RINGO: You speak with forked tongue.

TWO-HUNDRED-YEAR-OLD WOMAN: Nothing to fight for? Why you little selfish punk. Don't you know it takes a village?

WRITER: I know you slept with a village.

(Don Ringo slaps the Writer upside the head.)

TWO-HUNDRED-YEAR-OLD WOMAN: The once mighty California grizzly shorn of his place to roam.

(Kyle lets out a primal scream.)

KYLE: Aaaaahhhh . . .

TWO-HUNDRED-YEAR-OLD WOMAN: I will not tolerate a lazy writer unable, unwilling to use his or her imagination as the weapon it was meant to be. Nothing to fight for? Why we got more prisons than schools.

DON RINGO: We got *pinche* Minute Men patrolling the border.

TWO-HUNDRED-YEAR-OLD WOMAN: We need stem-cell research, bucko!

DON RINGO: The State is in a state of emergency!

TWO-HUNDRED-YEAR-OLD WOMAN: And not one more lump of coal from West Virginia if it costs the life of another miner. Rise up, rise up, lazy, bloated, Hispanic.

WRITER: Please don't call me Hispanic.

TWO-HUNDRED-YEAR-OLD WOMAN: What do you stand for, Mister Writer?

WRITER: I don't remember.

(Kyle roars.)

"This Chicano is beyond therapy!" Don Ringo (Herbert Siguenza, left), the Writer (Richard Montoya, rear), Kyle the Bear (Ric Salinas) and the Two-Hundred-Year-Old Woman (Sharon Lockwood).

(*Bewildered*) This must be Hell. I have nothing to fight for, lady!

TWO-HUNDRED-YEAR-OLD WOMAN: Nothing to fight for?

WRITER: I would rather party!

TWO-HUNDRED-YEAR-OLD WOMAN: Rise up, rise up, I say!

WRITER: I don't like the way the bear is looking at me.

(*Kyle starts to put a bear bib on.*)

TWO-HUNDRED-YEAR-OLD WOMAN: Eat 'em, Kyle! Unmask this pile of horse shit!

(Mexican band music. Kyle the Bear chases the Writer. Mayhem. They all dance-chase the Writer. The Two-Hunderd-Year-Old Woman and Don Ringo exit, putting a DO NOT DISTURB *sign on the door, leaving Kyle to bear-slam the Writer, landing on top of him on the bed. Kyle humps him. The Writer looks mortified. The curtain comes down.*

As we go to blackout, the Writer screams:)

WRITER: Put on a bear condom for fuck sake!

KYLE: Roar!!!!

(Music up: "Bare Necessities.")

| ACT TWO |

The Grateful Dead's "California" plays. All or part of the song could be played just so long as we hear: "California . . ." As the house lights dim, Disney's Zorro theme song is heard as if coming from a small, 1950s TV.

TV VOICE:
>Out of the noche
>When the full luna is bright
>Comes a horseman known as Zorro.
>The bold renegade carves a "Z" with
>His blade, a "Z" not for
>Zenophobia.
>Zorro, the fox so cunning
>And free . . .

(Two boys, Billy and Tommy, enter. Billy is dressed as Davey Crockett, Tommy is dressed as Zorro, circa 1950.)

LIL' DAVEY: I'm Davey Crockett!
LIL' ZORRO: I'm Zorro!

White Angel Zorro (Joseph Kamal) arrives to take Little Zorro's spirit (Herbert Siguenza) to the big rancho in the sky.

LIL' DAVEY: Euuuuu . . . he's a Mexican.

LIL' ZORRO: No he's not, stupid, he's Spanish.

LIL' DAVEY: Mexican!

LIL' ZORRO: Spanish!

LIL' DAVEY: Mexican!

LIL' ZORRO: Spanish!

LIL' DAVEY: Wetback!

LIL' ZORRO: Spanish!

LIL' DAVEY: Greaser!

LIL' ZORRO: Spanish!

LIL' DAVEY: Taco vendor, beaner, spick.

LIL' ZORRO: Ohhh, I'm telling!

LIL' DAVEY: Davey Crockett kills Injuns.

LIL' ZORRO: So what. So does Zorro.

LIL' DAVEY: Does not.

LIL' ZORRO: Does too. Only if they're bad Indians, so there.

LIL' DAVEY: Indians are alcoholics.

LIL' ZORRO: Are not.

LIL' DAVEY: Are too.

LIL' ZORRO: Shut up!

LIL' DAVEY: You shut up.

LIL' ZORRO: Euuu, you have a squirrel on your head.

LIL' DAVEY: No I don't

LIL' ZORRO: Yes you do.

LIL' DAVEY: It's not a squirrel, it's a 'coon.

LIL' ZORRO: Ooooh, I'm telling.

LIL' DAVEY: Besides, I can shoot you on account I got my daddy's gun.

LIL' ZORRO: Cannot!

LIL' DAVEY: Can too!

LIL' ZORRO: You're a sissy.

(Lil' Davey takes out a real gun that he can barely hold up.)

Ha! That's not a real gun.

LIL' DAVEY: Is too!

LIL' ZORRO: Is not!

LIL' DAVEY: Is too!

LIL' ZORRO: Shoot me then, sissy.

LIL' DAVEY: OK.

(A loud gun blast. Lil' Zorro falls to the ground, dead.)

Uh, oh.

WOMAN *(Voice-Over)*: Billy, what was that?

LIL' DAVEY: Mommy! Mommy!

(Lil' Davey runs off, scared. Lil' Zorro lies dead in a pool of blood—a large red "Z" made from a light special. Angelic music. Heavenly light shafts down to our little hero. An Angel, a handsome man dressed in a white Zorro outfit with wings, descends from Heaven and stands over our dead little Zorro.)

ANGEL: Tommy? Tommy? Tommy, get up now, lil' partner.

LIL' ZORRO: Gee, mister, I thought I died.

ANGEL: You did die, little fella.

LIL' ZORRO: I did?

ANGEL: Sure you did Tommy.

LIL' ZORRO: Hey, I know you who you are. You're Guy Williams! The Disney Zorro!

ANGEL: That's right.

LIL' ZORRO: Boss!

ANGEL: I'm here to take you where every little Zorro goes.

LIL' ZORRO: To Burbank, California?

ANGEL: No Tommy, that's Hell. I'm taking you to the big corral.

LIL' ZORRO: Are we going to the big rancho in the sky?

ANGEL: Why yes, little partner.

LIL' ZORRO: Where's Tornado?

ANGEL: Why here he comes now.

LIL' ZORRO: Yipeeeeeee!!!!!!

(A stick pony descends from above.)

Say, Tornado's awfully skinny, mister.

ANGEL : Don't you worry about that, Tommy. Just hop on!

(As the Angel and Lil' Zorro gallop off, the lyrics to the following song are projected onto a scrim, complete with a bouncing sombrero so the audience can sing along.)

C'mon, little cowpoke,
Jump on Tornado
We're heading up, up to a place,
A place that is safe and far away,
C'mon, little 'pokie, let's
Ride ride ride and we'll see you on
The other side . . .

(We turn back to the El Camino Real Inn. The lobby is in full swing as the Two-Hundred-Year-Old Woman and El Músico sing. Kyle the Bear keeps rhythm on a pair of snazzy bear bongos.)

TWO-HUNDRED-YEAR-OLD WOMAN: Let's pick it, fellers!

(The Cowpoke song becomes a faster, more raucous version of itself. They all jam punk-rock style. Then the song comes to a big finish.)

Lovely guitar picking, Señor Músico!
EL MÚSICO: Gracias, Doña.
TWO-HUNDRED-YEAR-OLD WOMAN: Hey, play that Green Day song now.

(El Músico rips into "American Idiot" with the old woman wildly air-drumming like Aynsley Dunbar from Journey, circa 1978.)

DON RINGO *(Concerned)*: Do we have the rights?
TWO-HUNDRED-YEAR-OLD WOMAN: I nailed Billy Joe Armstrong a million times—hit it!

ALL *(Singing)*:
Don't want to be an American Idiot . . .

(The Writer enters as the music subsides.)

TWO-HUNDRED-YEAR-OLD WOMAN: That was radical. How ya
feeling there, Mister Writer?

WRITER: A little tender, thanks to a certain bear.

(Don Ringo enters.)

DON RINGO: What bear?

(They laugh at the Writer's expense.)

WRITER: How long have I been sleeping?

TWO-HUNDRED-YEAR-OLD WOMAN: You've been hibernating
nearly a week now, must have been bitten by the brown
recluse spider.

WRITER: I kept having this dream.

KYLE: That you were a lil' Zorro shot by Davey Crockett and
taken to Heaven by Guy Williams?

WRITER: How did you know that?

(Kyle the Bear rises to face the Writer.)

KYLE: All Chicanos have that dream.

WRITER: Come in my room again and I'll be loaded for bear, you
furry freak.

KYLE: See, it was all an effort by the Doña to conjure up your
creative mojo, to get you writing, off your Chicano pity
potty. You should read my blog.

WRITER: Great.

DON RINGO: You should be thanking her.

TWO-HUNDRED-YEAR-OLD WOMAN: Just trying to kick down
the knowledge, fool.

KYLE: Word. See, your dream, it is a self-hate dream: a mani-
festation of you endlessly trying to fit into a society that
doesn't accept you unless you're light-skinned or Spanish.

DON RINGO *(Making quote marks with his hands)*: Tú eres mi otro
yo. You are my other self, even if I hate my "other."

(Pause.)

KYLE: Well said, Don Ringo. Well, I gotta go take a shit in the woods.

(Kyle and El Músico exit.)

WRITER: Please tell me that bear got his distemper shots.

DON RINGO: What bear? Ooooeeeeweee . . .

WRITER: That bear is real . . . he nearly broke my back mounting me.

TWO-HUNDRED-YEAR-OLD WOMAN: Come over here, boy.

(The Writer ambles over.)

Have you ever tried to put your anger aside for a single moment? To stop your bleeding from the self-induced paper cuts just long enough to marvel at the past generations of gringo children from Nebraska to New Jersey who donned the mask and cape as their parents did before them? And all those little boys, fat or skinny, wanting to save the world from evil. You see, they were thinking locally but acting Zorro-ly. Your play will help new generations recapture the Zorro dream. Don't you wanna save the world, sonny?

WRITER: No. I'd like to save my health insurance.

TWO-HUNDRED-YEAR-OLD WOMAN: Just because they lack in pigmentation don't mean we should deny their desires. God bless the lil' Zorros I say.

DON RINGO: God bless the little gringos one and all.

WRITER: God bless the little culture vultures you mean?

TWO-HUNDRED-YEAR-OLD WOMAN: Hate the game, not the players.

DON RINGO: Simón.

TWO-HUNDRED-YEAR-OLD WOMAN: Who will pick up the sword tomorrow and defend the powerless?

DON RINGO: The voiceless.

TWO-HUNDRED-YEAR-OLD WOMAN: The planet?

(The Writer is stumped.)

So you see, I view those little Zorros as something very powerful.

DON RINGO: *Revolucionarios.*

(Don Ringo gently fusses over the Two-Hundred-Year-Old Woman's favorite Zorro quilt. She pulls the Writer's script out of her pocket.)

TWO-HUNDRED-YEAR-OLD WOMAN: By the way, I read the first act of your opus.

WRITER: You read my pages?

DON RINGO: Me, too.

WRITER: How could you go in my room and read my script behind my back? What did you think?

TWO-HUNDRED-YEAR-OLD WOMAN: Take a knee, son. Here's a little heads-up, you've got a real problem with possessives and mixed metaphors.

WRITER: I *am* a mixed metaphor.

DON RINGO: I have notes, too.

TWO-HUNDRED-YEAR-OLD WOMAN: My momma used to make a simple roux using fat and flour.

WRITER: A roux?

TWO-HUNDRED-YEAR-OLD WOMAN: Yes, sir, something to bind the whole darn dish together. You need to find your roux, boy.

DON RINGO: *Órale.*

TWO-HUNDRED-YEAR-OLD WOMAN: When Daddy whittled on his piece of wood, he would carve away the possibilities allowing for something beautiful to emerge. Simple is better I say.

DON RINGO: *Órale* again.

WRITER: The committee has spoken—I suck.

TWO-HUNDRED-YEAR-OLD WOMAN: Look there, I wrote down copious Lit notes in the margin.

WRITER: Did you go to Yale Rep?

(The Writer grabs his script from her.)

TWO-HUNDRED-YEAR-OLD WOMAN: Hell, I built the place!

WRITER: Any distortion of my text is not unlike murder.

TWO-HUNDRED-YEAR-OLD WOMAN: My friend Freud said that.

(Coyote howl.)

DON RINGO: Muchacho, don't be discouraged with her comments about your script. La Doña has very high literary standards. I remember the day she made Tony Kushner cry. *Toma.*

(Don Ringo hands him a drink.)

WRITER: What is it?

DON RINGO: Homemade mescal, be sure to eat the worm.

WRITER: But I only eat soyrizo. From Whole Foods.

DON RINGO: Go on, it will ward off any potential viruses from the bear.

WRITER: What bear? Oooooweeeeoooo . . .

DON RINGO: You're catching on, *ese.*

(The Writer takes a pull then spits it out.)

WRITER: My mouth is on fire! Who on earth could drink this stuff?

TWO-HUNDRED-YEAR-OLD WOMAN: Murietta drank it by the gallon.

WRITER *(Throat burning)*: Joaquín Murietta?

DON RINGO: He could handle the fire water, can you?

WRITER: The famous Californio poet/bandit?

TWO-HUNDRED-YEAR-OLD WOMAN: Bandit to some, hero to most.

WRITER: Don't tell me Murietta stayed here.

DON RINGO: In the very room you are in now, muchacho.

TWO-HUNDRED-YEAR-OLD WOMAN: Same bed in fact.

WRITER: The literary gods are surely smiling upon me now.

DON RINGO: If you're lucky.

TWO-HUNDRED-YEAR-OLD WOMAN: Salud.

(Their glasses touch as they share a drink of mescal. As she speaks, the Two-Hundred-Year-Old Woman starts to slip into a touch of melancholy. Soft guitar music.)

Oh, Joaquín, he was as handsome as he was a great writer. When first I met him he was wearing a black hat, with a black crow feather and a black cape. All I could see were those dark *Sonoran* eyes. They said his heart was as black as his hair. No. I mean to tell you this man floored me, and I had 'em all: woodsmen, mountain men, orchard men, trappers, coachmen and troubadours who would serenade me with songs fanciful and sorrowful. The poets, the capes, the swords—how could a young girl resist? They used to say you could measure a man by the way he stacked wood. Today, we don't know what the measure of a good man is. *(She holds out her glass, Don Ringo knows what to do)* There was a man, long ago, he had a long switch made of a weeping willow branch. This fellow, you see, could find water hidden below the earth. That weeping willow switch became the envy of every goldminer and prospector north of Mount Diablo. Where there was water there could also be gold. Yes, sir, men died for that switch, men cried for that switch. When the fellow finally parted with it, he did so for the price of a girl, the daughter of a wealthy *Haciendado*. So, what was the measure of a man? What was the measure of a woman? What was the measure of that young girl?

WRITER: Were you that young girl, Doña?

(Don Ringo nods.)

TWO-HUNDRED-YEAR-OLD WOMAN: . . . with a bucket of tallow and a primrose in my hair. Life, fast and cheap. *(Softly)* My Californee. Her rich fertile soil had seen many a transgression. I shall do as my Murietta told me to do: I will not yield one inch of my land, my home, my soul to the greedy land-grabbers. Where is my Joaquín? I want to see my Joaquín!

DON RINGO: Cálmese, Doña, tranquila.

TWO-HUNDRED-YEAR-OLD WOMAN: But I long for him so, Don Ringo.

DON RINGO: Yo sé, Doña, yo sé.

TWO-HUNDRED-YEAR-OLD WOMAN: Yo quiero, mi Joaquín . . .

DON RINGO: Ya, Doña, ya . . .

(The Two-Hundred-Year-Old Woman pulls back a small red curtain and a large painting of Joaquín Murietta comes to life.)

MURIETTA: Aquí estoy, mi amor. Aquí estoy.

TWO-HUNDRED-YEAR-OLD WOMAN: Joaquín, Joaquín, you possess my love unadorned.

(Murietta: dusty, handsome, bullet belts across his chest, approaches the old woman like a true gentleman.)

MURIETTA: May I have this baile, señorita?

TWO-HUNDRED-YEAR-OLD WOMAN: Por supuesto, señor.

(The Two-Hundred-Year-Old Woman extends her hand to him.)

WRITER: Don Ringo, is she talking to . . .

DON RINGO: Joaquín Murietta, he hasn't appeared here in years.

WRITER: The Joaquín Murietta?

DON RINGO: The one and only.

WRITER: Like Patrick Swayze in *Ghost*.

DON RINGO: Shut the fuck up.

WRITER: Where's my pen and paper?

DON RINGO: Don't write down a thing. Watch. ¡Silencio!

MURIETTA: The gringos, they tied me up, they raped my wife and hanged my brother. I could only watch, Doña, unable to help them.

TWO-HUNDRED-YEAR-OLD WOMAN: I know, Joaquín, yo sé.

MURIETTA: They butchered my familia.

TWO-HUNDRED-YEAR-OLD WOMAN: They had no call to harm the women and children.

MURIETTA: Cowards! Grim, white men.

TWO-HUNDRED-YEAR-OLD WOMAN: But you never gave up, mi caballero.

MURIETTA: Nunca. Hasta la muerte.

TWO-HUNDRED-YEAR-OLD WOMAN: To the death.

MURIETTA: I remember each of their faces, each pair of eyes looking at me, laughing, spitting whiskey at me. By the light of the moon, I wrote each of their names on the walls of the cave where I hid like the fox.

DON RINGO: Ever the trickster.

MURIETTA: I swore on the swollen belly of my dead wife, in the name of our unborn child, that I would kill each of them.

TWO-HUNDRED-YEAR-OLD WOMAN: But how could you get close enough to them?

MURIETTA: I would disguise myself.

WRITER: Dual identity.

MURIETTA *(Slow, every word counts)*: Terror, real terror was in the haunted eyes of the young Washoe Indian brave who befell the strange and horrific sight of the Donner Party in the summit. Terror was the gringo vigilantes of Kit Carson, who stretched the black necks of men hanging from the torrey pines. I have seen the Chilean goldminers slaughtered in the Sierra sloughs, my Chinese and Filipino brothers shot three, four at a time. I would have to outsmart, outfox my enemy. I taught myself to talk like them, drink and walk like them, but I never murdered like them.

TWO-HUNDRED-YEAR-OLD WOMAN: How dare they call you a savage, a common horse thief.

MURIETTA: From the greedy rich, I took their money. From the poor I took off my hat.

DON RINGO: He was justice.

WRITER: He was gorgeous.

(Loud voices and pounding are heard outside the inn.)

VOICES *(Offstage)*: We know you're in there, Murietta! Mexican!

TWO-HUNDRED-YEAR-OLD WOMAN: The back door, quickly, Joaquín!

(Murietta tenderly kisses her on the lips.)

(Softly) Will you ride to your lover up in the hills?
MURIETTA: What lover?
TWO-HUNDRED-YEAR-OLD WOMAN: What hills?
MURIETTA: Touché.
TWO-HUNDRED-YEAR-OLD WOMAN: Go.
MURIETTA: Mujer, yo quiero quitarte la máscara.
TWO-HUNDRED-YEAR-OLD WOMAN: Yo quiero quitarte el sombrero . . .

(The lovebirds continue to slowly, lovingly counter each other.)

MURIETTA: I never thought possible that I would love an Americana such as you.
TWO-HUNDRED-YEAR-OLD WOMAN: Don't you mean a *gringa* such as I?

(More pounding at the door.)

MURIETTA: The jackboots may tear down the doors of this inn, but they will never scale the heights of my *corazón* as you have, mi gringa.
TWO-HUNDRED-YEAR-OLD WOMAN: Beautiful words, Joaquín, but you are risking your life to speak such poetry to me now. Go, man, go.
MURIETTA: My poems, my words, they are my life and my death.
WRITER: He's a phantom.
TWO-HUNDRED-YEAR-OLD WOMAN: He was no phantom.
MURIETTA *(Turning to the Writer)*: You!
WRITER: Huh? *(Startled, he backs up)*
MURIETTA: So, you are the chosen one, eh? Make every word count, cabrón. *(He is very close to the Writer now. He reaches into his inside coat pocket)*

(There is pounding at the door.)

VOICES *(Offstage)*: Murietta!

MURIETTA: This pen ... *(Produces a pen)* ... was mightier than my avenging sword could ever be. *(Hands the Writer his sacred feathered pen)*
WRITER: Whoa.

(Murietta is gone.)

TWO-HUNDRED-YEAR-OLD WOMAN: Once upon a time in California. There lived a good man named Joaquín Murietta ...

(Don Ringo reaches behind the reception desk and pulls out a jar covered with a cloth. He carefully places it on the desk.)

... the vigilantes cut off his head and put it in a jar of whiskey.

(Don Ringo removes the cloth revealing the severed head of Joaquín Murietta. The lights dim as the jar glows in the dark. The Writer gets very close to the jar. Murietta's eyes pop open.)

WRITER: Ah!!!
THE HEAD OF MURIETTA *(Turning to him)*: Got *cojones?*

(A beat.)

Ha! Ha! Ha! Ha!

(Don Ringo carefully puts the jar back behind the reception desk. The echo of Murietta's words, and what has just happened, fills the room.)

WRITER: Murietta was talking to me, he was talking to me, Doña!
TWO-HUNDRED-YEAR-OLD WOMAN: But were you listening?
WRITER: It's all clear to me now. I can't write about Zorro, I have to write about Murietta. I don't want to be Zorro. I want to be Murietta!
TWO-HUNDRED-YEAR-OLD WOMAN: But are you man enough, boy?

WRITER: Of course I am! What kind of silly question is that? Did I just sound gay?

TWO-HUNDRED-YEAR-OLD WOMAN: You might be able to write about it but could you live it? *(Nailing him)*

WRITER: Not a problem.

TWO-HUNDRED-YEAR-OLD WOMAN: Could you live it, boy!?

WRITER: Yes, Doña, I am Joaquín!

DON RINGO: Here, put this on.

TWO-HUNDRED-YEAR-OLD WOMAN: Say it again!

WRITER: ¡Yo soy Joaquín!

(The Writer falls to his knees.)

¡¡¡YO SOY JOAQUÍN!!!

(Music. Suddenly there is a large pistol pointed to the Writer's head. Freeholder Fella cocks the pistol. The Two-Hundred-Year-Old Woman and Don Ringo are gone.)

FREEHOLDER FELLA: Murietta? Well, well, well, I finally caught up to ya, Murietta. Why, you son of a bitch. Now go on, real slow like, off your knees.

WRITER: Uh, Don Ringo?

FREEHOLDER FELLA: Ain't nobody can help ya now, Joaquín. You's mine, all mine. You'll fetch quite a bounty in Calaveras County I'll wager.

WRITER *(Pleading like a pussy)*: Yo no soy Joaquín.

FREEHOLDER FELLA: That's not what I just heard.

WRITER: Nah, I'm just a writer, truly.
See? A fake bandido. Hee-hee.

FREEHOLDER FELLA: Murietta's got a fine hand for poetry.

WRITER: Well I ain't Murietta.

FREEHOLDER FELLA: Ya know what we did to Three Finger Jack, don't ya?

WRITER: Sí.

FREEHOLDER FELLA: Cut his fingers clean off.

WRITER: I'm gonna need all my fingers.

FREEHOLDER FELLA: Can't believe I drew nigh to ya. Ain't nothing faster than a Mexican on a horse, faster yet a stolen horse. Man, I'm good.

(Freeholder Fella still holds his gun to the Writer's head.)

WRITER: Sir, I haven't stolen anything except maybe an idea or two. That's it.

FREEHOLDER FELLA: Followed you through Squaw Valley, shadowed you on the banks of the Feather River and Putah Creek, terrorizing the white folk along the way.

WRITER: I'm telling you that wasn't me.

FREEHOLDER FELLA: What are you anyway, boy?

WRITER: What am I?

(Freeholder Fella sniffs closer to the Writer.)

FREEHOLDER FELLA: Always wondered what yer made of, Murietta. Part Mexican, Spanish daddy with an Injun mamma? Prairie nigga roots maybe. What is the going price on a Mexican head these days?

WRITER: Dead or alive?

FREEHOLDER FELLA: Makes no never mind. The only good Mexican is a hangin' Mexican. See, boy, I'm the White Devil you've always feared.

WRITER: Oh, I thought you were a Riverside County sheriff's deputy.

FREEHOLDER FELLA: Ha ha ha ha ha, that's real humorous! Pow!

(Freeholder Fella backhands the Writer, causing him to hit the ground. Freeholder Fella looks out over the audience as he waxes:)

What was that Chinaman worth I strung up on Telegraph?

WRITER: You can't put a price on another human being for God sakes, mister.

FREEHOLDER FELLA: Captain Jack, the Modoc Chief up the Bear River, fetched a sack of buffalo nickels, don't you know.

"I followed you through Squaw Valley . . . shadowed you through Putah Creek!" Freeholder Fella (Joseph Kamal, background) and the Writer (Richard Montoya).

WRITER: Sir, for the last time I am not Murietta. I'm a play-wright who specializes in multicultural voices.

(Freeholder Fella takes a wanted flyer from his pocket.)

FREEHOLDER FELLA: You don't look much like Murietta. You sure don't sound like Murietta. Hell, you ain't got the cajones to be Murietta.

WRITER: That's right.

FREEHOLDER FELLA: You know, they say the pen is mightier than the sword.

WRITER: That's what the old lady says.

FREEHOLDER FELLA: But I say, the sword . . . *(Brandishes a knife)* . . . cut's a might deeper.

(Freeholder Fella bends down, getting close to the Writer. He flicks his knife at the Writer's nose, causing a trickle of blood.)

WRITER: Oh my God, I'm bleeding!

FREEHOLDER FELLA: Ha ha ha ha . . .

WRITER: Aaaahhhh!

FREEHOLDER FELLA: Hell, you don't bleed like Murietta.

WRITER: Show mercy!

FREEHOLDER FELLA: You don't smell like Murietta.

(Freeholder Fella gets even closer, sniffing the Writer.)

You smell like bear.

WRITER: Bear?

FREEHOLDER FELLA: You disappoint me something terrible. I hate to waste a single bullet on a so-called playwright.

(Freeholder Fella puts his gun back to the Writer's head.)

WRITER: Maybe you should save your bullet for a screenwriter.

FREEHOLDER FELLA: Hold steady now while I put you down. Like a dog. Adiós, Pancho.

(We hear a rifle cock.)

TWO-HUNDRED-YEAR-OLD WOMAN: Let the boy go.

FREEHOLDER FELLA: Huh?

TWO-HUNDRED-YEAR-OLD WOMAN: Turn the boy loose I said.

FREEHOLDER FELLA: Easy, missy.

TWO-HUNDRED-YEAR-OLD WOMAN: Back on outta here White Devil fella, lest you're ready to meet your maker.

FREEHOLDER FELLA: Why no, ma'am.

TWO-HUNDRED-YEAR-OLD WOMAN: I'll put a cap in your ass right quick like. Ya feeling me, dog?

FREEHOLDER FELLA: I feel ya plenty, ma'am.

TWO-HUNDRED-YEAR-OLD WOMAN: Now tell your posse to get off my land unless'n they want a buttload of birdshot in the keister. Move 'em out!

FREEHOLDER FELLA *(Getting up; yelling offstage)*: Uh, nobody up in here boys! *(More to himself)* Nothin' but goddamned phantoms.

TWO-HUNDRED-YEAR-OLD WOMAN: The jig is up, git I said!

(Freeholder Fella kicks the Writer in the stomach and flees.)

FREEHOLDER FELLA: Pussy. *(From offstage)* Yee-haa!!!!!

(The sound of horses galloping away. Thunder and lightning.)

WRITER: That was not a fair fight.

TWO-HUNDRED-YEAR-OLD WOMAN: There ain't a context for fairness where that Freeholder Fella came from.

WRITER: He had no call to cut me.

TWO-HUNDRED-YEAR-OLD WOMAN: Let me break it down so a child could understand. You can't write about things that you have not lived. So you got a little blood on ya? Ain't the end of the world, son.

WRITER: I almost died, Doña.

TWO-HUNDRED-YEAR-OLD WOMAN: It was good for you. Got you outta the box.

WRITER: I've got to get back to my writing.

TWO-HUNDRED-YEAR-OLD WOMAN: No more writing, no more thinking, time to live it, darn it!

WRITER (Over-dramatically): I don't understand.

TWO-HUNDRED-YEAR-OLD WOMAN (Mocking): "I don't understand . . ." Don Ringo!

(Don Ringo enters in white fencing garb and a Karate Kid headband. He tosses the Writer a sword. He forces him to fight.)

DON RINGO: Defend yourself.

WRITER: Huh?

(In an instant Don Ringo advances on the Writer, his sword to the Writer's throat. Everything stops for an instant.)

Ow-ee, motherfucker! You cut me, Don Ringo!

TWO-HUNDRED-YEAR-OLD WOMAN: Stop your bellyaching. Again! (A clap of her hands for punctuation)

WRITER: This ain't fun no more . . .

DON RINGO: Ya! Do as I do.

(Don Ringo and the Writer are side by side now. Don Ringo elegantly paries across the stage with the Writer a half step behind. Spanish guitar music punctuates their lunges.)

TWO-HUNDRED-YEAR-OLD WOMAN: Bueno.

(The two come back across the stage as Don Ringo talks.)

DON RINGO: A caballero never gives up.

WRITER: Jouquín's words.

(The Writer stops and moves his sword slowly over the audience.)

DON RINGO: Always hold your sword as you would una mujer.

WRITER: What's that?

TWO-HUNDRED-YEAR-OLD WOMAN: A lady.

DON RINGO: Hold her gentle, yet firm, and always with respeto.

TWO-HUNDRED-YEAR-OLD WOMAN: Always with respect.

DON RINGO: Steady, breathe, mijo, calm like a bomb. Now lunge, cabrón!

(The Writer lunges.)

TWO-HUNDRED-YEAR-OLD WOMAN: Think as the fox does, deadly and precise as he strikes his prey.

DON RINGO: No wasted movements. The sword, an extension of your body.

TWO-HUNDRED-YEAR-OLD WOMAN: An appendage.

DON RINGO: It is part of you now. You are the sword. ¡Patinando!

(The Writer is put through the paces. They stop.
The Two-Hundred-Year-Old Woman puts a blindfold on the Writer.)

Concentrate, my Chicano grasshopper.

(Asian flutes. Don Ringo executes an elaborate move in seconds. The Writer deflects all, and advances on Don Ringo. Everything stops as the Writer's sword is suddenly at Don Ringo's throat. Beat.)

WRITER *(Softly)*: Touché?

(The Writer removes his blindfold.)

TWO-HUNDRED-YEAR-OLD WOMAN: Touché.

DON RINGO: ¡Excelente! You were born for the sword, cabrón.

WRITER: You are an amazing swordsman and teacher, Don Ringo.

DON RINGO: Órale.

TWO-HUNDRED-YEAR-OLD WOMAN: Oh that was nothing, check this out . . .

(Don Ringo and the old woman quickly move a small table into place, as if suspended in mid-air à la Matrix, but not. She

helps Don Ringo slowly fall back on the table. He lays on his back, pointing his sword skyward as she twirls him around several times.)

WRITER *(Astonished)*: Whoa!

TWO-HUNDRED-YEAR-OLD WOMAN: Just like *The Matrix!*

(Don Ringo bounces up, energized.)

DON RINGO: I will show you el punto reverso!

WRITER: Punto who?

DON RINGO: Así, mira.

(Don Ringo plants himself facing the Writer. He expertly does the punto reverso. It is lovely and potentially deadly as he strikes the Writer just above the calf in a nonlethal way.)

WRITER *(Startled)*: OK. Didn't see that coming.

TWO-HUNDRED-YEAR-OLD WOMAN: They never do.

(As she speaks, the Writer limps, but slowly executes the punto reverso.)

Properly executed, your opponent will run off holding his tendons in his hands, eventually succumbing to infection or bleed to death.

WRITER: Not so cool.

(The old woman raises a deadly serious and pointed finger toward the Writer.)

TWO-HUNDRED-YEAR-OLD WOMAN: There is nothing cool about the battle, nothing nice about warfare. Nothing. Understood?

WRITER: Understood.

TWO-HUNDRED-YEAR-OLD WOMAN: Never gloat, even when the enemy is unraveling.

WRITER: Oh.

TWO-HUNDRED-YEAR-OLD WOMAN: It is your noble obligation.

DON RINGO: Obligación noble.

TWO-HUNDRED-YEAR-OLD WOMAN: You don't see me yelling from the mountaintops just because Arizona sheriff Joe Arpaio is a whore, do ya!?

WRITER: Woo-hoo! Uh, no, ma'am.

(The Two-Hundred-Year-Old Woman prances around the parlor.)

TWO-HUNDRED-YEAR-OLD WOMAN: You don't see me prancing around the parlor just because Dick Cheney had another heart attack, do ya?

WRITER: You do seem a smidge happy.

TWO-HUNDRED-YEAR-OLD WOMAN: Well, sir, I ain't. Rest assured. Knowledge trumps the rapier most every time. He with the sword does not always possess the power. 'Course it don't hurt to have a little backup if you know what I mean.

WRITER: Yes, ma'am.

TWO-HUNDRED-YEAR-OLD WOMAN: Talk less, mister writer, a quiet man requires less of the world, and therefore he is more respectful of her.

WRITER: Can I respond to that?

TWO-HUNDRED-YEAR-OLD WOMAN AND DON RINGO: No!

TWO-HUNDRED-YEAR-OLD WOMAN: ¡El punto reverso!

(With a sharp single clap of her hands the Writer does the move involuntarily striking Don Ringo's calf.)

DON RINGO: ¡Ay chingado!

TWO-HUNDRED-YEAR-OLD WOMAN: ¡Exquisito!

WRITER: Don Ringo, sir, where did you learn all this?

DON RINGO: I was a mere boy when I trained under the command of the great Pio Pico himself.

WRITER: ¿Gobernador Pio Pico?

(Coyote howl.)

TWO-HUNDRED-YEAR-OLD WOMAN: The one and only.

DON RINGO: I fought along side the hombres. Have you ever fought for anything, muchacho?

WRITER: I'm fighting T-Mobile right now over roaming charges. I will yield them no quarter, sons of bitches.

TWO-HUNDRED-YEAR-OLD WOMAN: Well, that's a start.

DON RINGO: When we fought the invaders at San Pedro, we routed their navy. We captured men at Chino and fought to the death at San Pascual, but, alas, we could not fend off the onslaught and horror to come.

TWO-HUNDRED-YEAR-OLD WOMAN: They sent men to match mountains, Don Ringo.

DON RINGO: We were a worthy opponent, Doña.

TWO-HUNDRED-YEAR-OLD WOMAN: You were the true Prince of California, Don Ringo.

WRITER: A direct descendent of the culture of resistance, Don Ringo.

(Don Ringo nods proudly. The Writer bows to him.)

I am honored to have been in your sacred dojo.

DON RINGO: I am the first Chicano!

TWO-HUNDRED-YEAR-OLD WOMAN: Yeah, yeah, we know that already!

(Both men slowly face the audience. The Two-Hundred-Year-Old Woman instructs softly:)

Hearts.

(The men respectfully place their swords over their hearts.)

Sky.

(The men point their swords to the sky.)

Mother Earth.

(The men cut down across the floor.)

La tierra. Our *tierra.* Defend, guard her. Always.

(The Writer bows to her.)

Well then, a touch of nobility from our angry Chicano after all.

DON RINGO: Finalmente. Perhaps our writer is ready, Doña.

WRITER: Ready for what?

DON RINGO: Ready to star in the movie, pendejo.

WRITER: Uh . . .

TWO-HUNDRED-YEAR-OLD WOMAN: You don't wanna be a Sleepy Mexican your whole life, do ya?

WRITER: Well . . .

TWO-HUNDRED-YEAR-OLD WOMAN: I render you worthy to be in your own motion picture.

WRITER: What movie? Ooooweeeeoo, right? C'mon, what movie, Don Ringo, right?

TWO-HUNDRED-YEAR-OLD WOMAN: This movie, bonhomie!

(The Two-Hundred-Year-Old Woman grabs a movie director's bullhorn, ascot and leather rod from offstage. Again the film projector comes down.)

Lights, camera, action!

MAN *(Voice-Over)*: High in the hills of San Mandolito, in a mysterious cave, Yaqui savages gather around a golden shrine!

(The shrine and savages appear. Then doors at the front of the shrine slide open, like on a flying saucer, and sitting there on a golden altar is:)

YAQUIS: Don del Oro, Don del Oro, Don del Oro . . .

DON DEL ORO: Silence!

(Don del Oro is a robot-looking figure with a big funny Aztec mask. He breathes like Darth Vader.)

My loyal savages, the gold train to Mexico City leaves tomorrow. We must not allow it to leave the station at San

Juan Capistrano. You men there, go wait in the dark near the Mission, bring me the fat Friar Felipe. You men there, go wait at the train station and do what I told you, not that other thing I told you yesterday . . .

YAQUIS: Don del Oro, Don del Oro . . .

(A single enthusiastic Yaqui voice:)

YAQUI 1: Don del Oro, Don del . . . sorry . . .

DON DEL ORO: Silence! The rest of you, is there any more of you?

YAQUIS *(Offstage):* Over here, Don del Oro.

DON DEL ORO: Good. You must stop the legion of men that are meant to stop us. Be on the lookout for Diego la Vega, he is a tall and strapping fellow who favors color-coordinated Spanish casual wear. Kill him on sight. Also look out for El Zorro.

The evil Don del Oro (Herbert Siguenza), appearing from the shrine, instructs his hapless Indians, (from left to right): Vincent Montoya, Ric Salinas and Joseph Kamal; the Two-Hundred-Year-Old Woman/Lupita (Sharon Lockwood) is center.

YAQUIS: Zorro, Zorro, Zorro . . .

(One enthusiastic Yaqui voice:)

YAQUIS: Zorro! Zorro! . . . Sorry.

DON DEL ORO: Silence! El Zorro is also a tall and strapping fellow who favors black leather. Spank him on sight. Spank the little bitch but good. Nothing will stop us from having our gold. Remember, before the Spanish, before the Mexicans, before the white man, this land belonged to you!

YAQUIS *(Singing)*: "This land was our land, now this land is your land, from California to the . . ."

DON DEL ORO: Silence! Now go! Go, my little brown ones!

YAQUIS: Don del Oro, Don del Oro, Don del Oro . . .

(The Yaquis exit in a trance.)

MAN *(Voice-Over)*: This is a voice-over to indicate a passage of time. The Yaquis return . . . a-hem . . . I said the Yaquis return!

YAQUIS *(Entering)*: Don del Oro, Don del Oro, Don del Oro . . .

(The Yaquis carry blocks of gold, a tied-up Friar Felipe and the Spanish señorita, Lupita.)

DON DEL ORO: Silence! Very good, my savages! You came back quickly. You have brought me the gold and this rabble-rouser of the church!

FRIAR FELIPE: Release me, you golden monster! *(Singing)* "Please release me and let me go . . ."

DON DEL ORO: Silence! We found hidden weapons in the church. They were surely for the purpose to overthrow my friend El Gobernator.

FRIAR FELIPE: Yes they were. Because like you, he is nothing but a tyrant!

DON DEL ORO: Who lit the flaming "Z" in the hills above Mandelito?

FRIAR FELIPE: I lit the flaming "Z," you hunk of fool's gold.

DON DEL ORO: Why, you flamer! For that you will get twenty lashes.

(The Yaquis whip the tied-up Friar Felipe; he goes from pain to ecstasy.)

FRIAR FELIPE: Ahhh! Mother of God! ¡Ay Dios mío! ¡Qué rico! ¡Más! ¡Más! ¡Más Papi!

DON DEL ORO: Sadomasochistic clergy! Away with him, get him outta here! Throw him off Mount Diablo!

YAQUIS: Mount Diablo! Mount Diablo!

(The Yaquis take Friar Felipe offstage and throw him off Mount Diablo. The Friar's screams start loudly and fade away as he nears the depths of the mountain:)

FRIAR FELIPE: Ahhhh! Ahhh . . . aaaa . . . aaa . . . aa . . . a.

LUPITA: If only Zorro was here to save us! *(Long pause)* I said, if only Zorro was here to save us! Pssst, that's your cue, Writer!

(The sound of a whip and a huge shadow is cast. The Writer enters dressed in a black Zorro outfit: sword and mask.)

ZORRO/WRITER: What the hell am I doing here?

LUPITA: Thank God, you are here to save us, Zorro!

ZORRO/WRITER: Zorro? But I'm not . . .

LUPITA: Help!

ZORRO/WRITER: Huh? Look, I am only . . .

YAQUIS: El Zorro, El Zorro . . .

(Pointing to Zorro/the Writer.)

ZORRO/WRITER: Really? Are you serious?

YAQUIS: El Zorro, El Zorro . . .

ZORRO/WRITER: OK, fine. Unhand her I say! Release the gold at once or answer to my rapier!

DON DEL ORO: Attack him!

YAQUIS: Kill Zorro, kill Zorro . . .

ZORRO/WRITER: Stop! Alto!

(The Yaquis stop in their tracks.)

My Yaquis brothers, what has happened to you guys? You were once a peaceful people, docile and, well, let's be honest, a little lazy. Now this false golden idol has turned you into mindless savages! Look how you live in your spider holes. You used to be concerned with ethnic diversity, multiculturalism, and you had a solid "No Yaqui Child Left Behind" policy.

(Lupita clears her throat.)

Who wrote this crap?

(All point to him.)

ALL: You did!

ZORRO/WRITER: Right! I mean, renounce this hunk of scrap metal or perish, to Hades you will go. Ride with me—Zorro—and I will see to it that you each receive your driver's licenses!

DON DEL ORO: Do not listen to him! Savages attack!

(The Yaquis move in classic finger-snapping fashion, à la West Side Story's Jets vs. Sharks.)

ZORRO/WRITER: Stop again!

(Yaquis quickly stop again.)

I will fight you Yaquis, all one hundred of you, but one at a time if that's OK.

YAQUIS: OK! Oooooo! Oooooo!

(The Yaquis attack. One Yaqui brother reenters from the wings several times to create a sort of revolving door of blood-lusty

Yaquis. Finally a Yaqui dummy flies on to Zorro/Writer. They both wrestle to the ground. Zorro/The Writer spins him over his head and throws him offstage. Zorro/The Writer defeats all the warriors.)

ZORRO/WRITER: Are there any more of you Yaquis left?

YAQUI WARRIOR *(Offstage)*: No, that's pretty much it.

ZORRO/WRITER: Good.

(Zorro/the Writer confronts Don del Oro who stands on his golden perch.)

DON DEL ORO: "Danger, danger, Will Robinson! Danger!"

ZORRO/WRITER: Don del Oro, you must answer for the death of Don Ramón de la Vega, who you killed with golden arrows.

LUPITA: What sort of animal kills with a golden arrow!

ZORRO/WRITER: Your evil plan has failed.

LUPITA: He must be in cahoots with the Gobernator!

ZORRO/WRITER: Of course he is, Lupita. That's because he is . . .

(Zorro takes off Don del Oro's Aztec mask.)

ALL: El Gobernator!

(The Gobernator from Act One is revealed.)

ZORRO/WRITER: Don Alejandro de la Vega will once again be our Gobernador. Don del Oro's weapons of mass adobe destruction—if we find them—will be kept safely under lock and key.

LUPITA: Señor Zorro, how can I ever repay you? You have restored order to California.

(Meanwhile the Gobernator is sneaking out.)

EL GOBERNATOR: "Hasta la vista, baby."

LOLITA: Señor Zorro. You are my hero.

EL GOBERNATOR : I'll be back. *(No response)* I said . . . I'll be back!

(Still no response) Ah, fuck it.

(The Gobernator gives up and exits. Don Ramón de la Vega with a golden arrow stuck in his head enters.)

ZORRO/WRITER: Uncle Don Ramón de la Vega? I thought you were . . .

DON RAMÓN DE LA VEGA: Dead? No, the golden arrow you see lodged in my cabeza narrowly missed my lower lobe. Sure, there are things from that region of my brain that I long for, I can no longer taste manchego cheese or speak Spanish anymore.

ZORRO/WRITER: Lo siento.

DON RAMÓN DE LA VEGA: Huh. My motor skills are shot, and finding hats are a bitch. *(Then brightly)* But I am here now! And ready to serve as a Californio.

ZORRO/WRITER: Sweet.

LUPITA: Shall I dress your wounds, Don Ramón?

DON RAMÓN DE LA VEGA: No gracias, señorita, but I'll take a shot of morphine with a tequila chaser if you have it.

(Don Ramón de la Vega turns and reveals several more golden arrows in his back.)

If only my nephew Diego had half the courage you possess, señor Zorro, I would be a proud uncle, a proud uncle with arrows stuck in me but proud still the same. Where was that boy when we needed him?

LUPITA: Probably hiding under his satin sheets.

ZORRO/WRITER: Or perhaps, Lupita, he is hiding under a mask.

(Zorro/the Writer takes off his mask. Spanish guitar flourish.)

DON RAMÓN DE LA VEGA: By the saints! Diego! My nephew? You are Zorro?! I thought you were a . . .

ZORRO/WRITER: Writer? Never mind. Lupita, will you honor me? Give your hand in marriage, together we will raise fat Hispanic-Negro children and watch our vineyards grow?

LUPITA: As long as you're tested and there's a prenup.

(*They kiss.*)

ZORRO/WRITER: I must fandango! ¡El Pollo Loco!

(*Zorro/the Writer dances a wicked fandango. When he stops:*)

Ave Maria! While I was fandango-ing, Don del Oro . . .
ALL: ESCAPED!!!!!

(*They all run out. The Writer is left onstage alone, studying his Zorro mask.*)

WRITER: I did it, I did it. I became him. And in the final analysis, Zorro it seems is an honest amalgamation, a paradox sure, a fabrication maybe, but made up of Indian, Spanish, Sephardic, Mexican and American cloth. I would have never gotten any of that, not felt it deep in my bones had I not participated in this fantastically horrendous movie.
TWO-HUNDRED-YEAR-OLD WOMAN (*Entering*): What movie?
WRITER: Oooooweee, the "movie" right?
TWO-HUNDRED-YEAR-OLD WOMAN: This ain't a movie no more!

(*Sound of a bulldozer.*)

WRITER: What is that sound?
TWO-HUNDRED-YEAR-OLD WOMAN: It's a bulldozer and it's getting closer!
WRITER: Closer to what?
TWO-HUNDRED-YEAR-OLD WOMAN: Closer to stealing my land for the mini-malls and condominiums. More disharmony caused by man!
WRITER: Don't worry, Doña, I'll save the inn!
TWO-HUNDRED-YEAR-OLD WOMAN: Atta boy!

(*The Writer strikes a heroic pose. Suddenly an electric mini golden Hummer convertible with a bulldozer scoop crashes through the walls. Driving the Hummer is the Gobernator himself: Arnold Schwarzenegger!)*

EL GOBERNATOR: You can't stand in the way of progress. Get out! Get Out! California is mine!

(The Writer runs off scared. The bulldozer stops. The Gobernator and the Two-Hundred-Year-Old Woman surround the Writer. The Gobernator removes his head—it's Don Ringo!)

DON RINGO: The little chavala ran away.

TWO-HUNDRED-YEAR-OLD WOMAN: I still think he's the One.

DON RINGO: I hope it was all worth it.

TWO-HUNDRED-YEAR-OLD WOMAN: We shall see, Don Ringo. We shall see.

(A dramatic transition back to the interrogation room from the beginning of the play. The two Agents slowly enter and stalk the Writer, still dressed as Zorro in a straitjacket.)

AGENT 1: So let's recap what you just told us. You checked into the El Camino Real Inn?

WRITER: Yup.

AGENT 2: At this so-called inn you were greeted by an extremely horny two-hundred-year-old broad?

WRITER: Howoooooo!

AGENT 1: And it was here that you met the granddaddy of all Chicanos?

WRITER *(Like a coyote)*: Simón.

AGENT 1: You also talked to a Sleeping Mexican actor made of adobe?

WRITER: Sí, señor.

AGENT 2: You met a couple of outlaws that stored stolen loot in a safe behind a painting of dogs playing poker?

WRITER: It was destiny manifested, yes, sir.

AGENT 2: You fornicated with a therapist grizzly bear named Kyle?

WRITER: ¡Fornicando con el oso sí!

AGENT 1: And the governor of California tried to bulldoze, with his mini Hummer, the inn that housed the pickled head of Joaquín Murietta?!

WRITER *(Arnold voice)*: Swear to God!

AGENT 1: In all my years . . . I've never heard such horse shit!

AGENT 2: Did you fall off the wagon, kid?

WRITER: The wagon is in the garage! It's all true, it's all true. You can go to the El Camino Real Inn, talk to the two-hundred-year-old lady, talk to Don Ringo! I saved them! I saved them! I slept with Murietta, I mean in his bed.

(Both Agents laugh.)

Why do you laugh at me so?

AGENT 2: The El Camino Real Inn does not exist.

WRITER: It does!

AGENT 1: It burned down following the Mining and Mineral Act of 1872.

WRITER: They must have rebuilt it!

AGENT 2: They did.

WRITER: You see then . . .

AGENT 1: And Uncle Sam snatched it to build the Hollywood Freeway.

WRITER *(Realizing)*: Eminent Domain . . . ?

AGENT 1: Like a speeding train, across the plain, again and again . . .

WRITER: The 101, El Camino Real . . .

AGENT 2: One in the same.

WRITER: Are you saying . . .

AGENT 1 *(Soft, creepy slow)*: In the barrio streets of your feeble Chicano mind all chuck-hole lined.

WRITER: Doña!!!

AGENT 1: Thanks to the Patriot Act Part 4, the byline "terrorist who assaulted an elected official," has been added to your writer's bio.

WRITER *(Weakly)*: What about my civil liberties?

AGENT 1: Civil liberties?

(The Agents laugh hysterically, really losing it, rolling around on the ground. They go nuts with delirium, play patty-cake, a tour de force. Then they recover for a serious deadpan:)

Detainees and douche bags have no civil liberties.
AGENT 2 *(Arnold voice)*: "Hasta la vista, Zorro!"

(The Agents exit.)

WRITER: Sir? Sir? Would you come back please? I'd like to, uh, talk about the charges. I am an American, sir, I am one and I'd, uh, be willing to, you know, talk about the extreme laws in Arizona—and all that stuff . . .

I'll support closing the borders and pretend it will make for a more secure America, even though Al Queda is already in Fremont and we should put glory holes along the border fence so that we may keep an eye on our amigos to the south. I'd like a lawyer please. Anybody? I think domestic wiretapping is a good idea, if we don't do it the tourists win.

I'd like a lawyer please. Representation. Somebody rescue me! Doña? Don Ringo? I must be at Burning Man. Scary skies, tombstone skies. Where are those slightly mean, entitled Park Slope and Silver Lake hipster sleeper cells I find a certain comfort in? Thank God for myspace.com. Detainees? Deportees? Intellectual properties. Don't fence me in. My Pentecost or my purgatory? I'm sitting shiva over here in a dark place like a West Virginia coal miner. My God I got off the Red Road, I got off the Red Road, brother.

(The Writer sings a corrido, guitar backs him up.)

Mi casa es su casa . . .

Oh, my God we are so screwed.

(The Writer begins to sob. A Latino Janitor enters pushing a large broom. He wears a jumpsuit, a San Francisco Giants' cap. He is listening to an iPod. He gets close to the Writer.)

JANITOR: Pssst. Pssst. Mister, Señor Zorro, Señor Zorro, I am here, amigo.

WRITER: Who the hell are you?

JANITOR: I am the janitor who works here. And I am here to liberate you!

WRITER: You better go before you get deported.

JANITOR: I cannot get deported, señor, I have dual citizenship.

WRITER: Dual identity?

JANITOR: I also have a Costco membership card. (Shows the card)

WRITER: Who's he?

(A rather large Anglo "Z" Fan Boy, with a crude white "Z" scrawled across his faded Star Wars T-shirt, enters. He wears a mask and dons a latex cape.)

"Z" FAN BOY: OMG! Zorro, I'm your biggest Fan Boy. OMG, SMD! MFM!

WRITER: I think Phish broke up, dude.

"Z" FAN BOY: You don't understand, you are my hero!

WRITER: I'm not Zorro, I'm zero kid. My pistol shoots blank bullets.

"Z" FAN BOY: No. Your bullets are real, Zorro, because yours are bullets of the imagination . . .

WRITER: OK . . .

JANITOR: We must go now, El Zorro.

WRITER: I am not Zorro. Zorro does not exist, he's just a fantasy.

JANITOR: We are all entitled to our fantasias. When I was a little boy in El Salvador, me and my little brother were Zorro. Mira, I still have my máscara.

"Z" FAN BOY: Me too!

WRITER: Awkward.

(The Janitor pulls out a Zorro mask and puts it on, so does "Z" Fan Boy. They slap happy hands. The Janitor starts to sing:)

JANITOR:

En su corcel cuando sale la luna,
Aparece el bravo Zorro

A los hombre de mal, se los va castigar
Marcando la zeta del Zorro
Zorro, Zorro, Zorro . . .

WRITER: Enough, look, man, Zorro is dead!

JANITOR: Al contrario, señor, Zorro vive! Anderson Cooper said that a man dressed like Zorro spray-painted a large black "Z" on the White House.

"Z" FAN BOY: President Obama wears a mask! Michelle looks hot in hers!

WRITER: La Casa Blanca?!

JANITOR: That was the spark! The mash!

WRITER: The mash?

JANITOR: Sí the mash.

"Z" FAN BOY: That single ember ignited everything, dude.

WRITER: Oh, the match! One man, one match . . .

JANITOR: La gente marching. It was the Million Mask Man March to Wacheengton!

"Z" FAN BOY: Even Charlie Sheen marched, with his dad Martin and his brother Emilio!

(Projection images of a large "Z" on the White House and people protesting, all wearing Zorro masks.)

The People!

WRITER: ¡La gente!

JANITOR: Nurses, teachers, janitors, firefighters, big union white guys from Wisconsin, even pupusa vendors from Daly City, por la gran puta! The people are pissed again!

"Z" FAN BOY: "Most men live lives of quiet desperation."

JANITOR: Henry David Thoreau said that! And he went to jail like Murietta. Because they believed, they stood for something.

WRITER: You guys are smart.

"Z" FAN BOY: Your play exposed the true evil of El Gobernator Terminator!

WRITER: I actually finished the play?

JANITOR: Claro que sí! Don't give up. Never give up! Just like the Giants!

WRITER: That's what the Doña always told me, amigo.

"Z" FAN BOY: The Doña is hot in that Doña way.

WRITER: Yeah, like Helen Mirren.

(A guitar flourish, the screen flies away. The Two-Hundred-Year-Old Woman and Don Ringo appear on each side of the Writer, "Z" Fan Boy and the Janitor.)

TWO-HUNDRED-YEAR-OLD WOMAN: Remove the blindfold that covers your eyes.

DON RINGO: Remove the chains that bind your hands.

TWO-HUNDRED-YEAR-OLD WOMAN: Rise up in the spirit of Murietta!

DON RINGO: Rise up in the spirit of Crazy Horse!

JANITOR: Rise up in the spirit of all immigrants!

DON RINGO: Rise up for pro-choice and health care!

"Z" FAN BOY: Art school is the new law school.

WRITER: What? This is the "rise up section"?

"Z" FAN BOY: My dad. Rise up for cool gabachos!

WRITER: OK!

TWO-HUNDRED-YEAR-OLD WOMAN: Rise up for medical marijuana!

"Z" FAN BOY: Sweet.

DON RINGO: Rise up against the war!

TWO-HUNDRED-YEAR-OLD WOMAN: Bring back our boys!

DON RINGO: And fuck the Tea Party!

TWO-HUNDRED-YEAR-OLD WOMAN: Who are you?

DON RINGO: I am the first Chicano . . .

TWO-HUNDRED-YEAR-OLD WOMAN: Not you, Don Ringo. Him!

DON RINGO: Oh.

WRITER: Me?

TWO-HUNDRED-YEAR-OLD WOMAN: Yeah, you!

WRITER: Huh?

TWO-HUNDRED-YEAR-OLD WOMAN: Who are you?

DON RINGO *(Whispers)*: Who are you?

JANITOR: ¿Quién eres?

WRITER: I am . . .

"Z" FAN BOY: Who are you, dude?

TWO-HUNDRED-YEAR-OLD WOMAN: Say it, son!

WRITER: I am . . . I am . . . I am Zorro! Defender of justice and equality, protector of the poor! Champion of the oppressed and the undocumented!

JANITOR: ¡Zorro vive!

"Z" FAN BOY: Right fucking on!

(The Janitor helps the Writer get out of his straitjacket as the Writer steps downstage.)

WRITER: And I shall call my fuel-efficient Prius, El Tornado! *(Turning to the Janitor)* Thanks to you, my Mexican brother . . .

JANITOR: I'm Salvadorean.

WRITER: Whatever . . .

"Z" FAN BOY: Exactly.

WRITER: Thanks to you both I'm going to kick down the knowledge fool!

TWO-HUNDRED-YEAR-OLD WOMAN: Word up on that Z!

WRITER: Come save the world with me, my brother.

JANITOR: Maybe later, I have to clean the whole theater when this play ends. *(Exits yelling)* ¡Todos somos Zorro, todos somos Zorro!

WRITER: I must go!

"Z" FAN BOY: I'll go get my Sting-Ray bike!

WRITER: No time!

(The Writer leaps from the stage directly into the audience.)

Rise up, California! Rise up, citizens! Comrades put on your masks! Put them on for God's sake. They're right in your program! If not, ask an usher to give you one! Rise up, amigos, rise up! Rise up for our queer brothers and sisters.

(El Janitor and "Z" Fan Boy kiss on the lips and run off. The Writer then speaks to an audience member:)

Sir, I see that you don't wanna wear a mask? Keep paying four bucks a gallon at the pump—your choice, fucker!

(The Writer climbs up to the balcony.)

Thank you, Doña Ghostwriter.

TWO-HUNDRED-YEAR-OLD WOMAN: Keep running up the swollen river, boy!

WRITER: Yes, ma'am.

DON RINGO: "The dream of one man, is the memory of all."

WRITER: Borges rocks! Argentinians are cool.

DON RINGO: ¡Córrale cabrón! Shahh!

TWO-HUNDRED-YEAR-OLD WOMAN: Follow the tributaries into the *Heart of Darkness.* And don't forget to eat the naked lunch I packed ya special.

WRITER: I shall abide, ma'am. Rise up, Californians, rise up for properly executed agitprop theater. And if you didn't care for our fair and balanced Tea-Baggers comment . . . well then drive safely back to Iowa!

(Suddenly Agent 1 enters and takes aim and fires a shot at the Writer.)

AGENT 1: Freeze!

(The Writer falls . . . but after a beat he pops back up.)

WRITER: You missed! But you're gonna hit a wealthy subscriber if you're not careful!

(Agent 1 is about to shoot again when, out of nowhere, Kyle the Bear/Therapist attacks and chases Agent 1 offstage. Kyle then reenters.)

KYLE: Rooooaaaarrrrr!

WRITER: Job well done, Kyle.

KYLE: Roooaaarr!

WRITER: Well told right, my four-legged amigo.

KYLE: Zorro lives forever.

WRITER: Yes, he does, thanks in no small part to you, it's time you rest for winter, you earned it, return to your land, return to nature. Be an animal. ¡Hasta la Victoria Siempre!

(The Two-Hundred-Year-Old Woman, Don Ringo and Kyle wave good-bye to the Writer.)

TWO-HUNDRED-YEAR-OLD WOMAN AND DON RINGO: ¡Hasta la Victoria!

(The Writer responds with a dramatic fist to the air, then turns to an audience member:)

WRITER: Who the fuck is touching my cape? Never touch Zorro's cape, what's wrong with you people?

(Lights out. The curtain comes down as "Clandestino" by Manu Chao is reprised. The curtain rises. After the cast bows, they put their "fake swords" in hand, place their hands over their hearts, point their swords to the sky, then swoop them down to the earth, in an instant each cutting a "Z" in the air with a swooshing sound-effect. Bravo!)

END OF Z! PLAY

Since 1984, **CULTURE CLASH** has stormed the stages, bars, holding cells, churches, dives, whorehouses, safe houses, colleges and occasional synagogues, creating works that matter—hopefully—morphing and becoming theater artists with satirical fangs, but also artists with the ability to listen, record and steal. 2010 saw three world premieres—they write fast, in these speeded-up times—not chasing the culture, but also making it. Their books of plays (published by TCG) were recently banned in Tucson high schools by the Arizona Attorney General—the case will be heard in the Federal 9th Circuit Court. Culture Clash continues its struggle and the struggle to give voice to those who now also find themselves targets of extreme laws and attitudes as old as the hills in Gold Country. Our arrows are sharpened by fifteen stage plays and three decades of creating theater in America!